*The Foundations
of Mao Zedong's
Political Thought*

The Foundations of Mao Zedong's Political Thought 1917–1935

BRANTLY WOMACK

The University Press of Hawaii • *Honolulu*

COPYRIGHT © 1982 BY THE UNIVERSITY PRESS OF HAWAII
ALL RIGHTS RESERVED
MANUFACTURED IN THE UNITED STATES OF AMERICA

Publication of this book has been assisted by the Andrew W. Mellon Foundation.

Library of Congress Cataloging in Publication Data

Womack, Brantly, 1947–
   The foundations of Mao Zedong's political thought, 1917–1935.

   Includes bibliographical references and index.
   1. Mao, Tse-tung, 1893–1976—Political and social views.   I. Title.
DS778.M3W65   320.5'323'0924   81–16317
ISBN 0–8248–0752–9   AACR2

*For Tang and Yi-chuang,
and Ann, David, and Sarah*

Contents

	Acknowledgments	ix
	Introduction	xi
1	Mao before Marxism	1
2	Mao, the Party, and the National Revolution: 1923–1927	32
3	Rural Revolution: 1927–1931	84
4	Governing the Chinese Soviet Republic: 1931–1934	144
5	The Foundations of Mao Zedong's Political Thought	188
	Notes	205
	Index	233

Acknowledgments

The most pleasant task of a scholar is acknowledging the various *sine quae non* of one's research. Two in particular stand out. First, the guidance of Tang Tsou, who has been my mentor since I began to study China at the University of Chicago. The direction and quality of this research owe as much to him as to me. Second, the very high quality of existing research concerning Mao. Without Takeuchi Minoru's *Collected Works of Mao Zedong* the search for texts would have made my research either incomplete or impossible. Just as importantly, the work of Benjamin Schwartz, Stuart Schram, Jerome Chen, Frederic Wakeman, and many others have created a starting point for current studies which is already much higher than any single scholar could attain on his own.

On the more personal level, the friendship and encouragement of my colleagues have helped me persist in this project. A number of friends were helpful specifically with this book: Frederic Wakeman, Philip Lilienthal, John Starr, Peter Lee, Bob Bradley, David Chu, Murray Leaf, William Liu, Ed Hammond, Stuart Kiang, and Lowell Dittmer. It has been made more readable by the editing of Don Yoder, and owes its index to John Owens. The project was originally undertaken as a dissertation, and it owes its initial encouragement, shaping, and survival to Tang Tsou, Philip Kuhn, and Leonard Binder, who composed the dissertation committee. The research has been partially supported by the Center for Chinese Studies at the University of California, Berkeley, and by a research grant from the University of Texas at Dallas.

The sacrifices of Ann, David, and Sarah for the book are beyond recounting.

Introduction

This study traces the development of Mao Zedong's political thought from his earliest writings to the beginning of the Long March. It thus covers the first forty-two years of Mao's life, during which he participated in the May Fourth Movement of 1919, helped found the Chinese Communist Party, originated his political-military strategy of base areas, and administered the government of the Chinese Soviet Republic in Jiangxi. Although overshadowed by his later accomplishments, these experiences and activities were of considerable importance in themselves, and they were accompanied by writings which reflect Mao's judgment of their significance. The arguments, values, and methods revealed in his writings helped shape Mao's contributions to Chinese politics and are indeed themselves a significant part of his contribution.

  The purpose of the study is to draw upon the practical nature of Mao's writings and their political context in order to produce an interpretation of his early political thought *in vivo*. I attempt to present emerging political concepts with their original referents and to discuss the subjects which Mao depicts as urgent and important in terms of the practical decision points he was facing as a political actor. This approach is particularly well suited for Mao because his theoretical concepts tend to emerge from a course of practical experience rather than an abstract program. Mao's explicit theorizing was a reflection of his experience, and the gestation of his concepts in practice provided the referents and the connotative significance of his more theoretical statements. This can be seen in the style of his theoretical discussions after 1949, in which he constantly refers to his own experience and belittles any role which theory might play apart from such practice.[1]

Attention to the unity of theory and practice is the basic principle of Mao's political thought, and I have argued elsewhere that this is also a major innovation within both the Chinese and the Marxist political traditions.[2] Thus the primary task in understanding Mao's thought is grasping its practical context. The secondary tasks of logical interpolation and extrapolation, formulation of history of ideas, and comparison with other thinkers depend on this type of *in vivo* interpretation. To view Mao simply as a theoretician, or to abstract his theory from his political life, not only runs a serious risk of distorting Mao's views by taking them out of context. It also presumes the incorrectness of one of Mao's fundamental tenets—that theory and practice are inseparably interwoven.

Mao's theoretical development has never been simply an explication of earlier convictions; developing experience and shifting political contexts have led to continual recastings of his thinking. Hence a study of any particular period of Mao's thought cannot be a survey of all the roots of all his thought; to be comprehensive, therefore, this study would have to continue to 9 September 1976. The reason this is not attempted here is primarily practical: the development from alpha to omega of Mao's thought in its political context is too vast a subject. The period covered in this study is the first of three major periods. I call it the "foundations of Mao's political thought" because it was during this time that most of his important political concepts germinated. His subordinate role in the party at this time did not require Mao to make official, comprehensive pronouncements, but his practical political tasks induced the development and confirmation of a distinctive epistemology, political thought, and political style.

In the next major period, 1936–1940, Mao's new responsibilities of general leadership required him to state his views authoritatively. Mao's confidence in his own correctness vis-à-vis the Stalinist ideologues in the Comintern and the party was greatly strengthened by the lessons of the Chinese Soviet Republic in Jiangxi, but the transformed political context of the Anti-Japanese War required an abstraction of his political principles from their practical roots. The results of this abstraction and reapplication are Mao's theoretical works of the late 1930s ("On Practice" and "On Contradiction" are the best known) and his strategic analyses of the war and the Second United Front with the Kuomintang. As the war persisted, the rectification of the party and the political economy of the communist-controlled areas required new authoritative statements on matters of revolutionary administration. Most of these statements also have clear precedents in the "foundations" period. Finally, in the civil war the accumulated revolutionary experience and military power were applied to the task of final victory in China.

The third period is that of the People's Republic of China (PRC). This stage is first characterized by Mao's relinquishing of active direction of the revolution (for instance, the establishment of "first and second" lines of leadership in the Central Committee). Mao had stepped down because of his assumption that the new postliberation stage would be radically different from his accumulated experience and because of his desire to continue the vitality of the revolution by allowing other leaders to develop their experience. But certain problems of the new China turned out to be quite similar to those of Mao's experience, and other truly novel problems were presented by the leadership to which he had entrusted the management of China. These developments led Mao to reintroduce the politics of revolutionary struggle (the Great Leap Forward and, most important, the Cultural Revolution) but with far more complex results than in the original struggle for liberation. Whereas Mao's leadership before 1949 prevailed because of the timeliness of his politics, his two major interventions into the politics of the PRC were of a different sort. The "revolutionary romanticism" of the Great Leap Forward and the Cultural Revolution involved a distinctive opposition of revolutionary will and the processes of history. The experiential foundations of Mao's values and policies are evident, but to a great extent they are the retrospective experiences of Yanan and Jiangxi attempting to preserve, shape, and push onward a revolutionary present. Mao's lifelong concern for the survival of the revolutionary movement shifted away from the pre-1949 problem of physical survival to the more difficult ethical and political ones of preserving revolutionary identity.

The "Gang of Four" brought the self-destructive tendencies of unlimited moral critique to a fever pitch and thereby contributed greatly to the ease of their own removal. Since the main ideological strength of the Gang of Four lay in their single-minded extrapolation of Mao's revolutionary values as expressed in the Cultural Revolution, Hua Guofeng has since emphasized the concern with socialist construction which was prominent in Mao's writings in the 1950s and Deng Xiaoping has emphasized the practicality of Mao's thought in order to provide a thread of continuity into the post-Mao era. But there is no easy solution to the political and ethical challenges of Mao's legacy, and the multistage movement to criticize the Gang of Four is testimony to this. The fruit of Mao's practical revolutionary efforts was the contradiction of a revolution in command. The struggle with this contradiction will continue.

It is my expectation that the basic values of Mao's politics, formed in his early activities, will prove to be a durable contribution to Chinese politics. Before Mao's death, such an expectation would have been considered too obvious to deserve mention, but the public criticism of Mao and the large-scale repudiation of his policies which have been increasing since 1978 require an investigation into the limits of "De-Maoization" and the prospects of his basic approach to politics. Briefly, I would argue that the foundations of Mao's politics have already been incorporated into China's political culture. During his last twenty years, however, Mao applied these principles in an egalitarian critique based on class struggle, and the current leadership repudiates this approach in favor of the more stable development of the "four modernizations." Reversing twenty years of Chinese politics creates a major political watershed at the expense of Mao, but his basic approach to politics remains influential even in the new era of post-Mao modernization.

In terms of political power, Mao did not pass from the scene until almost two years after his death. Until mid-1978, the legacy of Mao's political preferences and aversions was still a significant factor—although no longer a decisive one—in Chinese policymaking. The key effort of Vice-Premier Deng Xiaoping's forces in 1978 was to break decisively the inertia of policies identified with Mao as a result of his personal, radical interventions in Chinese politics from 1958 until his death.[3] Two related theses were essential to the effort: first, that China had entered a new period in which practical commitment to modernization determined the course of politics; second, that practice was basic to Mao's system of thought, and policy should be determined by practical considerations rather than dogma. Together these theses implied that China should rethink her politics on the basis of the practical needs of the new age and that those scandalized by the abandonment of Mao's policies were still suffering from the poison of Gang of Four dogmatism.[4] In short, yesterday's Maoism was today's anti-Maoism, and yesterday's "capitalist roaders" were rehabilitated as victims of dogmatist persecution.

The rollback of the Cultural Revolution was interpreted as a rejection of Mao because its radical policies had prevailed through his personal intervention and the ensuing chaos had been contained and legitimated by an unprecedented glorification of his wisdom and power. The policies of Mao which emerged in his last ten years had as their target the power and political predilections of China's intermediate leadership. Now the former victims were asserting the legitimacy of their privileges and the autonomy of their responsibilities.

On the other hand, Deng Xiaoping in his major speech on the subject made an excellent argument for the primacy of practice in Mao's thought,[5] and the research of this book supports his contention. Moreover, Deng Xiaoping's political style is closer to Mao's preliberation style than was that of the Gang of Four. Many of the current attempts to further material well-being and to increase popular control over officials—and the rationale behind these policies[6]—have precedents in Mao's base area activities.

To the extent that the political thought of Mao Zedong can be identified with the radical policies which succeeded because of his personal espousal and the superhuman image of the Great Helmsman, the reorientation of 1978 marked an attack on his influence. Since Mao in fact had been so identified during his last ten years, both within China and outside, the assumption is natural that the current phase is a complete displacement of Mao. From a longer historical perspective, however, the weakness of this assumption and the limits of the identification upon which it is based become apparent. Deng Xiaoping has returned to pre–Cultural Revolution (and in some cases pre-1957) positions, but he could not return to a pre-Mao position. Mao's preeminent contribution to Chinese history was his guidance of the Chinese revolution. The lengthy process of this revolution was also the process of creating the structures, values, and leadership cadre of the People's Republic of China. A Hong Kong supporter of the current changes expressed the relationship to Mao eloquently:

> Mao Zedong's thought is a spiritual treasure of the Chinese people; for years it has melded with the people and no one can reject it. The people can't reject it because they cannot reject their own revolu-

tionary past. They cannot throw aside the weapon with which they know and change the world. . . . Mao Zedong made mistakes, but the demand that the party completely and accurately grasp Mao's thought [the official formula under which his mistakes are analyzed] should not be regarded as a remonstrance against Mao Zedong the individual. It is self-examination *(fanqing)* by the Chinese people, their self-criticism and their self-evaluation.[7]

As a constitutive rather than a controversial contribution, Mao's preliberation politics forms the accepted framework of assumptions for Chinese Communist politics. The common ground and its origin are not called to the attention of the foreign observer, but if one does not devote special efforts to grasp it, the changes in Chinese politics must appear unintelligible. The Cultural Revolution was not a typical expression of Mao's politics. It was an extreme effort by Mao, using novel means, to correct what he perceived to be the drift of party leadership away from revolutionary ideals.[8] The leadership could not defend itself from this charge because Mao's constitutive role in the party, the revolution, and its ideology made his authority unimpeachable. The post-Mao rejection of the excesses of the Cultural Revolution is complicated not only by the fact of Mao's leadership of it but by the general desire to retain and reestablish continuity with the party's revolutionary past.

Because such a distinction between Mao's constitutive role in Chinese Communist politics and his specific political interventions since 1957 has been lacking in most understandings of Mao, his politics is assumed to be irrelevant (except as a target) to current Chinese politics, and hence uninteresting. The contrast with the attention to Mao of a few years ago is enormous, but, as the Chinese say, the periods have changed. For our purposes, however, it is worth reviewing the assumptions of Cultural Revolution studies of Mao. The tendency to replace the study of a whole communist polity with a study of its leader made an intensive study of Mao during his lifetime too easy to justify. This approach to Mao has been discarded rather than criticized; hence its assumptions tend to reappear—with much weaker grounding—in the analysis of the current Chinese leadership.

The cultural ideal of the Promethean revolutionary has provided a satisfying—but false—interpretive model for Mao's life. There are two equally basic errors in the presumption of this subjectivistic image. First, Mao's determination of purpose was at least as dependent on objective factors as it was on subjective preference. He aimed at correct action—the apt solution for the particular problem—rather than the implementation of a private notion of the good. The epigram of a German theorist-politician that "politics is the art of making necessity possible" is apt for Mao's approach.[9] Second, Mao's method of leadership—through practical models rather than through theoretical treatises, through struggle rather than through harmony, through collective action rather than through authoritative command—committed him to a process in which individual preferences were risked in the attempt to induce a communal movement. In what he pursued and how he pursued it, Mao was not merely an individual in relation to history: he was one immersed in history through a self-conscious dialectic of subject and object.

If Mao's presence in Chinese politics is grasped as a historical dialectic, one runs less risk of exaggerating Mao's influence in the study of China. Concentrating attention on the masses is also an eminently Maoist adjuration: "Comrades! What is a true bastion of iron? It is the masses, the millions upon millions of people who genuinely and sincerely support the revolution, that is the real bastion which no force can smash, no force whatsoever."[10] The resulting revolution is a collective accomplishment, and Mao makes his own role in it clear in his criticism of Lin Biao's "theory of genius"—the tendency to attribute all accomplishments to the power of Mao's thought which became prominent in the Cultural Revolution:

> It is not that I do not want to talk about genius. To be a genius is to be a bit more intelligent. But genius does not depend on one person or few people. It depends on a party, the party which is the vanguard of the proletariat. Genius is dependent on the mass line, on collective wisdom.[11]

Mao's preference for collective wisdom is shown even in the writing of his critique of the genius theory: "I wrote 'Some Opinion,' which specifically criticizes the genius theory, only after looking up some people to talk with them, and after some investigation and research."[12]

Mao's dependence upon colleagues and ultimately upon the masses clearly does not imply passivity on his part. The influence of colleagues occurred within the framework of promoting revolutionary tasks; the influence of the masses occurred within the process of popular mobilization. Despite the impression given by later canonizations of his thought, Mao's typical argument relies not on the intellectual appeal of a brilliant idea but on the urgency and practicality of a specific measure for popular mobilization. It is particularly clear in his earlier writings that a great deal of the quality of Mao's political thought comes from lessons from the masses gained in the processes of investigation and mobilization. It is also evident from Mao's conflicts with party leadership before 1935 that the process often mistakenly individualized as a power struggle between Mao and the "Twenty-eight Bolsheviks" who controlled the CCP from 1931 to 1935 was more importantly a process of a new political style emerging collectively (with Mao as its chief exponent) from the experience of revolutionary government in Jiangxi.

Mao's active reliance on colleagues, the masses, and changes in the objective political situation allows the study of his political thought to be more than biographical delving into the personal idiosyncrasies and brilliance of a leader. Such interdependence makes the popular question of Mao's individual innovations within Chinese political thought, Marxism, or social science both less significant and much more difficult to answer. By concentrating on Mao, this study inevitably gives a misleading emphasis both to his role in the events discussed and to his originality in politics. But if the problem of who holds the copyright on a particular idea is left aside, Mao's writings analyzed in context become a fascinating window to the politics and thinking of his China. Not only did the significance of Mao's China and his own personal weight within that sphere increase enormously, but his writings became the core of the official ideology—the orthodox definition of the meaning of the revolution. Thus the attempt to acquire an intimate understanding of the dialectical development of Mao's politics and thinking is also an approach to the roots of contemporary China's most prevalent self-understanding.

1 *Mao before Marxism*

Considering the small quantity of Mao's writings prior to his identification with the Chinese Communist Party and the relative insignificance of his precommunist political activities, the "early Mao" has received an unusual amount of attention from both Western scholars and Chinese biographers.

The three most prominent Western scholars who base their interpretations of Mao on circumstances or writings of this period differ widely in what they consider significant. Richard Solomon's psychological interpretation stresses biographical and autobiographical accounts of Mao's struggles with his father to indicate the root of a basic urge to struggle against authority.[1] Mao's revolution is thus the collision of this urge with a traditionally docile political culture. Frederic Wakeman's wide-ranging study *History and Will* attempts to establish the significance of Mao's thought by coordinating a presentation of the Chinese and Western thinkers who influenced Mao's intellectual development.[2] Certainly Mao has stated that he read and was influenced by these thinkers in his youth.[3] But Wakeman's intellectual historical approach and Solomon's psychological perspective both presuppose that the continuity between Mao's youth and his maturity is more important than any discontinuity or development. Stuart Schram, the major translator of Mao's pre-Marxist works into Western languages, has proposed the more complicated thesis that the ideas presented in Mao's early works submerge during his Marxist period (1922–1965) and surface again with the Cultural Revolution.[4] The truly Maoist periods in this view are youth and old age, when his own ideas were not subservient to Marxist ideology.

Chinese interest in Mao's early life has produced two very

useful biographies, Xiao San's *Comrade Mao Zedong's Boyhood and Youth* and Li Rui's *Comrade Mao Zedong's Early Revolutionary Activities*. These are supplemented by a number of historical articles and reminiscences including a 1979 essay by Li Rui entitled "The Ideological Trend of Mao Zedong in His Youth."[5] The period as a whole is viewed by these writers as the time when Mao's characteristic intellectual and political habits took shape. Hence their position is more similar to Wakeman's view than to Solomon's reductionist interpretation or to Schram's discontinuity thesis. Their emphasis, however, is more on Mao's political development than on the significance of his intellectual encounters.

From Mao's own epistemological standpoint, one would expect him to consider youthful experiences important but not determining, and indeed that seems to be the tone of his well-told autobiographical account. The conditions under which consciousness arises are of primary importance to a materialist. But for Mao this primacy has significance only in action, and his practical orientation is grounded in the conviction that any condition can eventually be overcome through persistent effort. Thus the dialectic between subjective and objective renders abstract statements concerning the priority of one or the other ("determinism" or "voluntarism") virtually meaningless. In one of his earliest preserved remarks, Mao writes:

> Although I am determined by Nature, I am also at the same time a part of Nature. Accordingly Nature can determine my strength, and I also can determine Nature's strength. Although my strength is small, it cannot be said that it is without influence on Nature.[6]

Our focus in this chapter will be primarily on Mao's pre-Marxist writings, because a careful reading of these works yields valuable information about Mao's intellectual and political starting point. But we will begin with a brief look at the context of Mao's childhood and youth, since Mao's energetic involvement with family and school provided a striking source and corollary to his theoretical and political disposition.

The Context of Mao's Youth

Although many other revolutionaries came from pleasant family situations, in Mao's case life at home was analogous in many respects to the society he was later to revolutionize. From his father he learned power, exploitation, and hatred; from his mother he learned compassion and love. It should be noted, however, that Mao's father was a "teacher by negative example": Mao's frontal and energetic opposition was a mirror image of his father's strongest trait, while the possibilities of alternatives were shown by his mother. Significant for his later activities outside the family, he learned that paternal authority could be successfully opposed. This victory in the struggle for recognition with his father was won by exploits of unusual courage which must have contributed greatly to Mao's early development of an independent and vigorous character.[7]

Two other aspects of Mao's family situation may have influenced his later behavior: its economic activities and its financial support for his studies. From an early age Mao imitated his mother's benevolence in dealing with needy people,[8] and he must have been disturbed by his father's callousness in expanding the family fortune.[9] Economic success came too late to spare Mao from a childhood of hard physical labor, but it did enable his family to provide the modicum of support which allowed him to pursue his studies. Mao's first acts of opposition to academic masters began at the same time as his disobedience to his father. Indeed, running away from school at the age of ten is the first act of protest Mao recalls, and it brought better treatment from both teacher and father. "The result of this act of protest impressed me very much. It was a successful 'strike.' "[10] Although he resented having to memorize the classics, he learned to deploy them to his advantage in arguments with his father.

Mao entered the environment of the large "modern schools" at the age of sixteen, and with a two-year interruption for army service and independent study, he continued his studies until he graduated from the Hunan First Normal School in 1918 at age twenty-four. Mao's experiences during this period were much more than merely a confirmation of habits developed within the family. They were a socialization into the turbulence of modern China which took place as a characteristically energetic dialectic between himself and his school environments.

Mao's most notable conflicts during his scholastic career were directly related to the structure and pedagogical assumptions of the modern schools. As Mao said in a later work introducing a new kind of school system: "The general root of the evil [of the modern schools] is causing the students to be passive, grinding away character and tearing down the soul. Timid ones become superficial followers of opinion and gifted ones hesitate to come forward."[11] The specific occasions for student protest were matters like the large number of required courses, the prohibition of political activities, and the lack of an adequate physical education program. Fortunately for Mao's occasionally threatened school career, some influential professors and many students agreed with him and either defended him or joined him. Without such peer support and approbation from respected superiors, not only would his early efforts at reforming his immediate society have met with complete failure, but he would probably have found introspective pursuits more satisfying.

As Mao promoted various constructive, critical, and educational movements among his classmates (occasionally reaching out to groups beyond—for instance, a night school for workers), he developed personal ties which were to assure future support for analogous activities under his leadership. This power to mobilize was enhanced beyond mere numbers by the prestige of students in general and by the reputation of the First Normal School in particular, where Mao was evidently the preeminent student leader. The high opinion which influential teachers like Yang Changji had of Mao's character and intelligence gave him a foothold in the national academic world of China, although the fracturing of this academic world by its politicization after the May Fourth Movement—and the parochial character of his arena—foreclosed the type of quick national fame made by many in the *Xin Qingnian (New Youth)* generation.

Not the least contribution made by the modern schools to Mao's general development and political behavior was educational: he acquired a deep acquaintance with Chinese culture, the ability to express himself with finesse and power, and a considerable knowledge of world affairs and history. His tutoring in moral philosophy by Yang Changji was not only of high quality but thoroughly in harmony with Mao's habits of independence, social concern, and action. Yang's interest in ethics and his syncretic method led him to emphasize the similarity of Chinese and Western moral concerns, so that Mao's study of Western philosophy was not a disorienting confrontation with completely alien ideas. Mao's attitude toward the Chinese classics developed past his earlier use of them as cultural weapons against his father. Both Mao's autobiography and his later writings indicate the breadth of ancient and modern intellectual influences which he absorbed during his school days in Changsha.[12] Yang Changji's emphasis on the harmony rather than the disparity of East and West undoubtedly contributed to Mao's later habit of using traditional Chinese examples to illustrate Marxist principles.

The provincial, national, and international political environments of Mao's youth were most influential in determining the content of his political activity. Political literature of the times introduced him to China's national plight. Personal experience of provincial affairs informed him about internal politics close at home:

> At this time [in 1906, when Mao was twelve] an incident occurred in Hunan which influenced my whole life. Outside the little Chinese school where I was studying, we students noticed many bean merchants, coming back from Changsha. We asked them why they were all leaving. They told us about a big uprising in the city.
>
> There had been a severe famine that year, and in Changsha thousands were without food. The starving sent a delegation to the civil governor, to beg for relief, but he replied to them haughtily, "Why haven't you food? There is plenty in the city. I always have enough." When the people were told the governor's reply, they became very angry. They attacked the Manchu yamen, cut down the flagpole, the symbol of office, and drove out the governor. Following this, the Commissioner of Internal Affairs, a man named Chang, came out on his horse and told the people that the Government would take measures to help them. Chang evidently was sincere in his promise, but the Emperor disliked him and accused him of having intimate connections with "the mob." He was removed. A new governor arrived, and at once ordered the arrest of the leaders of the uprising. Many of them were beheaded and their heads displayed on poles as a warning to future "rebels."
>
> This incident was discussed in my school for many days. It made a deep impression on me. Most of the other students sympathized with the "insurrectionists," but only from an observer's point of view. They did not understand that it had any relation to their own lives. They were merely interested in it as an exciting incident. I never forgot it. I felt that there with the rebels were ordinary people like my own family and I deeply resented the injustice of the treatment given to them.[13]

The figures who won Mao's sympathy were the rebels—common people driven to extremes who fought heroically, though in the end futilely, against the powers that were.

Upon entering school in Changsha Mao began his lifelong habit of voracious newspaper reading. He thus became intimately acquainted with the chaotic conditions of Chinese politics.[14] The republic which replaced the emperor quickly lapsed into tragedy and then farce. The 1911 revolution ended imperial power by dissolving the political center; political unity would not be completely restored to China until 1949.[15] The threat of actual dissolution was serious, and foreign debts grew astronomically. The sentence Mao remembered reading in 1910, "Alas, China will be subjugated," seemed just as appropriate in 1919, when the results of the Versailles Peace Conference induced the explosive growth of new antiimperialist forces in China. Mao became an eloquent and powerful voice of antiwarlord and antiimperialist sentiment in Hunan.

Because of its location, Hunan's sufferings during this chaotic period were especially acute. The struggles between northern and southern powerholders crossed Hunan several times. Moreover, the economic boom caused by European preoccupation with the First World War was over by 1917, and by 1919 provincial mining exports had declined to 1913 levels.[16] Mao's impassioned account of Hunan's oppression by the rest of China and his support of the Hunan self-government movement show the provincial-patriotic direction of his early political thought.[17] Mao's attitude toward Hunan was complex. He considered it backward; its politics did not know of "thorough solutions based on agreement, but only of private wars."[18] But it was a province with a glorious tradition of revolution and of revolutionary intellectuals, particularly in recent times.

Despite his rural beginning, Mao quickly caught up with the leading currents in Chinese progressive thought. Mao "worshipped Kang Youwei and Liang Qiqiao" at the Tongshan Upper Primary School.[19] At the Hunan First Normal School he became an avid reader and later a contributor to the influential New Culture Movement periodical *Xin Qinqnian (New Youth)*, and in the May Fourth Movement he became known for his political and intellectual contributions to the Hunanese student movement. To someone with this background, China seemed young in thought, antiquated in institutions, and almost hopelessly adrift in politics.

Mao's Early Works

Although Mao was an exceptional student and radical leader during his years in Hunan, it is safe to say that had his activities and writings ceased in 1923, when he was twenty-nine years old, the surviving works of the period would not have received widespread attention from Western scholars. This is not to say that they are (or were) insignificant in themselves, but that much of their national and all of their international significance depends essentially on the further career of their author. The major utility of these early works in this respect is that they help to establish Mao's political identity before he became exclusively involved in the affairs of the Chinese Communist Party. A close analysis of Mao's pre-Marxist or precommunist works is essential for determining the effect of this change on his thought.

Unfortunately for the purposes of periodization, neither Mao's political commitments nor his ideology were suddenly transformed. If Mao could say as his good friend Cai Hesen did, "Whatever my earlier thoughts, they are all mistaken and bad; hereafter I will fly in pursuit of [Marxism],"[20] then neither the dividing line nor its significance would be in doubt. But in Mao's case, "pre-Marxist," "precommunist," and "exclusive devotion to party tasks" could all indicate different points in time. Mao's autobiography is cautiously worded: "By the summer of 1920 I had become, in theory and to some extent in action, a Marxist, and from this time I considered myself a Marxist." Other communist reminiscences prefer to quote this remark rather than supply their own periodization.[21] Mao founded the Hunan nucleus of the Chinese Communist Party early in 1921, and he attended the First Party Congress in April of that year. But the CCP in its first years was heterogeneous in both ideology and organization,[22] and Mao, as the founder and leader of the Hunan provincial branch, was in a position to determine for himself the practical significance of his commitments to communism. Therefore I have shaped this chapter according to the continuity of Mao's political activities and viewpoint rather than by the date of his confessed allegiance to Marxism or the date of the organization of the CCP. Mao continues to be engaged in (and to write about) province-wide activities with a "populist" rather than a class appeal until the fall of 1921, when organizing labor (the main effort of the CCP at this time) becomes his preoccupation. Although Mao's Marxist-oriented activities started as early as the summer of 1920, for the following year they coexist with more broadly based efforts. There are writings by Mao in a three-volume anthology he edited in the early twenties, *Collected Correspondence of New Citizens Study Society Members*,[23] which would shed valuable light on this theoretical development, but unfortunately they are unavailable. The available writings for 1920 and 1921 all concern his public, political, and cultural activities in Hunan.

The incompleteness of the corpus of Mao's early works is a considerable hindrance to comprehensive research on this period. The editors of Mao's *Collected Works* list the titles of thirty-one works written before 1922 which are not available, including one from 1919 entitled "What Is Socialism? What Is Anarchism?" and articles on women's rights and the labor movement. Beyond these, the large number of school essays and notebooks written by Mao during his five years at the First Normal School would be extremely useful in specifying the significance of various influences on his intellectual development. Thus an analysis of what is available—some snippets from various sources, six articles or series of articles, four advertisements—should not be mistaken for a complete picture of Mao's intellectual activity. But they are important works about subjects important to Mao, and a close reading of them is not likely to be misleading. The small number of writings makes it possible to discuss the context and significance of each major group of texts separately.

The earliest available texts by Mao are citations in Li Rui's biography from a 1914 notebook and from Mao's extensive marginal commentary on Cai Yuanpei's translation of Friedrich Paulsen's *System der Ethik*.[24] Mao's first published work was "A Study of Physical Education" in *New Youth*, April 1917.[25] The next available complete works are announcements for the first and second semesters of a night school for workers which Mao organized in 1917. In the aftermath of the May Fourth Movement Mao wrote many articles for journals which he started. The "Opening Statement of the *Xiang River Review*" (14 July 1919) is a baptismal piece for one of his journals,[26] and "The Great Union of the Popular Masses" is a series of three articles published in the following three issues of the journal.[27] Mao's involvement with specifically Hunanese political and cultural endeavors is reflected in three items: first, four articles and one coauthored manifesto on the Hunan self-government movement of 1920; second, three articles on the founding and early operations of the Cultural Book Society; and third, an introductory statement on the Hunan Self-Education College which Mao started in August 1921.

Quotations from Early Notes

The fragments which Li Rui provides from Mao's earliest notebooks are useless for the purpose of intensive analysis because they are short comments from unknown contexts. The quotations from Mao's marginal notes to Paulsen's *System of Ethics* are somewhat more useful because they are generally enthusiastic comments on a known text. However, as Li remarks, these are casual notes determined by the flow of Paulsen's text.[28]

Friedrich Paulsen was an influential German educator around the turn of the century who also wrote vigorous and popular works in philosophy and ethics. According to him the task of philosophy is to build a "metaphysics from below" *(Metaphysik von unten)* by synthesizing the results of the sciences rather than meditating abstractly. The foundation and goal of all philosophy is ethics, he argued, because will is primary to intellect. This distinction is not a conflict, since in Paulsen's view the laws of nature are ethical and the laws of ethics are natural. Since will is essentially the purposeful behavior of the universe, there is no ultimate separation between subjective and objective. Inclination and custom, individual will and the will of the totality, tend by and large in the same direction.[29] This ethical scientific world view was an assimilation of Darwinism[30] and various aspects of philosophy into a well-developed structure; it thus appealed to the progressive intellectuals in China who were faced with their own mediation between modern knowledge and a valuable ethical tradition.

Mao's enthusiastic response to Paulsen's *System of Ethics* and the parallel between Paulsen's views and Mao's later philosophy make a comparison of Paulsen and Mao tempting.[31] However, the comparison would necessarily imply an intellectual connection for which there is insufficient evidence. A Paulsenian essay which Mao wrote, "The Strength of the Will," and Mao's copy of *System of Ethics* from which Li Rui quotes would be essential to such a comparison. The quotations given by Li are of course selected to demonstrate the continuity of Mao's thought, but it is noteworthy that since Li's biography was written in 1958 some of these continuities have continued to develop. Mao's youthful animus against those who consider anything old as good and reject everything that is modern *(shi gu fei jin)*[32] is reflected in later movements which "slight the past and emphasize the present" *(bo gu hou jin)* and "use the past for the present and the foreign for China" *(gu wei jin yong yang wei zhong yong)*. His denunciation of the "four demons"—religion, capitalism, monarchy, and the three bonds (between prince and minister, father and son, husband and wife)—is an enduring political stance, although the evil basis of the four was later conceptualized as class oppression rather than oppression of the individual. The interdependence of opposites is another theme which has an important role in Mao's later thought. Stuart Schram has pointed out parallels between Mao's 1959 dialectics and the following reflection on Paulsen:

> I say: concept is reality, the limited is limitless, the sense of duration is transcendence of duration, imagination is thought, form is essence, I am the universe, life is death, death is life, present is the past and the future, past and future are present, small is large, yang is yin, up is down, vile is pure, thick is thin. Speaking of essences, the many are one, change is constancy.[33]

This logic is directly related to Mao's view of society in his assertion that strength depends on resistance and in his reflection on the interdependence of natural determinism and free will quoted at the beginning of this chapter.

"A Study of Physical Education"

Contemporaneous with the two-year ethics course in which he read Paulsen's book, Mao became actively concerned with the state of physical education at the First Normal School and in China as a whole. At school this concern resulted in his administration of an after-hours physical education program.[34] His general reflections on China's needs in this regard led to his first article, "A Study of Physical Education," published in *New Youth* in the spring of 1917.[35]

The article challenges even the present-day reader with statements like this:

Those whose bodies are delicate and small behave flippantly. Those whose skin is flabby are soft and dull in will *(Xin)*. This is the effect of their bodies on their minds.[36]

The purpose of the article is to alert readers to the general neglect and mismanagement of physical education in China and to urge them, especially students, to begin effective exercise. Although these two foci are respectively critical and hortatory, the major part of the argument is constructive. The insufficiency of contemporary efforts by physical educators is made evident in a disquisition on the fundamental importance of physical education. The exhortation to exercise is given force and content by an emphasis on the primacy of subjective consciousness in improving the situation and by the provision of a program of exercise.

The study of physical education is important to the individual because health is important; it is important to the nation because its weakness and lack of martial spirit stem from neglect of physical training. A vigorous pursuit of virtue and learning requires attention also to the balanced development of the body through exercise. But physical development is more than the presupposition of all other pursuits. The specific goal of physical education from a social point of view is martial heroism, something sorely needed in China, and thus training which develops strength of will and fierceness is especially recommended.

The article encourages the reader to proceed from understanding to action in order to improve an urgent situation. Mao is merciless in confronting the reader with his obligation to start exercising immediately. There is nothing more important, it is never too late, any method will do, exercise enhances rather than detracts from cerebral activities, neglect of exercise leads to a short life, a weak will, and flippant behavior. The basic theme is the primacy of self-awareness: "Strength *(jianshi)* lies in exercise and exercise lies in self-awareness."[37] The consciousness emphasized here is not abstract potential or freedom of choice, but the concrete ability (hence responsibility) to proceed from correct understanding to successful action. Mao's thorough rejection of physical education programs concludes not with an exhortation to change these programs but with a reminder that the main thing is the individual's awareness of the importance of physical education and his commitment to self-improvement.

Mao's emphasis on subjectivity as the solution to physical development is balanced by an emphasis on practical results. A hundred exercise programs may be propounded, but if "one method or half a method" is sufficient, there is no need to bother about the rest. Talk about physical education is not important. What is important is actually doing it. Mao underlines the practical orientation of the article by concluding with a full set of exercises.

One striking characteristic of this article among Mao's works is its nonpolitical nature. Praise and blame are assigned on the basis of people's relationship to physical education rather than to politics. Thus the martial sports of Japan and the West are praised as well as robust figures of history: Yan Yuan, Mohammed, Theodore Roosevelt, Gu Yanwu, Zeng Guofan. Those berated most severely are the teachers and the educational system as a whole, both modern and traditional components, and, by implication, the students for allowing the system and group pressure to cause them to neglect their vital interests.

Although the single-mindedness of the article precludes a specific political viewpoint, the article does have political and social implications and displays traits which underlie Mao's later political activities. Mao's alternative ideas for education were not presented until the founding of Hunan Self-Education College in 1921, but his description of modern schools as detrimental to the physical well-being of students is a serious criticism of his immediate social structure. Just as important, however, is the theme of activism itself. "A Study of Physical Education" is the first and most basic of Mao's many efforts to stir an audience to movement. To awaken communal self-awareness and to develop communal strength and will through practical activity are enduring themes of Mao's social and political efforts. The potential attributed to conscious, disciplined activity is infinite. No one is too old or too weak, no obstacle is too great, for "the character of the body can change, the weak can become strong, body and mind can both be complete—this is not a matter of fate but is completely within human power." The metaphysical foundation of Mao's confidence in the metamorphosing potential of action is given with double emphasis: *"There is only movement in heaven and earth."*[38] This rejection of the immutability of the world, with its corollaries of the dialectical relativity of knowledge and the unlimited potential for action, reappears in the well-known allegory "The Foolish Old Man Who Removed the Mountains."[39] The specific character of this dialectical mode of exhortation can best be seen in contrast to its nondialectical counterpart, "Do your best." In the latter formulation, moral justification is attained through maximum effort, but horizons of potential are accepted. Mao's formulation concentrates rather on the persistence of effort and its effectiveness in transforming present limits.

The Workers' Night School

Mao's work in physical education was only one of an astonishing number of projects, political, educational, and even military,[40] which he engaged in before the May Fourth Movement. Originally most of Mao's organizational talent was spent in student affairs, although he also distributed leaflets against Yuan Shikai and developed his political and social views. But as the final year of school approached, Mao and his activist friends began work in Changsha and founded the New Citizens Study Society, "a society which was to have a widespread influence on the affairs and destiny of China."[41] The group had three main purposes: the maintenance of selfless devotion to national salvation; self-improvement through discussion, study, and exercise; and progressive community activities. Whereas Mao's vigorous support of student interests in the First Normal School sometimes led to serious confrontations with school authorities, the extracurricular activities of the New Citizens Study Society were not disruptive. In this respect their activities were considerably different from the antitraditional forays of the elitist and protected colleagues of Zhang Guotao, who recalls from his youth: "Thunderously we stormed temples, smashed images of the gods, and campaigned against medical cures dispensed by clay idols. Naturally we were in constant conflict with pious and religiously faithful people."[42]

Typical and most demanding of Mao's projects was the Night School for Workers which was started in late 1917. The registration announcements for the first two semesters of the school provide short statements of its purpose and program.[43] Claiming that the workers' greatest handicap was not being able to read, write, and calculate, the students of the First Normal School offered free courses at a time convenient to workers. The enterprise involved considerable effort. There were over 120 students, with classes meeting for two hours five days a week, and Mao managed the school and taught history.

Another important activity of the New Citizens Study Society was encouraging Hunanese participation in the work-study scheme for education in France organized in Peking by Wu Yuzhang and Cai Yuanpei. It was in connection with this activity that Mao made his first trip outside of Hunan, during which he stayed for several months in Peking working in the library of Beijing University. Exposed to the leading edge of Chinese intellectual and political progressivism, Mao became more political and more radical. He returned to Changsha via Confucius' birthplace and Shanghai a few months before the outbreak of the epochal May Fourth Movement in Peking in 1919.

Opening Statement of the Xiang River Review

The effect of the May Fourth Movement on Changsha is described in the opening paragraph of the *Xiang River Review*, written two months after the beginning of the movement:

> Since the call of "world revolution" and the onrushing movement to "liberate mankind" antiquated outlooks must be changed. Formerly we did not raise doubts on many problems, did not quickly adopt many methods, and out of fear shrank from saying many things. Now the undoubted is doubted, the unattempted is attempted, many feared things are no longer feared. No matter who the personage, he cannot escape its influence.[44]

Mao Zedong, recent college graduate and just returned from a stimulating trip to Peking, was a leader of one of the few activist student groups in China antedating the May Fourth Movement. He was thus in a preeminent position not only to experience but to direct the impact of the May Fourth Movement in Hunan. The significance of the May Fourth Movement cannot be reduced to the anti-Japanese movement or to the New Culture Movement. It served as a catalyst for a society which urgently needed a new form of political expression and a new map for political orientation. China, whose political life had traditionally been controlled and centralized, was shattered into shifting zones of power and mortally threatened by imperialism. Its social ordering, determined until the twentieth century by a centralized and open examination system, now left university graduates with an uncertain future. Lastly, the indomitable, unified, and progressive West to which China had grown accustomed had torn itself apart in the war and was now frantically on the defensive against new, even more progressive, popular forces epitomized by the Russian Revolution.

The founding of a newspaper was an appropriate May Fourth activity. Not only was the awakening of large groups of people to political action exciting and newsworthy but the rapidity of the movement's development led to optimistic prognostications of political transformation. Mao's *Xiang River Review*, although it lasted only four weeks before it was shut down by Hunan's warlord, Zhang Jingyao, was a successful and widely respected May Fourth publication.[45]

The "Opening Statement of the *Xiang River Review*" (14 July 1919) is more a call to enlightenment than to action. As Mao remarks elsewhere in the same issue:

> Of China's 400,000,000 people, approximately 390,000,000 are superstitious. They blindly believe in ghosts, they blindly worship unusual natural phenomena, they blindly believe in fate, they blindly believe in coercion *(qiang quan)*. They don't recognize that there are individuals, that there is a self, that there is truth.[46]

His message is that hunger is the world's greatest problem and that the masses united have the greatest strength. Mao tries to explain "how mankind should live." He says that democracy is the basis for all opposition to coercion.[47] The powers that be in the sphere of religion, literature, politics, society, education, economy, thought, and international politics must be struck down by the call for democracy. Moderate methods are preferred to violent methods, because the oppressors are also prisoners of the old society and their abuse of power is an unconscious error. Besides this compassionate motive, Mao notes that the end result of using coercion to strike down coercion is still coercion.

Within his general preference for moderate methods, Mao makes distinctions between different situations and the behavior appropriate to them. In the academic sphere he proposes thorough research that is not bounded by tradition or superstition. In society he advocates unity of the masses to launch a persistent movement to offer those in power "loyal advice" and to achieve a "revolution by appeals." This strategy is contrasted to "revolution by bomb" and "bloody revolution," which he feels merely result in great confusion. To resist the immediate threat of Japan, however, he suggests boycott of classes, suspension of commercial activities, strikes against factories, and boycott of Japanese products as effective measures. This concern for finding the appropriate methods for diverse social and political circumstances finds its theoretical form in Mao's later discourse on the particularity of contradiction.

The themes of awakening, fearlessness, and confidence in impending social transformation which pervade the article are expressions of a faith in the power of the united masses stimulated by popular ferment in China and the West. The May Fourth Movement served as the catalyst for fusing Mao's progressive political sentiments and his inclination toward practical activity into engagement in radical politics. Political engagement gave Mao's thinking a new starting point. From this time on, revolution is the focus of his theory and practice.

The content of Mao's May Fourth views is as interesting as their new political engagement. The orientation is universal and thorough: the call is "worldwide" to liberate "humanity," and the basic slogan is "achieve freedom from coercion."[48] Paradoxically, Mao's confidence in impending, thorough social transformation accounts for the moderate tactics he suggests. He does not see the new society as a desperate undertaking, so violence is not required. In fact, violence would taint the new order with the methods of the old.

A link between this work and the Night School advertisements is Mao's presupposition of enlightenment as a prelude to action. This attitude is best explained by an earlier comment on Paulsen:

> To say that knowledge has no impact at all on men's hearts is wrong; knowledge definitely has a great impact.... That mankind has had progress, revolution, and the spirit of correcting faults is completely due to activists *(huodong zhe)* who relied on the leadership of new thought.[49]

Although the dichotomies of teacher and taught, mover and moved, enlightened and ignorant are not explicit in the *Xiang River Review*, the overdrawn description of the backwardness of Hunan and the nature of the newspaper's project suggest that a leading group is necessary to awaken the masses.

"The Great Union of the Popular Masses"

The main political essay of the remaining three issues of the *Xiang River Review* is the three-part article "The Great Union of the Popular Masses," which elaborates the idea of the power of the unified masses into a general perspective on politics and the Chinese and international political situations. The high reputation of the *Xiang River Review* probably derives in large part from this article, which was reprinted in full in *Xingqiri* [Sunday], a Sichuan publication, and later was reprinted in Shanghai.[50]

The most striking stylistic characteristic of the piece is a recurring dialectical progression from extremely bad to extremely good, and a related emphasis on the basic identity of diverse phenomena. The fact that "the darkness of society has reached an extreme," internationally through the world war and nationally through the North-South War, is the precondition to political transformation. "Thus there arises reform, there arises resistance, therefore there is a great alliance of the masses of the people."[51] A similar transformation is expected for China. Although she now seems completely incompetent in political and economic affairs, in the future China will be preeminent among nations.[52] As Mao observes in a later work, the theme of transformation of opposites is both very Chinese and very Marxist. Marx's philosophical reason for suggesting the proletariat as the ultimate revolutionary group is that they are so oppressed that they are an anticlass rather than a part of bourgeois society.[53] A similar confidence in the transformation of opposites leads Mao to welcome the observation (which otherwise would be disquieting) that the principle of action he recommends, the "great union," has been the root source of power for the nobles, the powerful, and the capitalists throughout history. The technique of union, whose power comes from numbers, was perfected by the few against the many. From the resulting community of weakness and misery arises the greatest union to destroy its oppressors.

The "Great Union of the Popular Masses" is a theory of society, a methodology for social transformation, and a judgment of China's readiness for transformation. In the first installment Mao discusses the "possibility and necessity of the great union." The argument proceeds from the observation that "no matter what the type of historical movements, there are none which do not proceed from the union of some people."[54] He points out that the power-holding minorities using the advantages of education, money, and military strength have driven the masses of people to such extremes that they have an intimate knowledge of the methods of oppression and are becoming conscious of the incomparably greater power of a mass union. Only a great shout need be given, and the old society will crumble. In the second installment, Mao presents the method of building up to a great union by starting with groups of common interests. He gives examples of the common interests of various basic groups (farmers, workers, women, and the like) and suggests aggregating these groups in general unions. The third installment deals with China's readiness for such a movement. Mao presents the situation realistically, demythologizing the 1911 revolution but valuing the experience of provincial and county assemblies and of course the organizations blossoming as a result of the May Fourth Movement. He reasons that China's embarrassing performance in politics and economics is due to lack of political experience stemming from long oppression. He concludes that the very length and intensity of oppression will lead to exceptionally rapid development:

> Some day the reform of the Chinese people will be more thorough than that of any other people. The society of the Chinese people will be more glorious than that of any other people. The great union of the Chinese people will be successfully completed before that of any other place or nation. Gentlemen! Gentlemen! We must exert ourselves together! We must strive forward together! Our golden world *(shijie)*, our glorious and bright world, is right before us![55]

Mao's political horizons are indistinct in this article. The first part is dominated by a universal frame of reference and a call to imitate countries, like Russia, more advanced in their great unions. Since the second part deals primarily with small unions it is locally oriented, with Changsha in mind, but the suggestions apply to other localities. The last part deals with China as a whole and is nationally oriented. As Stuart Schram has pointed out, the article's conclusion (which is quoted above) is one of the most nationalistic passages in Mao's writings.[56] However, it would certainly be mistaken to ignore the internationalist tone of the first installment and the "Introductory Statement of the *Xiang River Review*," since internationalism constitutes an integral part of

Mao's argument. This seeming paradox of nationalism versus internationalism is partly explained by a difference in timing. For the present, China's task is to learn from countries which are more advanced in popular struggles against power. China's future transformation, once accomplished, will be as glorious as her oppression was severe, but this preeminence will exist in a transformed world order and thus will not constitute hegemony among competitive nations. Mao's patriotism for China's existing political order does not extend beyond faith in China's future and defensiveness vis-à-vis foreign encroachments. In his proposals on Hunanese self-government in the following year, Mao reviews the utter failure of central government in China since 1911 and concludes, "The best thing would be [for China] to split into twenty-seven countries *(guo)*."[57] Even this apparent provincialism is not as far from Mao's nationalism and internationalism as it would seem. Mao's reasoning leads him to this proposal through the principle of self-determination, which he establishes with international examples as a universal principle. Mao propounds this self-determination of China's subunits for the immediate good of the Chinese people and expects them in the future to be reunited in a single polity.

The deeper problem in categorizing Mao's stance in regard to national boundaries is that China's national experience in modern times has differed fundamentally from that of the West. Western nationalism was at its most characteristic in the discovery of collective cultural identities and the attempts to establish corresponding political entities. In some cases nationalism demanded the subdivision of culturally diverse empires; in others it involved the amalgamation of culturally similar but politically diverse polities. Western nations by and large defined themselves against each other, seeking to distinguish separate identity from a common heritage. China's national experience was instead a discovery of a world beyond herself. China found herself defined by the forceful incursion of cultures she would have preferred to ignore. In Kang Youwei's *Datong Shu* [The book of great harmony], China's retreat from the presumed universalism of her cultural significance to being one nation among many is linked to a general dissolution of national boundaries and establishment of a world community. Mao seems to share this self-confidence of cultural subsistence within a cosmopolitan framework, a position which cannot be described simply as nationalist or internationalist.

A further problem in interpreting this article arises from the following passage:

> As for the actions to be undertaken after the union [of the masses has been achieved], there is one very radical faction which uses the method of do unto others as they do unto you, and which does its utmost to cause trouble for them [the capitalists and the aristocrats]. The leader of this faction is a German-born person named Marx. The faction which is milder than Marx is not anxious to see quick results and begins with the understanding of the common people. All should have a morality of mutual aid and work voluntarily. If nobles and capitalists turn their hearts toward the good and are capable of working, are capable of helping people and not harming them, then they don't have to be killed. The ideas of this faction are more comprehensive, profound, and far-reaching. They want to unify the world and make it one country, unify humanity into one family, enjoy harmonious, happy, intimate, and good relationships—not the type of intimate and close relationship suggested by Japan—and together achieve prosperity. This faction's leader is a Russian-born person named Kropotkin.[58]

The question which of course arises from this passage is whether Mao was an anarchist at this time—or at any rate more of an anarchist than a Marxist. Mao relates in his autobiography that he discussed anarchism during his stay in Peking in 1918. It is evident from this quotation that the anarchism Mao has in mind is of a very mild sort. Richard Solomon's statement that "Mao himself, in student days, had toyed with the anarchist's glorification of violence for its own sake" is completely mistaken.[59] In China the content of anarchism ran the whole gamut from men of goodwill with an animus toward hierarchy to violent nihilists.[60] Mao's "anarchism" favors organization for political and social ends, but it opposes the use of violence in attaining them. If the question of political violence is disregarded, it could be argued that rather than Mao later converting to Marxism, Chinese Marxism came to Mao, since such characteristically Chinese Communist tenets as mass line, internationalism, and benevolence to transformed reactionaries roughly correspond to the virtues of anarchism which he enumerates in the article. Early Chinese Communists were not hostile to anarchism. They applauded its rejection of existing society and its communal ideal but considered it impractical and utopian as a political movement. As a 1921 article put it, "the anarchists are our friends but not our comrades."[61]

There are, however, some significant differences between the political viewpoint expressed in "The Great Union of the Popular Masses" and Mao's later Marxism. The most evident is his reluctance to consider violent means in confronting the powerholders. Instead of this means of confrontation, two methods are proposed: the immediate one of patiently building up basic groups and the ultimate one of the all-powerful "great shout together." Mao's pacifism is intimately related to the reliance on groups rather than classes—sociability rather than unequal relations—as the basic social unit.[62] The result is a cry for liberation rather than a call for revolution. In this sense it could be said that Mao's political views in 1919 were more utopian than anarchist, and his own description, "a curious mixture," is most accurate.[63]

The Hunan Self-Government Movement

With the political stimulation of the May Fourth Movement, Mao became involved in a variety of public causes. The most notable of his efforts were an attempt to unseat the Hunan warlord Zhang Jingyao and a flurry of articles on the status of women prompted by the suicide of an unwilling bride in late 1919. Mao lost the first round of his battle with Zhang when a general student strike against the warlord led to the suppression of the *Xiang River Review*. Mao went on his second trip to Peking and Shanghai in order to enlist the aid of influential Hunanese in the capital in removing Zhang. Mao's writings on the status of women helped stimulate a major discussion of this question in Changsha, but only fragments of these newspaper articles are currently available.[64] Mao's basic point was that traditional Chinese society had bound women in an "iron cage" from which suicide might seem the only escape. The same general sentiment is echoed in Mao's position of the 1950s that "genuine equality of the sexes can only be realized in the process of the socialist transformation of society as a whole."[65]

Zhang Jingyao was driven out of Hunan by July 1920. Although this event was due more to the vagaries of warlord politics than to the vigorous efforts of Mao, the New Citizens Study Society, and many other Hunanese to oust him, the situation presented an unusual opportunity for the war-ridden province to acquire some autonomy and freedom from military rule. In these circumstances a two-factioned movement for "Hunanese Self-Government" arose. The more conservative faction was composed of established politicians and favored a constitution written by a committee of provincial politicians and assembly members. The more radical wing favored a popularly elected constitutional assembly. Of the ten articles Mao wrote supporting the radical self-government faction, four (and a codrafted proposal) have been discovered by Angus McDonald.[66]

Mao's articles have two basic concerns: the first is the precondition of a successful and long-lasting self-government; the second is the possibility and desirability of self-government for Hunan. The basic requirement for successful self-government is that it have a popular basis, since self-government organized exclusively by gentry would be fundamentally misconceived. This popular basis can be achieved by real mobilization of the people. On the second point, Mao observes that the theory that only big nations are strong enough to survive is an imperialist lie disproved by revolutions all over the world. That autonomy would benefit Hunan is indicated by a long and impressive narration of the sufferings Hunan has undergone because she was part of China. The fifth work, "A Proposal to Convene a 'Hunan People's Constitutional Convention' by the 'Hunan Revolutionary Government' to Enact a 'Hunan Constitution' for the Purpose of Constructing a 'New Hunan,'" is just what its title implies. It was coauthored by Mao, the editor of the Changsha *Da Gong Bao*, and the president of the Hunan union of students, and was signed by 377 students, journalists, lawyers, and others. Although it cannot be considered an article which Mao wrote, it is a document to which he contributed.

The content of these articles can be fruitfully related to that of the "Great Union of the Popular Masses" written the previous year. To some extent we have here a "great unionist" at work, one not discouraged by starting small, engaging in patient work at the existing level of people's consciousness, insisting that a durable government needs a popular basis, and finding proof of the possibility of Hunan's self-government in international developments and the extremity of Hunan's suffering. Angus McDonald calls such activity "more Woodrow Wilson than Lenin,"[67] and the same scornful judgment from a radical point of view is made seven months after Mao's articles in the journal *Gongchandang* [Communist]: "If one day the warlords were overthrown by the gentry *(shenren)* class, the gentry class would immediately turn into the previous warlords, doing evil of the same kind and manner, robbing the common people."⁶⁸ Both these judgments confuse a concern for immediate activity with an acceptance of the politics of such a movement as abstractly necessary and sufficient—for that matter, they are considerably more rigid than the political tactics of Lenin or Marx. Mao had defended the "Oust Zhang Jingyao" and "Self-Government" movements to critical members of the New Citizens Study Group:

> The movement to oust Zhang was just a simple opposition to the powerholder *(qiang quan zhe)* Zhang Jingyao. The self-government movement is just a simple aspiration that Hunan could specially produce a method which would allow Hunan to become a relatively good environment. Within this environment we would like to pursue concrete preparatory work.
> These two movements are both only expediencies utilizing the present context . . . in order to achieve measures for basic reform.⁶⁹

On the other hand the tone is significantly different from that of his May Fourth work. Much of the energy of the May Fourth Movement seemed to have evaporated as quickly as it arose, and, although Mao took the long view rather than despairing, the lessons of the movement significantly affected his political outlook. The world and China had awakened, but persistent and practical movements drawing their strength from the people were replacing the political mechanism of the great shout. This recognition of the political power of organization and concrete programs is a natural and direct development from Mao's emphasis the previous year on organizing "small unions" around shared grievances. In his autobiography, Mao connects this realization to an incident in the self-government movement:

> I remember an episode in 1920, when the New Citizens Study Society organized a demonstration to celebrate the third anniversary of the Russian October Revolution. It was suppressed by the police. Some of the demonstrators had attempted to raise the Red Flag at that meeting, but were prevented from doing so by the police. They then pointed out that, according to Article 12 of the [then] Constitution, the people had the right to assemble, organize, and speak, but the police were not impressed. They replied that they were not there to be taught the Constitution, but to carry out the orders from the governor, Zhao Hengti. From this time on I became more and more convinced that only mass political power, secured through mass action, could guarantee the realization of dynamic reforms.⁷⁰

The Cultural Book Society

The self-government movement was not the only effort Mao made at this time to prepare Hunan for basic reforms. In 1920 Mao organized a Russian affairs study group and a work-study scheme for students going to Russia, a Marxism study group, a Hunan branch of the Socialist Youth Corps (one of the most successful provincial branches), and the Cultural Book Society. He was, moreover, director of the Primary School Section of the First Normal School and chairman of its alumni club.

Of all these varied activities, it is most fortunate that material has been preserved on the Cultural Book Society. Whereas the political relevance of his other activities is fairly self-evident, that Mao would operate a bookstore as a mission rather than as a means of support seems anomalous. The available documents on the society make clear the various educational functions of the enterprise.

The Cultural Book Society was a cooperative capitalized by members' contributions and run by an elected manager (Mao) who was obligated to make semiannual public reports. Its main purpose was "allowing all kinds of worthwhile recent publications to spread throughout the province, giving everyone the opportunity to peruse them."[71] This was done by operating a main bookstore and ordering service in Changsha and encouraging branches to be set up in all counties. Later plans were announced for setting up an editing and translation bureau and a printing department.[72] All persons contributing one yuan or more were considered equal members; contributions did not pay interest and could not be withdrawn; no profit was made by the main bookstore on branch society purchases; and the society's accounts were available for inspection to everyone, member or not.

These regulations already suggest some of the secondary motivations for the society, motivations which are made explicit in the report of April 1921 given just before Mao left for the First Congress of the Chinese Communist Party. The society was not just a bookstore trying to sell progressive books. It considered itself a semipublic provincial organ with a mission to make available "books of value" to everyone. Enhancing its semipublic character was its partially successful attempt to use county educational officials and facilities for organizing branch book societies throughout Hunan. Moreover, it was constructed as a model organization for Chinese social ventures: its business was open (contrasted to the Chinese penchant for secrecy in business); its capital was not threatened by the possibility of withdrawal; it was not an undertaking for individual profit (Mao castigates the excessive individualism of Chinese merchants in "The Great Union of the Popular Masses"); and its accounts were orderly and efficient. This "model enterprise" reminds one of Robert Owens' attempt to win British merchants to humane treatment of workers by demonstrating that his New Lanark factory was a financial success—except that Mao tried to do without either the primitive or the essentially capitalistic aspects of the entrepreneurial system.[73]

So far as its fate is recorded, the Cultural Book Society was a success. A coup was scored at its founding by getting Tan Yankai, durable Hunanese politician and then governor of the province, to supply his calligraphy for the signboard of the bookstore. By the time of the semiannual report, seven branches and seven school depots had been established and the society had sold 160 titles (including, according to Li Rui, *An Introduction to Marx's Capital*, *History of Socialism*, and *The Worker's and Peasant's Government and China*), 40 different magazines, and 3 newspapers. Perhaps Mao's success with an alternative enterprise encouraged him to attempt alternative education the following year.

The Hunan Self-Education College

Mao's last Hunan venture which did not presuppose a class viewpoint was the founding of the Hunan Self-Education College. Despite Han Suyin's claim that "the whole purpose of the college was actually the recruitment and training of cadres for the Communist Party,"[74] the "Introductory Statement of the Hunan Self-Education College" persuasively argues a broader case based on a participatory concept of education which can be traced in Mao's earliest works. The school in its original conceptualization does not seem to have been successful, however, and Mao himself had little time for it after the first few months.

The college was conceived as a quasi-public provincial institution by its founder—and with ironic justification in that it was indirectly supported by provincial funds. A public stipend of four hundred yuan per month to the Quan Shan (Wang Fuzhi) Society was diverted, legally, to the establishment and maintenance of the college. The college was dissolved in November 1923 for teaching rebellious doctrines, but in two months it reappeared as the Xiang River Middle School.

On 16 August 1921, the "Introductory Statement of the Hunan Self-Education College" was published in Changsha newspapers in order to explain the college and attract students. The article is a development of the theme clearly stated in the first paragraph: "Its [the college's] purpose lies in using the traditional academy *(shuyuan)* form to acquire the content of the modern schools *(xuexiao).*"[75] Mao goes on to criticize the career orientation of the traditional academies and, more interestingly, the structural and methodological faults of modern schools. After evaluating their respective good points, he describes their shared "nondemocracy" *(fei pingmin zhuyi):* entry is restricted by examinations and high fees, and an intellectual class *(jieji)* of academicians who isolate themselves from the people is established.[76] Finally, Mao argues, the province of Hunan needs the college because there is no Hunan University as yet and the Hunanese people need something to satisfy their spiritual needs and develop their cultural desires:

> Although in actuality it [the college] is unable to establish relations with every Hunanese, in spirit it must be made into a public academic organ of the Hunanese society; although it is impossible to say for sure that it will have very good results, if we advance energetically for many years and months, we believe that one day we will achieve our goals.[77]

An interesting feature of this article is that although Mao was the leader of the Hunan Communist Party by this time, the article's format, combining the good points of old and new educational systems, is the most moderate stance that Mao had taken toward existing conditions so far. The effect of the article was more radical, however, since Mao's trenchant critique of the modern schools was a basic attack on a progressively disposed and influential segment of the provincial elite.[78] His critique of the modern school is basically this: there is no intimate relation between teacher and student, only uniform and mechanical management; moreover, the system requires passive students and thus inhibits individual character from developing. The second charge is directly related to Mao's earlier criticism of the schools in "A Study of Physical Education" and "Great Union of the Popular Masses."[79]

The concept of class *(jieji)* makes its first strong appearance in this article,[80] but the "class of common people" is the major focus and the proletarian class *(wuchan jieji)* enters as "the so-called proletarian class." The most interesting use of the term is its application to academicians. They monopolize learning by making it mysterious, thereby isolating themselves from the society of common people and "developing the curious situation of a kind of intellectual class *(zhishi jieji)* using the class of common people as slaves."[81] The function of the term "class" here is to identify a group with its own interests vis-à-vis another group. Class is not defined by an individual attribute shared by all members but by a corporate behavior pattern in which all members take part. As used here, class is thus "class for itself" rather than "class in itself."

Shortly after founding the Self-Education College, Mao became very busy in organizing the Hunan labor movement in line with party policy before the 7 February 1923 Incident involving the killing of railway workers in North China. The Hunan labor movement, spurred by the successful Anyuan Coal Mine strike in September 1922, developed rapidly. Mao's leadership in the labor unrest made him a persona non grata with the governor, who ordered his arrest. Mao fled to Shanghai in April 1923.

Conclusion

Throughout all of Mao's early activities and writings the most striking characteristic is an energetic and selfless concern for public affairs. In his innumerable efforts to do something for the common good, Mao is the prototype of the main target of future CCP recruitment—the activist *(jijifenzi)*.

Mao's style consistently urges the reader to *do* something. The moral imperatives are neither abstract nor categorical: the discussion of the topic leads to a consideration of *what* to do which implies *who* to do it. In every article Mao identifies himself as one of those who see the problem and feel compelled to act. The pronoun "we" is far more important than "I," and its reference group is never exclusive and usually is the people.[82]

In the works discussed in this chapter, Mao's activism is expressed in the intimate relationship between theoretical concerns and practical activities. Every article contains a significant and plausible proposal for immediate action, and in most cases Mao already had been engaged in the endeavor he suggests. His concerns are thus about matters with which he is familiar, and he writes when he thinks successful action is possible. The question of where to begin is never left unanswered; in fact, it is sometimes used as a critical tool against alternative viewpoints.[83] As Mao remarked to his fellow New Citizens Study Society members:

> I feel that very many people talk about reform, but for them it is only an empty ideal. Where do they eventually want to get to with their reforms? What methods will they use to achieve it? At what point will they themselves or their comrades begin work?—there is very little careful research of these problems.[84]

Mao's practical orientation has a basic influence on his theoretical style. Since any theory proposed is expected to be workable in practice, Mao's chief concern is with the correctness of the theory at hand rather than an abstract comparison of alternative hypotheses. Mao wants to penetrate to the essence of the matter, using assumptions of unanimity ("everyone knows . . .") to establish his formulation of the problem and wide-ranging examples from Chinese history and modern nations to support factual judgments. The assumptions of unanimity are not so much self-evident propositions as assumptions necessary to the general orientation of the article. When in the "Report of the Affairs of the Cultural Book Society" Mao says, "Everybody understands that there is nothing more necessary than the propagation of culture, and the efficacy of cultural propagation should not be limited to the efficacy of a few schools,"[85] he is not stating the obvious. However, the article is not directed at anyone who would have serious reservations about this statement. Mao's constant use of examples is another sign of his practical orientation. This is especially evident in "A Study of Physical Education" and the "Hunan Self-Government" article. In the "Great Union of the Popular Masses," the dialectic of oppression and liberation is grounded in a wealth of examples from Western history. Since the Cultural Book Society and the Self-Education College are new institutions, there is little place for argument from example. But it is interesting that a significant part of Mao's motivation in promoting these novel institutions is the exemplary function he expects them to have. The importance of examples in his thinking adds significance to the founding of model institutions.

In these early writings the dialectical interdependence and flux of reality has an explicit centrality for Mao's thinking which begins to submerge in the Hunan self-government writings. This shift does not represent the displacement of dialectics by a more categorical approach. Rather, the limited, practical tasks of his later Hunan activities required only proximate practical justifications, and still later his party activities required only proximate ideological ones. It is not difficult to perceive a continuity in dialectical substructure in Mao's later writings. When the development of his political thinking demanded a major reorientation in approach, as in 1937 and 1956–1957, Mao reasoned from his basic dialectical viewpoint. But the more philosophical works expose the logical skeleton of his thinking; they are not temporary apostasies from an otherwise dogmatic Marxism. The anti-Marxist bias typical of Western scholarship on Mao has contributed more to the apparent woodenness of Mao's writings than did Mao himself.

Ultimately, Mao's justification for ideological commitment is utility. Mao argues for the New Citizens Study Society to become Marxist: "Unions of feeling *(ganjing de jihe)* should become unions of ideology *(zhuyi de jihe)*. . . . Ideology is like a banner. When the banner is raised, everyone then has something to hope for, something to run after."[86] The acceptance of ideology for its utility does not imply a merely tentative commitment, because the revolutionary action which it facilitates is the central task. Given a crisis of ideological leadership, however, it might be expected (particularly with hindsight) that development of the useful aspects of ideology and revolutionary organization would take precedence over submission to party dogma.

The chief characteristic of Mao's political viewpoint in these early works is what he calls democracy *(pingmin zhuyi)*. Although the expression is used in only two works,[87] it underlies Mao's orientation toward the general welfare and organizational nonexclusiveness which permeate his writings and activities and explains his procedural tenets of self-determination and openness in public and semipublic affairs. His democratic-populist orientation is based on the conviction, expressed in his May Fourth articles, that the united masses of the people are the strongest political force. A corollary developed by the first and second "Hunan Self-Government" articles is that a strong and viable government cannot be built without eliciting popular support:

> How can a matter in its inception, particularly when it is extremely important, be run successfully or well if there are not many persons

to engage in a movement to promote it, to inspect it from the side and to criticize it from behind?[88]

The Cultural Book Society and Hunan Self-Education College both assume a natural legitimacy from their democratic structure and populist missions. Both express, moreover, a quasi-governmental urge to be available to all the people within the provincial boundaries.

Mao's apparent shift of focus between provincialism, nationalism, and internationalism can be explained by changes in his political expectations. In each case Mao turns to the largest feasible unit. The optimistic May Fourth articles recognize no organizational limit to the power of the masses. By 1920 Mao did not think that mass politics could be achieved on a national scale, and his activities assumed provincial horizons. Thus his "provincialism" is not an enclosure of his political aspirations; it reflects a practical judgment that only a provincial movement could be attempted at that time. In all cases the well-being and discretion of subunits is respected, whether they are small unions, county assemblies, or branch book societies.

The developments in Mao's political thought during this period correspond to stages in Mao's political experience. The May Fourth Movement demonstrated to Mao that political institutions (analogous to paternal power and school authorities) were "paper tigers" when faced with a determined movement from below. The consequent politicization of his activities and attitudes was disciplined by the subsiding of the movement. His next attempt was within the framework of a political movement, admonishing its supporters to develop a popular base for their autonomous government. Not only were Mao's efforts unsuccessful, but the entire self-government movement soon became a political ploy of the new warlord, Zhao Hengti. Mao's activities then became less directly political. His study groups were aimed at raising the theoretical level of fellow activists; more general endeavors like the Cultural Book Society and Hunan Self-Education College attempted to enliven social consciousness throughout the population. In the meantime Mao's own political standpoint was becoming more thoroughly Marxist and he became more involved in his organizational role in the Chinese Communist Party. From 1921 to 1923, Mao took a leading part in organizing labor throughout Hunan. The slaughter of railway workers in North China in the 7 February 1923 Incident signaled a retreat in unionizing activities, and the situation of the Communist Party in Hunan worsened. After his forced exit from Hunan, Mao worked for the Party Central Committee in Shanghai and shortly afterward became involved in united front work with the Kuomintang.

The significance of Mao's pre-Marxist thought is perhaps best epitomized by a statement in "A Study of Physical Education": "The will *(yizhi)* is definitely the forerunner of a man's career."[89] Mao's early activities and writings reflect the establishment of his basic mentality and style, which become enduring components of his political identity. The continuities which are recognizable from Mao's earliest writings are not crystallized aspects of ideas or behavior, however; they exist in an active dialectic with changing political environments and developments in thought and experience. The basic continuities of Mao's thought can be generalized as follows. First is the continuity in form or specific patterns of thinking in spite of discontinuity in content. Preeminent among these patterns are attention to the immediate despite changes in "what is concrete" at any particular moment and the use of a dialectical logic in ethics and social analysis. Second is the continuity in basic assumptions in spite of discontinuity in methods. The primary assumption that "the united masses of the people are the strongest political force" remains the same despite basic changes in Mao's framework of social analysis (from group to class) and his framework of political action (from self-organized local associations to the Communist Party). Assumptions of the necessity of struggle and the importance of practice also remain the same despite transformations of their application. Finally, there is continuity in ultimate aspiration in spite of discontinuities in practical policies. Mao's goal of a China transformed to serve the people is ultimately behind such apparently compromising or mundane affairs as running a bookstore.

2 Mao, the Party, and the National Revolution: 1923-1927

The demarcation between Mao's democratic-populist activities and his commitment to the politics of the national revolution is the collapse of Mao's hope for Hunanese revolution. This change in orientation was not abrupt: as political conditions in Hunan restricted Mao's popular activities to cultural and educational ventures, his political enthusiasm came to be channeled into the politics of the working class and the Chinese Communist Party. But the final abandonment of a populist political style and of Hunan as an adequate revolutionary arena in 1923 is nevertheless a watershed of great importance for Mao's political development. Mao's next three years of CCP activities marked an irrevocable commitment to a new framework of politics. His concern with the peasant movement from 1925 to 1926 returned him to a direct concern with the problems of mass revolution, but despite serious tensions with the CCP leadership, his peasant-oriented populist empiricism remained within the Leninist party paradigm.

The consequences of the loss of Mao's native political base for his politics can be seen in a short piece Mao wrote just before leaving Changsha for Shanghai, "An Introduction to *New Age.*" The return to broader political horizons—"how the nation is to be recast, how politics is to be cleaned up, how imperialism is to be defeated, how military rule is to be overthrown, how the educational system is to be reformed, how literature, art and other fields are to be revolutionized and reconstructed"—is not due to a resurgence of May Fourth confidence in the immediacy of revolution. It results from the conviction, painfully acquired, that a democratic revolution within one province was impossible. And it indicates a change in political focus from the masses of the people to a group of colleagues with "an independent and self-strengthening spirit, a persevering and unbending will." This "state of scholarly refugees" *(xuewen shang di wangming zhi bang*—referring to the new periodical and its sponsors) does not have the natural legitimacy or ultimate political power of the masses; it is the auxiliary to future mass politics.[1] Its role lies precisely in the general unpreparedness of society for revolution. Its function is to "study the practically useful disciplines and carry out preparations for the reform of the society" and to be "an experimental standard." Some success in these tasks can be expected because of the spiritual qualities of the group: "Starting with such a purpose *(zixin feichang zhengque)*, and proceeding with such spirit and will, it necessarily has hope for success." Although the colleagues of whom this was written were involved with the periodical *New Age* and the Self-Educational College, the description is also quite appropriate for the Chinese Communist Party. The article's emphasis on theory—or, more precisely, on correct knowledge by which a dedicated group will pave the way for mass political activity—indicates a motif which runs throughout this period of Mao's politics and writings.

This chapter is concerned with the ideological aspect of Mao's development from 1923 to 1927 because ideology figures more prominently in Mao's thought after his commitment to communism. The conceptual framework of class struggle, the proletarian party, imperialism, learning from the Russian experience —all took the place of Mao's more global speculations of the May Fourth era on "how man should live" and the nature of political power. Although the values of Mao's pre-Marxist politics remained, the process of developing from the "good activist" into the "good cadre" involved basic political and intellectual adaptations. When the optimism of the May Fourth Movement proved unfounded, the focus of Mao's politics shifted from the metamorphosing instant of anarchist revolution and its ephemeral midwife, the great shout of the people, to more limited and feasible projects. The earlier expectation of a dimensionless moment of transformation required neither a revolutionary organization nor a strategy; the mission was a simple one of popular enlightenment— spreading the good news of the power of the aroused masses. With the dampening of hopes for a quick and painless transfer of power, popular revolution came to be regarded as the end product of a necessary process of revolutionary activity. A protracted struggle was now felt to be inevitable, one involving limited objectives and cumulative gains in a prerevolutionary environment.

The new significance of strategic ideology and political organization is based directly on the addition of the dimension of time to the revolutionary enterprise. With this realization, Mao entered the Leninist framework of a disciplined party guided by a scientific revolutionary strategy. Mao did not add his own characteristic dimension of revolutionary activity, that of space, until the defensive situation of the base areas after 1927 and the sustaining potential of the peasantry required it. From 1923 to 1927, Mao's politics and thinking were shaped within the Leninist paradigm of the ideological party creating and awaiting the revolutionary opportunity.

The innovations in Mao's political thought in the period under consideration in this chapter are thus primarily innovations of ideology and organization. The first major change is the transitional one of Mao's development into the party framework of activity. Since this was a complex and drawn-out process, let us highlight some themes of Mao's politics not stressed in Chapter 1. Mao's first contribution within the Leninist framework was his theory of party alliances. Mao's position on alliances was quite flexible, but it did provide some underlying principles for the hectic politics of the national revolution and the Northern Expedition, and eventually it became an essential part of the logic of united fronts. Mao's most significant contribution to the politics of the Leninist revolutionary party combined the question of rural revolution with that of the party's legitimacy. In the welling optimism and opportunities of the 1926 Northern Expedition, Mao's basic political values surfaced in his emphasis on the potential for popular revolution (necessarily including the peasantry) rather than on the chance for a merely partisan success. Confronted with the possibility of revolutionary breakthrough, the revolutionary organization (or at least the *really* revolutionary organization) must serve its purpose rather than simply serve itself. Mao's commitment to a political approach of populist empiricism rather than to the urban orientation of the Central Committee of the CCP put him in a serious conflict with party leadership which was only partially resolved by the collapse of CCP–Kuomintang cooperation in 1927. As Mao fought for survival in his remote bases after 1927, the challenge to revolutionary legitimacy which he saw in the peasant movement of 1926–1927 developed into a new rural political-military strategy.

The Growth of Mao's Marxism

There were changes in Mao's political style which are evident in "An Introduction to *New Age*"; moreover, there were changes in political commitments which involved going to Shanghai and pursuing a career of high bureaucratic posts in the Chinese Communist Party (and later in Sun Yat-sen's Nationalist Party, the Kuomintang). These changes have roots which go back to the beginning of Mao's political activities. Mao and Cai Hesen organized the New Citizens Study Society in 1917–1918 for reasons analogous to those for founding *New Age:* it was to be a group distinguished by its dedication to the task of national salvation—penetrating in its consideration of the problems of Chinese society and universal in its search for the most apt solutions.[2] These similarities are not so surprising when it is recalled that in 1918 revolutionary expectations had not yet been awakened by the May Fourth Movement, and by the spring of 1923 the cycle of popular initiatives in Hunan arising from the ferment of the May Fourth Movement had finally run aground. The New Citizens Study Society functioned as a core of leaders, organizing a wide variety of single-purpose, broad-based organizations according to its own political preferences and the opportunities which Hunan politics presented.[3] Originally, the politics of the society stemmed from petit-bourgeois idealism and patriotism, but it retained its role as the nucleus of revolutionary leadership in Hunan by continuously adjusting to the radicalizing lessons of active politics. The development of Mao's commitment to communism occurred within this political and ideological context which itself was undergoing successive metamorphoses.

The exact course of Mao's theoretical development is impossible to trace because the textual evidence of his precise relationship to various intellectual currents is insufficient. Although Mao showed an intense interest in a great variety of thinkers and political events, he did not feel impelled to engage in synthetic or critical theorizing. Among his friends he was better known as an activist than as a theorist. Li Weihan, a founding member of the New Citizens Study Society, recalled a slogan: "[Cai] Hesen is an expert on theory, Runzhi [Mao Zedong] is an expert on reality."[4] As Li instantly admits, the epigram is unfair to Mao's theoretical interests and abilities, but it is evident that at this time Mao neither considered himself nor was considered by others a teacher of philosophy. It is also evident from the independence and solidity of reasoning in his early works that he was nobody's disciple in theoretical matters. In addressing the practical problems he wrote about, Mao would pursue them to their root, but he did not digress on the universal themes this endeavor involved. Rather than a teacher or disciple in general theoretical matters, Mao was an informed reader and careful utilizer.

Nevertheless, as political and ideological ferment developed during and after the May Fourth Movement, the commitment to energetic, popular-democratic politics began to involve basic choices among emerging ideological positions. Mao witnessed this process at Beijing University on his second trip to the capital in the spring of 1920, and he himself made a preliminary commitment to Marxism after much reading and discussion. Upon his return to Changsha, Mao and the New Citizens Study Society assisted the founding of a Russian Study Club[5] in addition to Cultural Book Society activities and Hunan self-government politics, and somewhat later they founded Hunan branches of the Socialist Youth Corps and the Chinese Communist Party.

An indicator of Mao's ideological stance at this time of simultaneous democratic-populist and protoparty activities is Mao's relation to a sharp dispute between Marxists and reformists which in the summer of 1920 divided the members of the New Citizens Study Society who were working in France. The French branch held a five-day meeting in July which attempted without success to decide on a political program for "reforming China and the world." The Marxists were led by the eloquent Cai Hesen, who later became editor of *Xiangdao (The Guide Weekly)*, the major communist periodical in the twenties. The reformists were led by Xiao Zisheng.[6] The leaders of both factions appealed to Mao for his views, thereby indicating both Mao's prestige among his friends and also that he was not already identified with one side or the other. Mao's response to this dispute came in two letters written in December 1920 and January 1921. The letters are extant, but only commentary interspersed with excerpts is available.[7] In the excerpts Mao makes a strong case against education as a sufficient method of social change by pointing out its interrelationship with the rest of capitalist society. Ultimately, his doubts about anarchism, absolute liberalism, and even democracy *(demokelaxi)* rest on the same ground: although they are pleasant enough in theory, in reality they cannot be achieved. Thus Mao indicates enthusiastic agreement with Cai Hesen's Marxist viewpoint, whereas he "does not indicate agreement with the recommendations of Xiao Zisheng's group."[8] This cautious wording by the editor suggests that the blow to the reformists is softened by unquoted passages. Nevertheless, in comparison with Mao's May Fourth writings it can be said that Mao's ideological center of gravity had shifted toward Marxism under the influence of the disappointments of earlier, more anarchistic expectations and with increasing exposure to Marxist theory.

Mao was not alone in accepting communism after deciding that finer political ideals were impractical. The new Chinese Communists of the early 1920s did not disparage the ideal of anarchism, but they did question its realism. As one author put it in 1921: "[The anarchists] want to strike down all controlling classes, to overthrow all organizations of the old society—but ultimately what is the clever plan?"[9] Although this author concedes that the ideals of communism are not as deep as those of anarchism, he claims that any progress toward anarchism must pass through the stage of communism. The stubbornness of social evils requires a dictatorship of workers, and when one is starving, coarse food at hand should not be rejected because one dreams of fine food.

On the other hand, radical criticisms of the Kuomintang (KMT) before its reorganization in 1924 stressed its lack of ideology and its tendency to rely on military ententes rather than on popular movements in pursuing its political aims. These two factors were seen as interrelated, because the working relationship with warlords and imperialists necessary for the KMT's wars—the KMT did not yet have an army of its own—constrained their propaganda and hence the development and propagation of a radical ideology. In the new spirit of Chinese revolutionary politics, a critic of the KMT states: "A revolutionary political party relying on national antiimperialist propaganda can become a great force. . . . A truly revolutionary army can only be built using this propaganda, and this army would be definitely far superior to any hired troops of the Northern warlords."[10]

The apparent practicality of communism had many aspects. In the first place, the Marxist emphasis on the economic base of politics was plausible to those who had seen the ruling strata in China steady themselves after the May Fourth Movement and in some cases (most notably in Hunan) adopt democratic facades. Secondly, the success of the Bolsheviks in consolidating a new revolutionary order was quite persuasive. In 1911 the Chinese also had overthrown a traditional autocracy, but the progressive aspects of this event had quickly evaporated.[11] Evidently a dedicated political organization was necessary to achieve the revolution and secure its fruits. Thirdly, the conception of the communists as a workers' vanguard party preserved the mass orientation proved effective in the May Fourth Movement and at the same time promised greater stability and effectiveness by concentrating on a crucial modern class and by founding a professional revolutionary party. A fourth appeal of communism was its coherent and critical ideology, which however poorly understood at first provided a trusted portrayal of international dynamics and a scheme for domestic class analysis.[12] The emphasis of Leninism on the struggle against imperialism—and the promise that imperialism was the last and highest stage of capitalism—seemed particularly appropriate for China.[13] In the struggle against imperialism, nationalism was internationalism and vice versa.

Confirming the growth of a specific ideological commitment on Mao's part was his increasing involvement with communist activities in Hunan. Considering the not yet centralized character of the Chinese Communist Party in its first years, this involvement should not be mistaken for a categorical submission to orders as if he were joining a well-established organization. The CCP was from its beginnings a coordinated ideological group, but intimate accounts of its early functioning (such as Zhang Guotao's)[14] suggest that the leading figures of the major geographical branches of the party (Chen Duxiu in Shanghai, Li Dazhao in Peking, Mao Zedong in Changsha) had a remarkable amount of personal discretion in operations in their areas. An additional peculiarity to keep in mind is that the early Hunan Communist Party emerged largely from the circle of Mao's activist friends, especially his colleagues in the New Citizens Study Society. Thus the new party allegiance was in part only a change of labels and of national affiliations. Even so, Mao's increasing involvement in party activities was a basic change from his previous democratic-populist politics—a change that contrasted with his continuing but diminishing public cultural efforts, the Cultural Book Society and the Self-Education College. The primary task of the Chinese Communist Party until the massacre of railway workers by Wu Peifu on 7 February 1923 (from this date until Mao's eviction from Hunan in April the party was in shock) was organizing the proletariat. In Hunan this meant forming unions and calling strikes in the province's large mining operations, among the railway workers, and among Changsha's various trades.[15] Mao and his cohorts (including Li Lisan and Liu Shaoqi) were quite successful in all these interrelated efforts; the railway and mine strikes in September 1922 were the high point.

The theoretical innovations of Mao's party politics were his acceptance of class divisions as fundamental in society and his dedication to the interests of the proletariat. Neither of these novelties is without precedent: Mao's lengthy and sympathetic descriptions of the shared oppression of workers, farmers, women, and others in "The Great Union of the Popular Masses" appeal to a shared consciousness of oppression of various groups, and although the whole citizenry of Hunan was the ideal target of Mao's democratic politics, the people he reached tended to be urban and literate. The changes are significant nonetheless. The attention which the party directed at the proletariat was not an effort to set up one "small union" among many; it was an attempt to organize a group with special historical features. Oppression was no longer treated simply as minority coercion, but as capitalist exploitation. The immediate objects of this oppression would be the vanguards of the revolution. Revolutionary activity is still considered representative of society at large: it is still a revolution *against* special interests rather than one *for* special interests. But the view of the masses tends to be structured into leaders and beneficiaries, and the communists attempted to be the leaders of the leaders. This efficiency of revolutionary attention meant a concentration on the affairs of a minority in unusual circumstances. In the case of Hunan, class politics was not democratic-populist politics, although it did not contradict a more universal orientation. Moreover, it was not indigenous provincial politics to the same degree as previous efforts, since the party's activities were coordinated on a national basis and were not as flexible in exploiting local opportunities. The devastating effect of what was for Hunan the vicarious experience of the February Seventh Massacre proves the importance of the national linkage. And the national significance of Mao's party activities in Hunan enabled him to transfer to party work in Shanghai after his expulsion from Hunan.

The international framework of Mao's politics also became more prominent and specific within the communist paradigm. The most obvious instance is the increased importance of the Russian example. The expected global significance of the Chinese revolution became more specific, although not basically different, with the advent of theories such as Li Dazhao's which described China as part of the world proletariat within an imperialist order.[16]

The Revolutionary Tasks of the CCP

It is ironic that upon becoming a professional revolutionary Mao ceased to be active in his own right in politics. It is also largely coincidental, since leaving Hunan meant leaving both his employment as a teacher and his political connections. Mao worked for the Central Committee from his arrival in Shanghai until the Third National Congress of the CCP, held in Canton in June 1923. The Comintern-sponsored proposal of a united front with the Kuomintang for national revolution was the major resolution of this assembly, and thereafter Mao's main task was to coordinate the measures of the CCP and the KMT. During the six months between the approval of the united front and its implementation at the first KMT national congress in January 1924, Mao wrote several articles for *The Guide Weekly*. These articles are limited in scope, but they indicate the interrelation of Mao's new political role and his political orientation.

In some ways this new stage in Mao's politics is analogous to his concentration on provincial politics after the disappointment of his May Fourth hopes. It was basically a withdrawal from a larger scope of political activity to a framework within which immediate, practical work for the reformation of society could be carried out. A cause of the shift in orientation from a geographical unit to a group of dedicated revolutionaries was Mao's disappointment with the people's apathy. One article begins with Mao's dismay that there has been no public outcry concerning a treaty arranged with Great Britain which sacrificed Chinese sovereignty in a strategic location (Weihaiwei in the northeast corner of Shandong province); another is a bitter ridiculing of the Hunan warlord Zhao Hengti for pretending to be the defender of the Hunan Constitution, bringing shame on Hunan's inert population.[17] A contemporaneous author complains that popular spirit was weaker in 1923 than it was before the overthrow of the Qing dynasty.[18] The admitted necessity of a mass movement from which the strength of the revolution would spring was at variance with the low level of popular consciousness and organization. The revolutionary party was to be the resolving agent of this tension.

The party is not a small but still self-sufficient natural unit of society. Rather, it is a group constituted by its members' unity of purpose to transform society. Thus the revolutionary group is a radically non-self-sufficient social entity; it exists to affect a larger body. It has legitimate self-interests only insofar as its existence can contribute to the larger body. Mao's limited provincial efforts could be justified on a continuum of concentric circles: first Hunan, then China, then the world. A temporal continuum provides the party's framework of significance—what can be done now to produce a revolutionary situation in the future? Behind the transition from directly mass-oriented politics to the indirectly mass-oriented politics of a revolutionary group is the assumption of a protracted political struggle.

As a forerunner of the revolution, the party must survive and utilize a prerevolutionary situation. Its tactical tools for attaining its political ends are cooperation with other organized political interests to achieve specific objectives of mutual benefit and the partial mobilization of its own political base by mass organizations and propaganda. The specific arenas of both these activities give day-to-day party political decisions a certain flexibility. Since it is the instrument of the revolution, the party can legitimately pursue policies which are immediately aimed at its own organizational interests. But the line between prudence and opportunism can easily become blurred—certainly there is a tendency to displace the revolutionary goal as the real determinant of policy with the narrow group interests of the "revolutionary" party. In Mao's case, party-centeredness allows for considerable political flexibility, but it never contradicts the ultimate goal of popular revolution.

The political activity of the revolutionary group also concentrates attention on the correctness of ideology. An explicit ideology is necessary because the basic political act is no longer a general call for liberation but specific activity designed to establish the prerequisites of liberation. The politics of the party is instrumental action, not self-legitimating mass spontaneity; it is based on an explicit scheme of the dynamics of society and is justified by its success in achieving revolutionary objectives. Since party activity involves a common understanding of the hindrances to liberation in the present society and how these obstacles can be removed, an explicit paradigm must be available—a structure of general theses which relate the interpretation of political events and proposals for political action to the general goal of the party. The ideological formulation of the *path* to the distant goal of revolution replaces the goal itself as the referent of policy determination, and the actual relation of strategy and goal tends to become the domain of specialists in revolutionary theory. It could be said that the ideology constitutes the language game of the revolutionary group,[19] but only with the stipulation that the consensus on common conceptions is grounded on the conviction that they are objectively correct. The shared language game (seen as jargon by outsiders) is a constitutive element of the group, but both in general and in its particulars it is eventually at the mercy of individual judgments concerning its relation to reality.

This idea of the party is not explicit in Mao's Shanghai writings because his responsibilities did not include general formulations of ideology, but it is presupposed in the various antiimperialist editorial tasks he did undertake. The best example of Mao's new political approach is "The Beijing Coup and the Merchants."[20] Since this was apparently an assigned topic for the 11 July 1923 issue of *Xiangdao*, which is devoted exclusively to evaluating the political effects of Cao Kun's usurpation of power, one should attach no particular importance to the choice of topic. At first sight this article seems to be a continuation of Mao's democratic-populist politics: on the occasion of the Shanghai merchants' opposition to the Cao Kun coup, he urges merchants to unite in their resistance to the warlords' *lijin* (internal taxes on trade) and the low tariffs enforced by the imperialists.[21] He claims that "the work which should be undertaken by the merchants in the national revolution is more urgent and more important than the work which should be undertaken by other citizens."[22] Close analysis shows that this appeal is an indication of the new flexibility of party politics rather than a continuation of transclass populism. In Mao's earlier writings the merchants would not have been excluded from an appeal, but it would not have been addressed especially to them. The merchants are considered important owing to "the necessity of history and the imperatives of contemporary events"—meaning presumably the bourgeois-democratic character of the national revolution and the inability at that time of any other class to organize effective opposition. The following passage suggests the new role of the party in Mao's thought:

> We know *(women zhidao)* that semicolonial politics is the politics of dual oppression in which the warlords and the foreign powers are conspiring together to repress the citizens of the whole nation.

Under the double oppression of this rule naturally the entire citizenry suffers deeply, but the group which feels this suffering most acutely and most urgently is the merchants. Everyone knows *(dajia zhidao)* that the *lijin* and tariffs are the two questions of life and death for the merchants, and that their urgent demands for lowering *lijin* and raising tariffs express heartfelt desires. But the reduction of *lijin* and the raising of tariffs are definitely not easy things to achieve, because the reduction of *lijin* harms the interests of the warlords and raising tariffs harms the interests of imperialism.[23]

Besides containing the main point of the article, this argument has an interesting structure which does not occur in Mao's earlier political writings. In all the writings analyzed in the previous chapter, with the partial exception of the advertisements for the Workers' Night School, Mao attempted to identify himself with his audience in order to persuade them; in this work, however, the reference group with which he identifies is not the merchants. The "we" of "we know" in the preceding quotation shares a specific ideological framework—the double oppression occurring in semicolonies—which is the viewpoint of the communists and later of the KMT (Sun Yat-sen's "hypercolony" metaphor), but not that of merchants in general. In another article Mao boasts about the correctness of "our" analysis of imperialism in Chinese politics.[24] By contrast, what "everyone knows" is much more palpable and is not stated in an ideological framework. The point here is not that Mao deliberately chose his pronouns to emphasize the exclusive knowledge of the CCP, but that his pattern of expression is a clear symptom of the new importance of the ideological revolutionary group for his politics. This disjunction between "we" and "everybody" is the basis for a dichotomy between "we" (the revolutionaries) and the merchants which runs throughout the article and establishes a distance between author and subject which is new to Mao's writings. The merchants' revolutionary potential is explained in the third person and their earlier avoidance of politics is ridiculed. When the merchants are addressed in the conclusion of the article, it is the experienced revolutionary "we" warning the politically naive merchants that revolution is difficult and includes democratization. The natural elitism behind Mao's populist mission has shifted from the May Fourth presumption of a mission of enlightenment to a party-centered presumption of knowledge and dedication.

Mao's insistence that the merchants pursue popular, open politics in their opposition is a clear link between his earlier politics and his party tactics. Chen Duxiu's contemporary article on the dominant political role of capitalists lacks this recognition of the importance of interclass dynamics within the revolutionary united front.[25] Mao's continuing preference for open and democratic political movements perhaps explains some aspects of his quick adjustment to the politics of the reorganized KMT, since the Three People's Principles (nationalism, democracy, and people's livelihood—*San Min Zhuyi*) of Sun Yat-sen[26] correspond closely with the style of Mao's earlier political involvement. But Mao's personal experience with the failure of nonclass progressive politics in Hunan and the spotty record of the KMT assured that Mao's participation in the KMT was alliance politics rather than total commitment.

Alliances and the National Revolution

The strategic formula under which the CCP operated until the break with the KMT in 1927 was that of the national revolution (*guomin geming* or *minzu geming*). This was conceived of as a revolution in two directions: antiimperialist and antifeudal (which generally meant antiwarlord). The primary emphasis was on antiimperialism, a goal which was shared at that time even by groups outside the KMT–CCP alliance.[27] The native targets of the national revolution, the compradores and the warlords, were seen either as groups directly dependent on imperialism or as symptomatic of the effect of imperialist intervention in China. Thus an all-class alliance of the citizenry could be called for to achieve the national revolution, and the bourgeois and proletarian parties, the KMT and the CCP, could join in a united front. The KMT's tendency to deny the importance of class struggle within China and the CCP's hope for a later proletarian revolution against the bourgeoisie were not immediately relevant to this objective because, as Chen Duxiu put it, "in the present economic situation the warlords and the capitalists have definitely split but the capitalist/proletarian division is not yet a complete break."[28]

The idea of a national revolution as the next step in the revolutionary process—a limited but possible revolution—is a major Leninist concept. It is based on the recognition, present even in Marx's earliest writings,[29] that there would be significant stages in the revolutionary process. The notions of bourgeois-democratic and socialist revolutions were refined through vigorous debates between Mensheviks and Bolsheviks. Using the notion of revolutionary stages within the framework of his analysis of imperialism as a world capitalist system, Lenin set the national revolution as the immediate task of radical parties in colonial and semicolonial countries. The national revolution was one in which all classes not dependent on feudalism and imperialism had an interest. Native capitalists wanted to throw off the restrictions of dependence, and for the proletariat it was a blow at the world capitalist system. Thus the political strategy appropriate to the national revolution was a united front of all nationalist parties.

In China the CCP's interpretation of the national revolution was expressed by Chen Duxiu in a December 1923 article, "The Chinese National Revolution and the Various Classes of Society."[30] The article's tone (peculiar for the leader of the CCP) is defensive on behalf of the bourgeoisie and critical of those who propose leading roles for the peasantry, the intellectuals, or the proletariat. Chen notes the awakening political consciousness of the bourgeoisie and stresses that economic development will inexorably lead to confrontations with imperialism. Despite the important roles of the petit bourgeoisie, the workers, and the peasants, the bourgeoisie is expected to play the leading role in the national revolution. Chen reasons that the development of the proletariat as a class must necessarily lag behind that of its employers,[31] and he finds evidence for this prediction in the feudal mentality of most Chinese workers. The article is undoubtedly intended to soothe the KMT on the eve of the declaration of the KMT–CCP united front. Only at the end of the article does Chen sound a worrisome note for his new allies. The victors in the national revolution will definitely be the bourgeoisie, but what will happen next is unclear. A good example, he notes, is that of the bourgeois-democratic revolution of March 1917 in Russia, followed by the socialist revolution of October.

In retrospect, Chen's understanding of CCP participation in the national revolution shows the theoretical roots of his rather passive dependence on the KMT alliance in the crises of 1927. The leading role ascribed to the bourgeoisie makes necessary the first sentence of the April 1927 Joint Declaration by Chen and Wang Jingwei: "In this time of the gradual approach of victory in the national revolution, the solidarity of our two parties is especially necessary."[32] But Chen's limiting conception of the national revolution was not the only possible one. The concept of the national revolution answered the strategic question of where to begin. By provisionally constricting horizons it broadened the scope of political tactics and permitted strategic alliances. The national revolution could be seen as the first practical step in an uninterrupted revolution rather than a preproletarian stage defined by economic parameters.

Although Mao first systematically elaborated his own idea of national revolution in his "New Democracy" writings of 1940,[33] this second view of the national revolution helps explain the enigma of Mao's participation in the first KMT–CCP united front, in which he was both an enthusiastic collaborator and (in 1927) a major problem. It also focuses attention on Mao's view of alliances, a subject to which he devotes careful thought in some usually ignored articles he wrote for the KMT in 1925. These thoughts on alliances are the first appearance of the principles of Mao's alliance politics. Not only do they lie behind the later development of his united front strategy,[34] but they also play an essential role in the logic of internal mobilization in the base areas.

Mao was active at the First National Congress of the reorganized KMT in January 1925 and was elected an alternate member of its Central Executive Committee. He worked for most of 1924 as the secretary of the organization department of the Shanghai KMT. This was evidently a frustrating experience, for Mao resigned early in 1925 on the pretext of a "brain illness" and retired to his family home in Hunan until summer 1925. Upon his return he was put in charge of the central propaganda department under Wang Jingwei, and in this capacity he began to edit *Political Weekly (Zhengzhi Zoubao)* for the KMT in December 1925.[35] The significance of the concept of a limited immediate objective for alliance politics is evident in Mao's contributions to this periodical.

Political Weekly was political in the sense of relating to the KMT as a political force among the other political forces in China. Its specific purpose was to counter misinformation about the Guangdong political situation by presenting the facts and by counterpolemic. Mao promised in his initial editor's message, "The style of *Political Weekly* will be 90 percent narration of practical affairs and only 10 percent debate concerning the propaganda of counterrevolutionary factions."[36] His own contributions were mostly counterpolemical, however, with the major exception of "The Chinese KMT's Propaganda Outline for the Anti-Feng [Fengdian] War," an official evaluation drafted by Mao. Adopted by the KMT's Central Executive Committee, this work analyzes a major struggle among the North China warlords and evaluates the significance of this struggle for KMT diplomacy.

If there are two principles underlying Mao's thought on alliances, they are that they should be as broad as possible and that urgency sharpens every hostility into two camps with no middle ground. On the second, Mao points out to the middle-of-the-roaders that their position is comfortable in quiet times, but when both camps start their mutual bombardment all the guns will be trained on those in the middle.[37] Pacifism, the suppression of conflict, and damning the extremes do not in the end represent a third alternative. These viewpoints are ridiculed not because they are moderate but because they attempt to evade the inevitability of struggle.

Alliances are necessary if political victories are to be won when the revolutionary forces are comparatively weak. Since the object is to win, the alliance should be as extensive as the balance of interests will allow. Political conditions can lead to a nesting of alliances—narrow, long-term groupings operating within larger, temporary ententes. This situation is exemplified by the alliance strategy evident in the "Anti-Feng Propaganda Outline." A major ally in the war against the Fengdian clique of Zhang Zuolin is the Zhili clique of Wu Peifu and Sun Quanfang. In fact, it is actually their war; the KMT is only an interested outsider. The KMT is allied with Zhili despite the imperialist backing of both camps (America with Zhili, Japan with Fengdian, and England ultimately with whoever wins, though at the time supporting Fengdian). The reason Fengdian is the enemy while Zhili is an ally is that the direct targets of the May Thirtieth Movement,[38] England and Japan, had united behind Zhang Zuolin in gratitude for his suppression of the Shanghai mass movements. Although in previous warlord struggles of this sort the public had been apathetic, in this case popular sentiment is rightly against Fengdian because of its Shanghai actions. But since Zhili and Fengdian are basically the same sort of warlord powers, there are two important limitations on the KMT's involvement. First, it is an alliance with the military power of Zhili, not with its imperialist, comprador, and landlord backing. Hence the political factions supporting Zhili (Research Clique,

New Diplomacy Clique, and so forth) are condemned. Moreover, union in the war against Fengdian is not support for Zhili's victory. It is to be emphasized in the propaganda that Zhili should not simply replace Fengdian.

It might thus be deduced that the anti-Fengdian war (from the standpoint of the KMT) is only the first phase of the anti-Fengdian, Anti-Zhili struggle.[39] This is evident from the next level of alliance, which is with Feng Yuxiang's National Revolutionary Army (NRA–Guominjun), a group which received no support from the imperialists. The NRA can thus be a true ally: "The people *(renmin)* in distinguishing between friends and enemies consider only whether or not they have relations with imperialism. If anyone at any time has relations with imperialism, the people will thereupon not recognize them as friends." The KMT has a much closer relationship with the NRA because it has the potential for opposing the imperialist roots of both Fengdian and Zhili and can be expected to be a direct collaborator in the national revolution. All this goodwill for the NRA exists in spite of the fact that "for the present because of strategic necessities [the NRA] has not yet broken with Zhang Zuolin."

The final alliance, that between the KMT and the people, seems inseparable. "The true leader of the people is the Chinese Kuomintang. The true government of the people is the Guangzhou National Government." Since the propaganda outline was written for KMT cadres by Mao in his capacity as head of the propaganda bureau and it was approved by the Central Executive Committee of the KMT, this attitude is to be expected. But Mao does suggest that the close relationship between the KMT and the people is up to the people: "The whole body of the oppressed masses of the Chinese people *(Zhongguo quanti minzhong)* are the masters of all of China's problems. In the present anti-Feng war, the people should be the general commanders."[40] The KMT's popularity is thus not a blind dependence on KMT leadership but a reliance on this leadership's commitment to the people's interests. The foundation of Mao's democratic-populist politics—his belief in the ultimate political power of the masses—emerges here as the final touchstone of alliance politics. The principles of the KMT's commitment in the current situation are the establishment of a representative people's government and a representative assembly to resolve the unequal treaties problem. Moreover, the freedoms of assembly, speech, and organization are to be guaranteed.

Mao philosophized in the same issue of *Political Weekly*:

> In today's world, no matter whether things are animate (like people) or inanimate (like newspapers), they should not be viewed too rigidly. Since the "revolutionaries" and "counterrevolutionaries" have now divided the family estate, those animate and inanimate things can today be in this group and tomorrow be in that group.[41]

This is an apt description of Chinese politics, particularly KMT politics, from the death of Sun Yat-sen in the winter of 1925 until the final expulsion of the communists in the summer of 1927. The antiimperialist upsurge of the May Thirtieth Movement in 1925 particularly benefited the CCP, making the KMT right wing even more anxious about the "communization" *(chihua)* of the united front. Moreover, with the KMT's unification of Guangdong in late 1925, some neighboring warlords began to consider joining forces with the revolutionaries. Tang Shengzhi, a militarist who helped Mao's old enemy Zhao Hengti become governor of Hunan and had defeated Tan Yankai's KMT-backed attempt to retake Hunan in 1923, was converted to the People's Three Principles in the fall of 1925.

With political identity in such a state of flux, the question of alliances was correspondingly fluid. But Mao's writings indicate a difference between alliance politics and opportunism. Alliance is cooperation for a goal. As we have seen in the anti-Feng piece, the more limited the goal, the more extensive the alliance. Opportunism is the sacrifice of purpose for immediate advantage. In criticizing the attempt of the rightist KMT Western Hills clique to transfer the base of KMT operations to Peking, which was then controlled by the warlord Duan Qirui, Mao describes their basic policy as "to be able to hold public meetings under warlords and under imperialism."[42] This policy compromises any possible significance in their antiimperialist and antiwarlord slogans. As Mao explains:

> In places controlled by the enemy, the organization and meetings of a truly revolutionary party are completely secret, but their propaganda and recommendations are public. In order for the party's organization and meetings to emerge into the open or enemy territory, first an understanding with the enemy is required. Hence there have to be some points where it is to the enemy's advantage to

reach a tacit understanding or to guarantee protection.... This is only possible for the enemy's friends, not for a revolutionary party which wants to overthrow the enemy's mandate.[43]

This argument is part of Mao's counterattack against the anticommunist rightists who were trying to disrupt the Guangdong KMT–CCP alliance, but its attempt to identify hypocrisy and opportunism by counterposing the responsibilities of a truly revolutionary party introduces a theme which was shortly to become important in the very different context of Mao's writings on the peasantry.

The Peasantry and the National Revolution

From 1925 to 1927 Mao developed an emphasis on the importance of the peasantry for the national revolution which was significant both intellectually and politically for communist participation in the First United Front. With the CCP's severance of ties with the KMT in mid-1927 and the failure of various communist efforts to seize control of urban areas, the rural orientation of Mao's 1926–1927 politics provided an essential transition to the rural strategy of the first guerrilla bases. The uniqueness of Mao's views on the peasantry has long been overemphasized,[44] but the centrality of the peasantry for Mao's revolutionary politics from 1926 to 1949 is unquestionable.

At the time of the May Thirtieth Movement, Mao Zedong was in temporary retirement at his family's rural home in Hunan. Mao's six-month retreat was not only the longest time he had spent in the countryside in his adult life; it was also a unique vantagepoint for viewing the national effect of the antiimperialist upsurge. As Mao recounted to Edgar Snow:

> Formerly I had not fully realized the degree of class struggle among the peasantry, but after the May Thirtieth Incident, and during the great wave of political activity which followed it, the Hunanese peasantry became very militant. I left my home, where I had been resting, and began a rural organizational campaign. In a few months we had formed more than twenty peasant unions, and had aroused the wrath of the landlords, who demanded my arrest. Zhao Hengti sent troops after me, and I fled to Canton.[45]

Mao's experience with rural activism in the summer of 1925 was undoubtedly important for his view of the peasantry, although it is claimed that Mao conducted rural investigations as early as the summer of 1921,[46] and Zhang Guotao remembers Mao's rural emphasis as early as the Third Congress of the CCP in June 1923. According to Zhang, "Mao Zedong stressed the importance of the peasant revolution. He went on to point out that the forces of the KMT lay only in a corner of Guangdong Province and that the CCP should concern itself with the broad masses of peasants throughout the country."[47] Although Zhang credits Mao with being the major official advocate of the peasantry at this time (and the Third Congress was the first party congress seriously to consider the peasant question), others were also directing attention to rural conditions. Peng Pai had begun his work among the peasants of Hailufeng in September 1922, and in July 1923 Chen Duxiu published a careful class analysis of the peasantry.[48] But the first and one of the most interesting CCP articles on the peasantry was published in *The Communist* in April 1921.[49]

The earliest communist article on the peasantry contains many of the themes of Mao's later studies. The anonymous author maintains that urban radicals do not understand the misery and revolutionary potential of the Chinese peasantry, who "are no less miserable than the Russian peasants." He gives a detailed picture of the varieties of peasant oppression drawn from his own observation and ends the article with an egalitarian appeal to the peasantry which is so stirring that it could have been used as an introductory speech by rural organizers from 1927 to 1949. The author also notes that the peasantry and the party need each other for the success of the social revolution:

> If they [the peasants] become class conscious and arise in class struggle, our social revolution, Communism, will be assured. Therefore since they have this tendency, waiting for their natural, slow progress is not as good as using some man-made methods to accelerate them, thereby enabling them to become class-conscious a day earlier and avoid a day of suffering.[50]

The official communist position as elaborated in Chen Duxiu's "The Chinese Peasant Question" of July 1923 is considerably more restrained than this early exuberance. Chen begins by stating that in contrast to Russia, Chinese peasants are hard to organize because of the large proportion of landholders. He finds the peasant's troubles caused more by a price squeeze due to imported goods and the devastation of warlord struggles than by the oppression of a local elite.[51] Although Chen concludes his class analysis of the peasantry by recommending that various peasant associations be formed, the tone of the article is in keeping with Chen's general emphasis on the leading role of the bourgeoisie.

But these pre-1925 communist discussions of the mass base of the national revolution were mostly hypothetical. There were only 950 CCP members in early 1925.[52] It was only after the upsurge of the May Thirtieth Movement had multiplied this number by ten and the consolidation of KMT political and military power in Guangdong had made a march northward to Peking look possible that peasant policy became a practical question. With his emphasis on the peasantry in 1926-1927, Mao confronted an urban proletarian party with the necessity of organizing a dispersed and backward countryside, and he challenged a party coalition hungering for national victory with the uncomfortably radical demands of a class making no immediate contributions to the political-military struggle. Mao had not suddenly turned utopian. Through his experience and analysis of the peasant movement, he had become convinced that a meaningful and lasting victory depended on a transformation of relationships in the village and, conversely, that the countryside contained a latent revolutionary strength which would make victory inevitable.

Mao's firsthand experiences in Hunan in the summer of 1925 were to prove a watershed in his political thought. His reestablishment of familiarity with rural conditions, his participation in successfully organizing a peasant response to national events, his perception of the warlords' function as guarantors of the landlord's interest—all provided a practical foundation for a fundamental rethinking of the objectives and forces of the national revolution. This foundation was not immediately utilized, however. Mao's chief assignment upon arriving in Canton was to run the KMT propaganda bureau, which had been stagnating under the nominal leadership of Wang Jingwei and more directly under Wang's brother-in-law Chen Qunpu. It was in this capacity that he founded *Political Weekly* in December 1925. Meanwhile Mao was becoming known as an expert on peasant affairs. In January and February 1926, he published two general articles on the peasantry in the first two issues of *Zhongguo Nongmin* [The Chinese peasant]. The Second National Congress of the KMT, held in January, placed great emphasis on peasant support of the national revolution. As a result, the peasant department received the largest budget of any department, 18,000 yuan per month. Mao was named director of the Peasant Movement Training Institute in Canton with a monthly budget of 5,000 yuan.[53] The sixth class of the Institute, whose term ran from 5 May to 10 October 1926, was under his direction and was by far the institute's largest and most intensively trained.[54] There were over 320 students from twenty provinces. The method of instruction was quite reminiscent of the Hunan Self-Education College. Independent research was expected, and the fruit of that research was a book: *China's Peasant Problem*, the first factual study of the whole peasantry from the point of view of the national revolution.

Mao's first article on the peasantry is "An Analysis of the Various Classes among the Chinese Peasantry and Their Attitudes toward Revolution."[55] The purpose of "Peasant Classes" is to specify a peasant strategy for the revolutionary "we." A peasant strategy depends on the inclinations and disinclinations toward revolution which exist within the villages; Mao claims that there are classes common to all Chinese villages. The suggested strategy springs immediately from the class descriptions—namely, to organize the petit bourgeoisie, semiproletariat, and proletariat, to ask the landlords to retreat but be prepared to struggle and smash the worst elements, and to encourage the "vagrant proletariat" *(Youmin, Lumpenproletariat)* to join the revolution by pursuing a solution to the unemployment problem. Mao's descriptive analysis which eventuates in this strategy is a presentation of the archetypical economic, social, and psychological situations of the different "kinds of people" *(zhong ren)* in rural China and an estimate of how many people are in each situation. For all the generalization involved in such a survey, the class descriptions are quite precise and undogmatic. Mao excels at describing the misery peculiar to each class from owner-peasant to vagrant. Even the small landlords have occasionally felt the oppression of the big landlords and warlords and thus have some feelings of opposition, but as a class they have an exploitative relation to the peasantry. The great majority of the owner-peasants feel the weight of worsening economic conditions, and those who are steadily getting poorer suffer their relative deprivation acutely: "The agony of spirit felt by this type of person is greater than that felt by anyone else because they have the contrast between past and present."⁵⁶ The rural semiproletariat—those who rent part of the land they farm (semiowner-peasants), those with tools but without land (sharecroppers), and poor peasants completely at the mercy of their landlord—are one-half of China's rural population and lead lives of bare survival in degradation. The condition of the rural proletariat, which is primarily farm laborers, is worse than that of the workers with regard to hours, pay, and treatment. At the bottom of the list are the vagrant proletariat: soldiers, bandits, thieves, beggars, prostitutes. "In all of humanity, their lives are the most unsettled." To win them to the revolutionary cause, their specific problem, that of joblessness, must be taken as one of China's most serious problems.

This style of description is reminiscent of the middle section of "The Great Union of the Popular Masses." Shared misery is the primary theme, and this theme is intimately related to potential for revolutionary consciousness, both of which are grounded on the class's economic relations and condition. Since the class framework in which the descriptions are presented is more general than the "small union" framework of the May fourth article, it is more useful as a policy referent for a national revolutionary party and less amenable to completely unencumbered spontaneity. It is noteworthy that the specific theme of inequality (the landlords are X percent of the population and own Y percent of the wealth) is absent here. The dominant themes are direct oppression within village society, deteriorating economic conditions, and lack of the necessities for survival among the poor.

The landlords are the enemies of the peasantry because of oppression rather than mere possession:

> [The big landlords'] interest is built upon the severe exploitation of five kinds of peasants: owner-peasants, semiowner-peasants, full tenants, poor peasants, and farm laborers. They have five methods of exploitation. (1) Heavy rents. From 50% to 80%. For the semiowner-peasants, full tenants, and poor peasants this form of exploitation is exceptionally widespread and horrible. (2) High interest rates. Monthly interest is between 3% and 7%, yearly interest between 36% and 84%. This is also exploitation of the semiowner-peasants, full tenants, and poor peasants. Occasionally the evil of this type of oppression exceeds that of heavy rents; often there are cases of people driven to complete bankruptcy in a few

years because of debts and mounting pressure. (3) Heavy local taxes. This is using a type of pressure to require the owner-peasants and semiowner-peasants to pay charges according to holdings for the expenses of the township defense department *(tuan fang ju)*. This department . . . is the armed forces of the landlord class, a necessary setup for putting down peasant uprisings and for maintaining the exploitative system of the landlord class. (4) The exploitation of farm labor, that is, the exploitation of their surplus labor. But in China there is still not much capitalist agriculture; the big landlords do not manage their land personally. As a result there are still more small landlords than big landlords practicing this type of exploitation. (5) Cooperating with warlords and greedy, corrupt officials to pay in advance the peasant's land taxes and to demand heavy interest the following year from the taxpaying peasants. How these five forms of exploitation altogether cause the misery of the peasantry is beyond description. Therefore China's big landlords are the mortal enemy of China's peasantry, they are the real foundation of imperialism and the warlords, they are the only fortress of the feudal, patriarchal society, they are the final cause for the development of every sort of counterrevolutionary power.[57]

The peasant movement to counter this oppression cannot be merely a distant echo of urban antiimperialism; the countryside has its own intense class struggle, the immediate targets of which are individual local landlords. The relationship of the rural class struggle to the national revolution lies in the function of the landlords as the basis for the larger systems of warlord and imperialist oppression.[58] The peasantry is thus more than an ally in the national revolution; it is a distinctive mass basis for the antifeudal, antiimperialist struggle. Implicit in the leadership opportunity Mao describes in this article is a leadership responsibility for a truly revolutionary party.

Mao's next article, "An Analysis of the Classes in Chinese Society,"[59] is peculiar in that it appeared in the issue of *The Chinese Peasant* following "Peasant Classes," yet it repeats verbatim the descriptions in the earlier article of most of the rural classes (although the description of the big landlords is left out). The new elements in "Classes in Chinese Society" are its orientation, particularly its introduction and conclusion, and its inclusion of urban classes. The differences in orientation are significant, and the repetitions are explained by Mao's recollection to Snow that it was originally written for *The Guide Weekly* but was rejected by Chen Duxiu.

Structurally the article centers on the question of "who are our enemies and who are our friends," which is considered basic to proper tactics *(celue)*. The body of the article is a class analysis that is introduced as a gloss on the manifesto of the First National Congress of the Kuomintang.[60] After analyzing the various rural and urban classes in terms of numbers and attitudes toward revolution, Mao returns to the question of friends and enemies and suggests that it is only necessary to get the oppressed classes, the 395 million (out of 400 million) true friends, to unite. In obvious juxtaposition to the tactics of Chen and the rest of the CCP Central Executive Committee, Mao maintains that it is not essential to concentrate on winning over the middle class (small landlords and national bourgeoisie). In fact, such a strategy might only confuse true friends.

This article is a significant advance over the previous one because it completes the class analysis of China and makes explicit the relationship between the class analysis and the policy of the revolutionary party. In this article, the tactical question "who are our enemies, who are our friends?" is a litmus test for the identity and legitimacy of the truly revolutionary party. The premise of this test is also the premise for Mao's earlier criticism of the Western Hills clique: "If one does not distinguish clearly between enemies and friends, then one cannot be a revolutionary element." In this case, however, the problem is not to expose a hypocritical group by describing the principled action of a truly revolutionary party, but to remind the revolutionary party of its true mission. The responsibility, legitimacy, and ultimate political power of the revolutionary party lie in unifying the masses for revolution against the oppressors. That Mao felt it necessary to remind "the revolutionary party" (presumably the Guangdong KMT and the CCP) about such a basic point is a symptom of the quickening maelstrom of Northern Expedition politics; that Chen refused to publish it in *The Guide Weekly* verifies its timeliness. Mao poses the problem in harsh terms:

> The reason the Chinese revolution has had so little success in its thirty years is definitely not due to errors of aims *(mudi)* but is completely due to errors of tactics *(celue)*. The so-called tactical error is just this, not being able to unite true friends in order to attack true enemies. . . . We are all [members of a] revolutionary party, we all

lead the masses, we are all the guides of the masses. But we cannot help but ask ourselves, do we have this ability *(benling)*? Could it not be that we are leading the masses down the road to defeat? Can we definitely be successful? If we want to have the assurance of "not leading them down the wrong road" and of achieving "certain success," great care is necessary in important tactics. In order to determine these tactics, who are enemies and who are friends must first be distinguished clearly.[61]

The basic justification of a revolutionary party is its promotion of the revolution. This requires knowing who the masses are and who the oppressors of the masses are; it involves representing the interests of the former against the latter. The flexibility of party tactics is flexibility for a purpose. The party should not be misled by its special political role into thinking that it is self-justifying or that revolution is no more than its own controlled, reiterative efforts. "A revolutionary party is the guide of the masses." Therefore Mao describes the revolutionary masses, answering the question of true enemies and true friends and also indicating the "unerring path" and "certain success." The path is serious investigation of the real situation and interests of the masses, and certainty of success can be deduced from the revolutionary potential produced by the severe oppression of the overwhelming majority of the population. The article moves from fundamental queries at the beginning to revolutionary confidence at the end: "395 million people, organize!"

The more universal framework of class analysis in "Classes in Chinese Society" allows Mao to discuss some basic points not mentioned in "Peasant Classes." The general theory of class analysis and the comparability of Chinese classes to those in other countries is discussed in two paragraphs which preface the individual class descriptions. The theory of class divisions is represented quite oddly:

> No matter which country, it is natural that they all have three levels of people: upper level, middle level, and lower level. Carefully analyzed, however, there are five levels: the big capitalist class, middle class *(zhongchan jieji)*, the petty bourgeoisie, the semiproletariat, and the proletariat.[62]

The relationship between the three natural divisions and the five classes is impossible to determine with certainty, because Mao does not indicate the perspective from which upper, middle, and lower are decided. But the individual class analyses are generally divided into threes, and in these cases the division is formally on the basis of economics and coincidentally demarcates receptivity to revolutionary propaganda. The attitudes of the Chinese classes toward national revolution are regarded as almost exactly the same as those of classes in capitalist countries toward the social revolution. This is due to the unity of world revolution:

> The revolutions of the modern age are basically one revolution; their aims *(mudi)* and methods *(shouduan)* are the same, namely the same purpose of smashing international capitalist imperialism and the same method of uniting oppressed nationalities and oppressed classes to fight. This is the present revolution's most important peculiarity, unique among all revolutions in history.[63]

Mao's emphasis on the peasantry increases significantly between the "Peasant Classes" article and "Classes in Chinese Society." The concentration on the peasantry and the critique of the big landlords is more explicit in the first article, but the general significance of the analysis is left ambiguous. Is the peasant policy an opportunity to be exploited, like the anti-Feng war, one policy among many, alongside a merchants' policy and an overseas Chinese policy? Or is it something more basic? In the second article, the specific theme of rural revolution is played down, but the centrality of the revolutionary party's representation of the oppressed classes is forcefully emphasized. Seven months after "Classes in Chinese Society," Mao wrote another general article, "The National Revolution and the Peasant Movement,"[64] which is the culmination of the two themes of the importance of peasant movements and responsibility to the masses. In the intervening time, the Northern Expedition had been launched, Changsha had been captured, lost, and recaptured by the KMT-related forces of Tang Shengzhi, and an intensive training program of peasant movement cadres had just been completed under Mao's direction at the Peasant Movement Training Institute.

The manifesto-like vigor of the article is apparent from its first few sentences:

> The problem of the peasantry is the central question of the national revolution. If the peasantry does not arise and participate in and support the national revolution, the national revolution cannot succeed. If a peasant movement isn't quickly produced, the peasant

problem cannot be solved. If the peasant problem does not attain an approximate solution during the present *(xianzai)* revolutionary movement, then the peasants will not support this revolution. Up to the present moment there are still people even within the revolutionary party who do not understand these principles.[65]

In this passage and throughout the first part of the article, Mao emphatically argues that the litmus of party legitimacy—representing the oppressed—must include leading the peasantry in the struggle with the landlords. The peasantry must be identified with; it cannot merely be allied with. To restrict the peasant movement would be to restrict the foundation of the national revolution. Mao's confidence in the centrality of the peasant question is founded on the experience of the KMT in Guangdong. He attributes the thorough eradication of Chen Jiongming's rival government to the rise of the peasant movement in the areas under Chen's control, particularly in Haifeng. Not only did the peasant associations undermine Chen's position militarily, but they created a new, radically reformed atmosphere in the countryside. From this success story Mao deduces an eloquent reformulation of the national revolution:

> Hence [we] can know that the situation of the Chinese revolution is just this: Either the suppression of the peasantry by local bullies, bad gentry, avaricious officials, and corrupt clerks [forms] the foundation of imperialism and the warlords, or the suppression of the local bullies, bad gentry, avaricious officials, and corrupt clerks by the aroused peasantry forms the foundation of the revolutionary forces. The Chinese revolution only has this form, it does not have a second form. Every locality in all of China needs to move toward the situation of Haifeng; only then can the revolution be considered successful, otherwise no matter what the situation it can't be considered successful. Every locality in all of China needs to move toward the situation of Haifeng; only then will the foundations of imperialism and the warlords really be shaken. Otherwise they won't be.... From this [we] can know that those who disparage or dislike the peasant movement are in reality sympathizing with the local bullies, bad gentry, avaricious officials, and corrupt clerks; in reality they do not want to strike down warlords, they do not want to oppose imperialism.[66]

Among the key elements of this passage is the emphasis on local oppression as the target and inducer of revolutionary power. The revolutionary struggle at the village level does not take place in abstract terms. The peasant movement is a personal, local confrontation with known oppressors, and it draws its strength from hatred and the instinct for survival. The similarity of class conditions in every village makes possible the coordination of the rural struggle, and the function of the landlords as primary exploiters at the base of a system of secondary and tertiary exploitation enables the movement to have broader antiwarlord and antiimperialist dimensions. The leadership of the party in this context is not so much control as the evocation of the maximum strength and maximum participation of the masses in their own movement. Any other attitude implies suspicion of the peasant movement, and a suspicious attitude is only appropriate for its targets. The last clause of the passage is daring, since many of those who were cool to the peasant movement were active antiimperialists. This is a characteristically dialectical logic:[67] because of its relation with more primary forms of exploitation in China, antiimperialism cannot be a political goal to which all others are sacrificed. Effective antiimperialism must set itself first against the landlords. Mao specifies what he means by the landlords being the base of imperialism in his attack on the notion that the compradores and the landlords are equally significant targets. In Mao's scheme, the warlords are the "selected leaders" of the landlords, who are far more ubiquitous and financially important than the compradores. The warlords utilize the compradores to bring imperialism to their side.

Mao does not attempt to go beyond his vigorous defense of the peasant movement's role in the national revolution and present a comprehensive program for peasant activists. Although Peng Pai's experience in peasant organization in Haifeng is a vital demonstration of the possible success of peasant movements, this model alone is evidently insufficient for abstracting a general strategy for the agrarian revolution. The research task remaining is to make a comprehensive and detailed study of rural conditions throughout China. The practical task is to initiate peasant movements in as many places as possible. Mao's approach to the theoretical problem was typically frontal and thorough: a major assignment of his class at the Peasant Movement Training Institute in the summer of 1926 was to write *The Peasant Problem*, which included a comprehensive survey of rural conditions in each province, a study of peasant movements, and some material on foreign experience, particularly Russian.⁶⁸ "The National Revolution and the Peasant Movement" was written as a preface to this book. On the practical side, Mao emphatically recommends that more cadres get involved in the rural movement, although he cautions that this shift of attention must not be to the detriment of organizing workers, students, and middle and small merchants. But how can the peasant movement be organized and led without a comprehensive plan for rural work? Mao's answer to this question is the first clear prototype of the mass line:

> Go to a village you are familiar with or to a strange village. In summer dry out in the hot sun, in winter face the severe cold of the wind and snow, and, holding the peasants' hands, ask them their troubles, ask them what they want. From their misery and needs, lead them to organize; lead them to struggle with the local bullies and bad gentry; lead them to cooperate with the workers, students, and middle and small merchants in the cities and set up a united front; lead them to participate in the antiimperialist and antiwarlord national revolutionary movement.⁶⁹

This is not a regression of Mao's politics to May Fourth populism occasioned by the ferment and promise of the Northern Expedition. The distinction between party and mass and the self-consciousness of their relationship indicates that the dedicated group of revolutionaries had become the starting point of Mao's political thinking. The harmony he expects between the organization of the peasants' own struggle and the national policies of the party shows a confidence in the correctness of its general political paradigm. In this sense theory plays a much more explicit role than it did in his earlier politics. On the other hand, the party/mass interaction which Mao describes in this first "mass line" passage is just as far removed from the Leninist concept of agitation as a unidirectional transmission belt as it is from simple populism. The cadre following Mao's advice presumes the ultimate harmony of party interests and peasant interests, but he does not assume that he knows what the peasant's immediate interests are, and in several senses these interests are primary to his agitational effort. It is also assumed that the cadre will be the first politicizer of the peasants rather than the broker of established political interests. The path toward mobilizing the revolutionary potential of the peasantry begins with attentive responsibility to the peasant's immediate needs. It is remarkable that this basic principle of Mao's rural politics, which he eloquently restated on the basis of six years of guerrilla experience in 1934, antedates Mao's intensive involvement with peasant organizing and is a direct consequence of his already established intellectual and political style.

Many characteristics of these 1926 peasantry articles are strongly reminiscent of Mao's pre-Marxist politics. The enthusiasm and popular orientation of his discovery of the peasant movement seem closer in spirit to his May Fourth politics than to his 1923-1925 writings. Mao also displays a drive to penetrate to the root of the problem, something which is not prominent in the intervening articles except as a systematizing force in alliance theory and propaganda. Equally basic is a return to an unfettered empathy with the sufferings of the overwhelming majority of the population—in the confidence that this misery can be transformed by mobilization into an insuperable revolutionary force. Misery, rather than economics, is the basic criterion of Mao's class analyses, although of course the two are intimately related. A corollary of this return is Mao's fascination with the numerical superiority of the oppressed, indicating that he still believes the "greatest union" wins. In "Peasant Classes" and "Classes in Chinese Society" Mao is deeply disturbed by the problem of winning the vagrant proletariat, bandits, thieves, beggars, prostitutes, and soldiers for the revolution. He insists that their problem of joblessness is equal to the peasants' problem of poverty, although it is evident that the revolutionary potential of the vagrants is not comparable. This strong concern indicates that Mao's mass politics is not simply a matter of numbers; it is not lower-class oriented simply because of the arithmetical center of gravity: it builds up its overwhelming majority from the bottom—that is, from the most miserable.

Another important line of continuity in Mao's political thought is his reliance on actual investigations to establish his new viewpoint and his caution in generalizing a plan of action on the basis of inadequate material. Social science in the sense of a systematic and thorough study of social conditions is evidently a key element in his populist empiricism. But Mao's social science is not a detached effort to disclose the enduring truths of social life. Rather, it is aimed at specifying the revolutionary potential of society and establishing the context of the party's political behavior. As S. M. Miller has pointed out, political commitment does not preclude a concern for objectivity;[70] after all, the objective consequences of actions will materially affect the movement. Hence commitment to a political enterprise can serve as a corrective for ideological distortion or complacency. For Mao research is a survey of political resources rather than an attempt to discover general laws. The method of research is not a detached study of latent traits; it is empathy with the consciousness of the participants and the experience of the revolutionary movement. Despite its directive nature, investigation is not a preliminary to revolutionary action but emerges from struggle. Mao complains about the lack of information on the peasant movement and explains why this is so:

> The collection of this type of material naturally depends on the progress of the peasant movement. Since with the exception of Guangdong every place is just beginning, the materials are scanty.[71]

The Hunan Peasant Movement

The importance of the Haifeng peasant movement in ousting Chen Jiongming and the subsequent rapid expansion of peasant associations throughout Guangdong aroused the attention of both the KMT and the CCP. The expectation that peasant movements would play a significant role in the advance of the Northern Expedition led the KMT Central Executive Committee to expand greatly the funding and activities of its peasant department, although the elimination of local despots was the last item in the KMT program described in the manifesto of the Second National Congress of the KMT in January 1926. For its part, the CCP passed a resolution on the peasant movement at an enlarged conference of the Central Committee in July 1926.[72] This resolution was extremely mild. The economic demands were that peasants should not receive less than 50 percent of the harvest, that annual interest on loans should not exceed 30 percent, and that no advance taxes or exorbitant taxes should be levied. The political demands were for freedom of assembly and organization for peasants, election of county magistrates,[73] and prohibition of the arrest and adjudication of peasants by the local defense corps *(min tuan)*. The policy suggested to the peasants by the CCP was an alliance broad enough to include middle and small landlords. This policy, which opposed only big landlords with notorious reputations, was considerably less radical than the one implied in Mao's "Classes in Chinese Society," and according to Zhang Guotao, the resolution was opposed by the Guangdong district committee, which argued for greater support of the peasant movement. The agrarian policy of the KMT as expressed in its "Political Platform" of October 1926 was more radical than that of the communists in at least one point: they demanded a maximum annual interest of 20 percent instead of 30 percent.[74] In reality, however, many KMT progressives with roots in the countryside were becoming alarmed by the rapid growth of the peasant movement and the possible economic and political consequences of their demands. The situation can be illustrated with an excerpt from a letter to *The Guide Weekly* requesting the peasant movement to avoid "bloody incidents":

> A friend from my village who was quite revolutionary was particularly enthusiastic about the peasant movement. In June of this year [1926] at the time of the reduction of rents by the peasant associations he wrote his father and elder brothers saying, "Speaking of the present reduction of rents, it is spreading throughout Guangdong like a fast tide; it would really be impossible to stop it. My father and elder brothers see the daily misery of the peasants; my father and elder brothers should comply with and implement the peasant associations' announcement of rent reduction." His father and brothers were furious upon receiving this letter and wrote back, "What sort of books are you reading, and what revolution do you want to make? You have studied so much that you want to make revolution against us!" Immediately his father sent an urgent telegram to his son, which said approximately "We hope that upon receiving this telegram you will return home immediately. We are not able to continue paying the expenses which you incur in studying. If you are again disobedient your allowance will be cut off." When this revolutionary youth received the telegram, he was very sad and troubled. He was unable to continue his studies, so he went home.[75]

The CCP's concern with controlling the peasant movement was more indirect. They were generally enthusiastic about the explosive growth of a new segment of the mass revolutionary movement and about its civil revolutionary contribution to the progress of the Northern Expedition, but their (and the Comintern's) conception of the bourgeois nature of the national revolution made the maintenance of the united front the paramount concern. Underlying this priority was the view expressed by Chen Duxiu in 1923:

> Workers' movements, peasant movements, and student movements are all unable to separate themselves from political movements, because political freedom is a necessity to every movement. For instance, if Cao Kun and Wu Peifu don't collapse, then democratic government can't be secured, so where besides Guangdong can railway workers' unions and general student unions exist?[76]

The same point is made more succinctly by Zhang Guotao:

> If the influence of the peasants was to be made firm and the land problem was to be solved, the most essential need was for protection that could be provided by a government supporting the interests of the peasants.[77]

The more that political events in rural areas outran the united-classes, antiimperialist formula of CCP–KMT cooperation, the more the Central Committee of the CCP felt obliged to insist that the interests of groups involved with the Guangdong and later the Wuhan KMT be respected.[78] This attitude was parallel in many respects to the relationship of the Western Hills group to Duan Qirui which Mao had criticized the previous year, although the political content was entirely different. The mass revolutionary goals of the "really revolutionary party" were gradually sacrificed for the sake of maintaining party relationships with the KMT and the Comintern. The Central Committee began issuing critical words of caution to the peasant movement about "excesses" as early as September 1926.[79] The ultimate principle was the alliance. Insofar as it was controlled by the Central Committee the CCP became the party of the alliance rather than the party of the masses.

The explosive growth of peasant associations in areas under KMT control forced the CCP's agrarian policy to develop rapidly from diffident vagueness in mid-1926 to outraged frustration at peasant excesses by the spring of 1927. Total peasant association membership jumped from 981,442 in June 1926 to 9,153,093 in June 1927. As the peasant movement grew behind the leading edge of the Northern Expedition troops, attention shifted away from the older peasant associations of Guangdong to the rapidly proliferating ones of Hunan, Jiangxi, and Hubei. Of these, Hunan was the principal focus of hopes and anxieties about the peasant movement from the fall of 1926 until the Autumn Harvest Uprising of 1927.

The successes of the pioneering Guangdong peasant movement had bred by late 1926 a powerful and violent counterrevolutionary force in that province, and although the peasant associations continued to grow as late as January 1927,[80] the movement was preoccupied with this new and harsher phase of the rural struggle. "There is not a village without bloody atrocities.... It could be said that the peasant movement of the whole province has plunged into a difficult situation for the time being."[81] From June 1926 to June 1927 the membership of the Hunan peasant associations rose from 38,150 to 4,517,140; in Guangdong the increase was from 647,766 to 700,000—the rounded membership figure and conspicuous lack of detailed information in the latter census are ominous symptoms of deterioration.[82] In 1927 armed landlord counterattacks against peasant associations spread into Jiangxi and then Hunan. In Jiangxi, where the peasant associations had mushroomed from 6,000 to 50,000 members in the month of October, the antipeasant, anti-Bolshevik reaction began with the third session of the KMT's provincial assembly on 1 January 1927. A sharpening conflict between the provincial KMT government and the peasant movement led by Fang Zhimin culminated in June with the suppression of the peasant movement and an order expelling communists from Jiangxi.[83] In Hunan, growth of the peasant movement was more massive and repression was correspondingly more severe. On 21 May 1927, an army commander in Changsha violently suppressed the Hunan CCP and peasant association headquarters in Changsha. After initial plans of armed retaliation had been frustrated by Chen Duxiu's efforts at mediation, landlord forces attacked peasant associations throughout June, resulting in the deaths of over 10,000 people.[84] The landlord backlash against the communist-led peasant associations eventually provided the armed political base for the "new warlordism" of the anticommunist KMT.

The Hunan peasant movement was Mao's chief preoccupation during late 1926 and 1927. This attention by no means indicates a narrow provincial focus, however. Mao continued to be a high-level functionary in the CCP and the KMT during this time, and he even assumed the new duties of running a Central Peasant Movement Institute in Wuhan and organizing a national peasant association.[85] But Hunan was a national focus for hopes and fears concerning the peasant movement. Hunan had the largest peasant associations and provided a favorable context for peasant activism. On the threatening side, most of the military forces supporting the Wuhan KMT had their roots in Hunan, and these roots were with the terrified rural elite rather than with the peasantry. As we have seen earlier, Mao was involved in early peasant organization in the counties around his home in the summer of 1925. In 1926–1927, he actively participated in the first Provincial Peasant Congress in December, spent the month of January investigating local conditions in five counties, and in February and March made written and oral reports on his Hunan investigations to various groups in Wuhan. Central Committee bureaucrats like Zhang Guotao were undoubtedly right in their suspicions that the radicalism of the Hunan peasant movement and the Hunan Provincial Committee of the CCP was encouraged by Mao's sponsorship.

During Mao's December visit to Hunan, the "Manifesto and Resolutions of the First Congress of Peasant Representatives of All Hunan Province" was composed under his personal direction.[86] Befitting its representative character, the manifesto shows definite signs of having been written (or rewritten) by a committee. Its argument is much more orthodox than any of Mao's other writings on the peasantry, and its organization is looser. The initial theme is the harm done to China's peasantry by imperialism and its instruments, the warlords. The exploitation led to popular uprisings, but until Sun Yat-sen these lacked adequate organization. Now the peasant movement has made great contributions to the Northern Expedition, particularly in consolidating rear defenses and smashing local tyrants and bad gentry. These activities are important because exploitation at the village level is the real base of the warlords' power. Onto this already circuitous argument are attached three defensive points. The first shows that the liberation of the peasantry will benefit the whole country; the second argues that the chaos in the cities is due to war rather than to the peasant associations; the third contends that the extralegal measures of the peasants against the local tyrants and bad gentry are justified by the urgency of the struggle. This last point foreshadows the defense of peasant "excesses" which is central to the argument of the Hunan Report. But the perspective of this defense is slightly different because it centers its critiques on the nervous pacifism of the party officialdom: "If [the party] is afraid of 'quarrels' and has a suspicious or opposing attitude, then it can't be considered a revolutionary party."[87] The Hunan Report stresses instead the objective necessity of peasant actions which seem excessive from the distance of the cities. The central metaphor of the Hunan Report is *jiao wang guo zheng:* "Proper limits have to be exceeded in order to right a wrong."[88] The metaphor of the manifesto is the first usage of an equally famous Mao trope: "At this time either the east wind prevails over the west wind, or the west wind prevails over the east wind, so how can harshness be avoided?"[89]

The Hunan Report

In great contrast to the manifesto, the Hunan Report (Report of an Investigation of the Hunan Peasant Movement) is personal and eloquent.[90] It has become Mao's best-known article, but even from the start it was an important and controversial analysis of the peasant movement. It is claimed that Chen Duxiu would not allow the second and third sections of the report to be published in *The Guide Weekly* because of policy differences with the first installment,[91] but the report was quickly republished in various degrees of completeness in pamphlet form and in other periodicals.[92] The overwhelming majority of revisions in the 1951 official version of the report and in the elegant English translation of the *Selected Works* are stylistic;[93] the only really tendentious series of changes in the official edition is a cover-up of the report's united front origins by inserting "Communist Party" in appropriate places.

The Hunan Report is an extraordinary work of political persuasion aimed at the most crucial question facing the united front. The potential for political change through victory of the Northern Expedition seemed to be at loggerheads with the potential for social change evidenced by the peasant associations. The situation presented the leadership with a particularly acute form of the perennial question for Chinese radicals: *zou nei tiao lu?*—which road to take? Mao's answer to this question is fascinating both for its persuasive ingenuity and for the insight it permits into his political thinking.

Relying on his month-long investigation tour of rural Hunan, Mao preempts the discussion of possible trade-offs of political and social goals by assuming that the dilemma does not exist. Mao argues that rural social revolution is an irrepressible force, and he mercilessly confronts "revolutionary comrades"[94] with the choice of leading the vast revolutionary majority or siding with the rearguard of the landlords in the rural struggle. By building his strategic argument up from the peasant movement, Mao simply bypasses the prudential concerns of leaders like Chen Duxiu who reasoned down from the dual prerequisites of victory in the Northern Expedition and maintenance of the united front. The crucial step in this bypass is the nature of "peasant excesses." Mao interprets the question of excesses as whether or not unnecessary injustices occurred in the villages, and he rightly points out that the tales of atrocities heard in the cities were being fed by the partial accounts of fleeing landlords. But the question of village justice was not central to the Central Committee's anxiety about excesses. From the perspective of the leaders in Wuhan, any activity which strained the KMT–CCP alliance or jeopardized the forces of the Northern Expedition was excessive. Mao does not address this notion of excessiveness because to do so would dilute the persuasiveness of his argument—and, more important, because he does not believe that a legitimate revolutionary group could be hostile toward mass activism.

Mao achieves a vigorous encapsulation of the basic message and attitude of the Hunan Report in the first paragraph. This paragraph is so well written that a thorough analysis of it is the best introduction to the report:

> On this trip I made firsthand investigations of the five counties of Xiangtan, Xiangxiang, Hengshan, Liling, and Changsha. In the thirty-two days from January 4 to February 5, I called together fact-finding conferences in villages and county seats, which were attended by experienced peasants and by comrades working in the peasant movement, and [I] listened attentively to their reports and collected a great deal of material. Many of the hows and whys of the peasant movement were exactly the opposite of what the gentry in Hangzhou and Changsha are saying. There are many strange things which I have never seen or heard before. I believe that the same is true in all of China no matter what the province. Therefore all talk directed against the peasant movement must be speedily set right. All wrong measures taken by the revolutionary authorities concerning the peasant movement must be speedily changed. Only thus can the future of the revolution be benefited. For the present upsurge of the peasant movement is an exceptionally great issue *(yige jida di wenti)*. In a very short time, in China's central, southern, and northern provinces, several hundred million peasants will rise like a mighty storm, like a hurricane, a force so swift and violent that no power, however great, will be able to hold it back.

They will smash all the trammels that bind them and rush forward on the road to liberation. They will eventually sweep all the imperialists, warlords, corrupt officials, local tyrants and evil gentry into their graves. Every revolutionary party and every revolutionary comrade will be put to the test, to be accepted or rejected as they decide. There are three alternatives. To march at their head and lead them? To trail behind them, gesticulating and criticizing? Or to stand in their way and oppose them? Every Chinese is free to choose, but the lot of the present situation will force you to make the choice quickly. Therefore I have written my report and my views for the perusal of the revolutionary comrades.[95]

The argument of the paragraph is in two symmetric halves. The first presents the minimum message and content of the Hunan Report: Mao's investigation shows that the accepted picture of the peasant movement is wrong and that policies which derive from the mistaken view should be corrected. The second half is the maximum message: Mao's view *(yijian)* of the peasant movement as the central political force, whose needs are thus the criterion of revolutionary behavior. The relationship of the two halves is quite close. The first presents the facts of the rural situation and the second presents its dynamics; the first recommends that policy be readjusted to accord with the facts and the second suggests that revolutionary attitudes be readjusted to accord with the current trend. The argument of the second half is less self-evident because it is an estimate of the potential of the peasant movement; its policy conclusions are more radical because it demands a party and a personal empathy with and commitment to the relatively autonomous momentum of the movement. The relationship between the two halves is not factual versus interpretative but external versus fundamental. Both are essential to a revolutionary understanding of the peasant movement. Likewise the relation within each half between observation and recommendation is quite close. It would be irrational for the party not to adjust its policy in the light of a better understanding of the situation, and the description of the overwhelming force of the expected rural revolution actually preempts the "freedom of choice" mentioned near the end of the report.

Equally noteworthy in this paragraph is Mao's relationship to the party and to the peasant movement. Mao speaks in his own right as expert on the peasant movement.[96] His authority to speak on rural conditions, conferred by his lengthy on-the-spot survey, is mentioned at the beginning of each of the article's three sections and also in the important subsection, "It's Terrible or It's Fine." This self-confidence derived from personal experience is the missing element in "China's Peasantry and the National Revolution." The experienced "I" addresses a rather undefined group ranging from "revolutionary authorities" in the context of correcting policy mistakes to "every Chinese" in the context of presenting the basic political choices. Above all, Mao addresses his "revolutionary comrades." The decision whether to lead, follow, or oppose is put in personal rather than in party terms—not only because of the coldness toward the peasant movement manifested by the leadership of the KMT and the CCP, but also because the imminence of the revolution and the upsurge of spontaneous popular organizations (the village-level peasant associations in particular) imply that revolutionary politics is on the verge of passing out of its preparatory, party stage and that mass revolutionary leadership is needed. The subject of the report, the peasant movement, is presented as a spontaneous uprising of the broad masses of the oppressed. Mao's metaphors suggest that it is an irresistible natural force; to report on "a force so swift and violent" is not to present a case for judgment but to describe historical necessity. The alternatives of leading, following, or opposing are not only preempted as far as revolutionary content is concerned: as far as historical survival is concerned they are a choice between the wave of the future, insignificance, and suicide.

The introductory paragraph just analyzed constitutes the Hunan Report's first subsection, "The Importance of the Peasant Question." The rest of the "Rural Revolution" section details the organizational growth and politics of the peasant associations and attacks attitudes which are critical of the peasant movement. The growth of the peasant association is divided into two periods: from January to September 1926 and from October 1926 to January 1927. In the first period the peasant associations were small and underground. A peculiarity of the early phase was that organization preceded political action; struggle in the villages had not appeared and the primary political involvement was assisting the Northern Expedition. The second (and continuing) phase was that of revolutionary action. The earlier organization enabled a serious and successful rural revolution in many counties of central and southern Hunan, with the result that within four months one-third of the Hunan peasantry was organized and "a revolution without parallel in history"⁹⁷ was under way. More important to the sudden blossoming of the peasant movement was the conquest of Hunan by Northern Expedition forces. Although Mao does not mention this conquest, the events were fresh enough in the minds of his audience.

The primary target of the revolution is a personal one within each village—the former oppressors. The peasant associations are now all-powerful in their villages, and the targets are pursued with great gusto. With this reversal of oppression, the supporting culture of the landlords is also attacked. The threat which the "new world" of the peasant movement ultimately posed to the existing social order was felt with particular force in the cities as the rural landlords who fled there told of their experiences. According to Mao, the notion of a terrible rural situation was so pervasive that even revolutionary-minded people could only say that such situations were inevitable in a revolution. Mao's task is to show why even the violence of the peasant movement is "fine." Claiming that the overthrow of local tyrants, bad gentry, and lawless landlords was the real objective *(zhenzheng mubiao)* of the national revolution, Mao declares that "all revolutionary comrades should know that the national revolution needs a great change in the countryside, that the 1911 revolution did not have this change and therefore failed." In the present national revolution he estimates that the achievement of the city dwellers and military is 30 percent and that of the peasants 70 percent. There would be no question of considering the peasant movement terrible if all revolutionaries had had Mao's experience:

> If your revolutionary viewpoint is firmly established and if you have been to the villages and looked around, you will undoubtedly feel thrilled as never before. Countless thousands of the enslaved— the peasants—are striking down the enemies who battened on their flesh.⁹⁸

The first section of the Hunan Report ends with a discussion of another criticism of the peasant movement: "The Question of Going Too Far." This is a middle-of-the-road position because it accepts the necessity of the peasant associations but criticizes them for excesses. Mao does not deny the incidents; in fact, he gives examples of what could be considered extreme behavior. But they are not excesses. In the first place, the notorious peasant actions are against notorious oppressors; they are not random. Mao's second point, that revolutions require such actions, contains an eloquent statement of his view of revolution:

> A revolution is not a dinner party, or writing an essay, or painting a picture, or doing embroidery; it cannot be so refined, so leisurely and gentle, so temperate, kind, courteous, restrained and magnanimous. A revolution is an insurrection, an act of violence by which one class overthrows another. A rural revolution is a revolution by which the peasantry overthrows the power of the feudal landlord class.[99]

The "excesses" were necessary in order to make the landlords fear the peasantry. Since the peasant associations are seeking to transform society and politics in the village, they must have absolute power. There can be no remnant of landlord prestige or power. To criticize excesses is thus a position in the interests of the landlords.

In general the task of the first section of the Hunan Report is to describe the context of the peasant movement and to oppose an informed and revolutionary grasp of the rural situation to attitudes prevalent in the cities which are critical of the movement. The essential characteristics of the rural revolution are that it will prevail, that it is the just and final solution to thousands of years of feudal oppression, and that it must be complete. The specific mistake of the categorical denunciation of peasant activities is that it ignores the historic mission of the peasant movement. The specific mistake of the criticism of excesses is that it ignores the nature of revolution.

The second section, "Vanguards of the Revolution," analyzes the dynamics of the rural revolution within the village. The primary element is the poor peasants, who constitute 70 percent of the rural population; the corresponding counterrevolutionary theory is that the movement is led by riffraff.[100]

The origins of the antipeasant attitudes of the gentry are the antigentry activities of the peasants. These activities against the gentry occur because the peasant associations at the village level are run by poor peasants, and these activities are the base of the rural revolution. Hence the poor peasants are the vanguard and heroes of the revolution. "To deny their role is to deny the revolution. To attack them is to attack the revolution. They have never been wrong on the general direction of the revolution."[101] To support this judgment, Mao gives a class analysis of the village peasantry. The content of his class descriptions is basically the same as those of his writings of a year before. This time, however, the division is into three classes: rich, middle, and poor peasants. The poor peasants include the semiowner-peasants and those more destitute. The convenience of this division into three parts is that the parts correspond to attitudes toward the peasant association. The rich peasants are hostile or cold, the middle peasants are vacillating, and the poor peasants are the main support of the revolution. Just as they were despised because of their misery before the peasant upsurge, the poor peasants are feared because of their fierceness as its leaders at the village level. Mao's emphasis on the poor peasants became a cornerstone of his rural politics, but after 1927 his thinking about middle peasants and rich peasants underwent considerable change. In the Hunan Report rich peasants are described as unfriendly to the movement but not as an enemy. Middle peasants on the other hand are dismissed because of their vacillation. In the more serious class struggles of the base area period, winning over the middle peasants to active participation became a major policy focus and the rich peasants became a target of the village revolution.

Only after presenting a general grasp of the rural revolutionary situation and an understanding of intravillage dynamics does Mao detail the relationship of the peasants to the peasant associations in the last section, listing fourteen major achievements. The thorough reporting of this last section complements the previous two by describing the political, economic, and reconstructive efforts of the peasant associations. The political and reconstructive efforts are numerous and impressive; the economic demands seem mild by comparison. According to Mao the peasants were quite effective in destroying the prestige of the landlords, but they were not demanding that land be redistributed. One explanation for the absence of the land issue was seasonal—since peasants are consumers rather than producers in the winter, their measure of preventing the shipment of grain out of the village was of greater immediate benefit. Moreover, since the CCP had not yet arrived at a land policy,[102] the corresponding absence of this demand in the peasant associations can be taken as an indicator of the importance of central political leadership in determining the movement's direction. In retrospect, the most underdeveloped part of the Hunan Report is the discussion of the peasants' military power. Although the military power of the landlords had been overthrown, their armed bands merely switched their allegiance to the peasant associations. A new, purely peasant military force had come into being—namely the spear corps, which were 100,000 strong in one county alone—but the mass mobilization involved and the terrifying effect of these corps on the landlords is stressed more than their military effectiveness.

The Hunan Report ends with one last appeal to take the revolutionary commitment seriously and to support the achievements of the peasant associations. Empty revolutionary talk is condemned with a most apt allusion:

> To talk about arousing the masses of the people day in and day out and then to be scared to death when the masses do rise—what difference is there between this and Lord She's love of dragons?[103]

The peasant movement which Mao describes in the Hunan Report corresponds remarkably well with his prognoses of the rural situation of the previous year. Bitter class struggle within the villages was producing a political and social revolution in the countryside which was shattering the traditional feudal structures of landlord rule. But the peasant movement is not the central issue of the national revolution in the sense of being the key to victory in the struggles with Zhang Zuolin and the other warlords. Mao notes that in Hunan organization preceded revolution. The peasant movement did not emerge vigorously until after the conquest of Hunan by KMT forces. The importance of the peasant question, and the significance of the Hunan peasant movement, is its centrality to revolutionary legitimacy—to the purpose of the Northern Expedition—and to the stability of the succeeding regime. The reference to the 1911 revolution is instructive. This event was superficially successful but merely replaced one form of oppressive government with another. Militarily the function of the peasant movement was the not very urgent task of securing the rear area, but politically the ultimate justification for military advances was to expand the area where political transformation could take place.

Mao's optimistic assessment of the Hunan peasant movement was evidently unconvincing to both the KMT and the CCP, either because of a fear of dragons or because of a more pessimistic view of peasant power. And indeed the political events of 1927 seemed to support the doubters. The massacre in May was a great shock to the self-confidence and prestige of the peasant movement, and the failure of the Autumn Harvest Uprising completed the picture of rural organizations ineffective as political or military forces in their own right. When the political and military context of the peasant movement turned from benevolence to hostility it proved to be insufficiently resilient. A large part of the blame for this unpreparedness should be assigned to the CCP Central Committee —as the alliance deteriorated, the Central Committee worked frantically to prevent any defensive readjustment of the mass movements. But there are important structural reasons for the failure to be gleaned from the Hunan Report.

The principal structural defect is the contradiction between the demands of Mao's newly discovered source of mass politics and the interests of the established parties to which he appeals for support and leadership. For the urban and landed progressives of the KMT left wing and the labor and cosmopolitan revolutionaries of the CCP, his revolutionary understanding of the "new world" of the villages was simply not within the horizon of possibility. The idea of a world of hostile classes but without a proletariat contradicted the constitutive ideologies of both revolutionary parties, and the spontaneity of its development was a threat to their legitimacy. Most concretely, social revolution in the countryside threatened the multifaceted military situation of the Northern Expedition, since warlords who had only recently joined the KMT in order to share the spoils of the Northern Expedition were the main strength of the Wuhan KMT. These contradictions are evident in the report primarily as a suppressed tension. The contrasts between existing attitudes and what Mao proposes, between village peasant associations and county levels of every kind of organization, between uncompromising village politics and moderate village military and economic policies—all are understated in the Hunan Report but can be seen as the dark side of the peasant movement.

The suppression of these tensions indicates the Achilles heel of the 1926–1927 peasant movement. Just like the CCP, it grew as a movement politically and militarily dependent on the KMT and thus at its mercies in the event of a conflict. When the conflict became inescapable and the weakness apparent in the latter half of 1927, reorientation toward independent survival became the major leadership task.

It may seem strange that Mao's populist empiricism—that is, seeking the real potential for mass-oriented political action—would prove so tragically misleading about the strength of the peasant movement. But facts occur in a context of environmental conditions, and a change of context can render apparently well-founded expectations obsolete. Mao's lack of prescience consisted in his blithe extrapolation of the peasant movement's growth and his failure to see that peasant success would breed a powerful consolidation of antipeasant forces. His overoptimism is analogous to his hopes in 1919 for the efficacy of the "great shout of the popular masses," but it was not counterfactual at the time. Mao's experience proves a point he was to make ten years later in "On Practice": "Man's knowledge of a particular process at any given stage of development is only a relative truth."[104] The important thing is quick and accurate assessment of the new stage and a reorientation of policies. Mao proved equal to this task at Jinggangshan in 1928.

Conclusion

The most significant characteristics of Mao's writings and politics in the 1923–1927 period are essentially related to his commitment to the Chinese Communist Party. Mao by this time was no longer a May Fourth activist; he was a revolutionary cadre. In contrast to his earlier work, organization, both ideological and political, played an explicit and sometimes dominant role. The practical immediacy of Mao's May Fourth writings which voiced itself in nontheoretical, general calls to action was submerged in mundane party tasks until the upsurge of the Northern Expedition. Even Mao's return to mass politics in Hunan in 1926–1927 is not a return to his earlier political style. The significance of the peasant movement is established in Marxist categories of class struggle and the political activities of the peasant associations have to be reconciled with party authority.

But the populist revolutionary aims which led Mao into the Communist Party retained their importance as the final criteria of revolutionary legitimacy. In Mao's relationship to the CCP there is a blend, at times a suppressed tension, of unreserved commitment to the party and at the same time a grasp of the party's instrumentality to mass revolution. As Mao's class analysis located the main potential of the national revolution in the oppressed rural classes, his emphasis on the responsibilities of the "really revolutionary party," along with his emphasis on the counterrevolutionary character of suspicious attitudes toward the peasantry, became an indirect but serious criticism of the direction of CCP leadership. In turn, Mao's relative lack of concern with the politics of the Northern Expedition and his concentration on rural revolution must have seemed premature to many of his colleagues. But Mao's growing alienation from the Central Committee in 1926 and early 1927—signaled by Chen Duxiu's refusal to print Mao's "Classes in Chinese Society" and evident in Zhang Guotao's narration of the period—did not lead to a break with the party. The party, particularly in its idealization as the really revolutionary party, had become the essential framework of Mao's revolutionary action.

The uniqueness of Mao's attitude toward the party is most clearly seen in contrast with other theories of revolutionary organization. Suppose we compare Mao's position with the views of three prominent European Marxists: Georg Lukacs, Karl Korsch, and Antonio Gramsci. The reception of Bolshevism in China and Europe was similar in that the practical success of the October Revolution was the key to its appeal.[105] But the florescence of Leninism in Europe occurred in a fundamentally different political context, because the existence of large, officially Marxist, social democratic parties in Europe made the question of revolutionary legitimacy a bone of contention between parties within a general Marxist framework. Rejection of Bolshevism (because of traces of tsarist authoritarianism and anarchist voluntarism) became the new integrating ideology of the German Social Democratic Party (SPD),[106] while the frustration of radicals with the opportunism of the established workers' parties led them to promote Lenin's "revolutionary *Realpolitik.*"[107]

The most elegant and coherent Leninist view of the party is given by Georg Lukacs in his 1922 essay "Methodisches zur Organisationsfrage."[108] Lukacs stresses the dialectical interrelationship of revolutionary theory, party, and class, with the party's practical activity as the central mediating moment:

> The correctness of revolutionary Marxism in an objectively revolutionary situation is much more than the merely "universal" correctness of a theory. Precisely because it has become completely actual, completely practical, theory must become the director of every single daily step. But this is only possible if theory completely abandons its purely theoretical character and becomes purely dia-

lectical . . . thereby practically overcoming every opposition between theory and praxis.[109]

The party's concentration on practical revolutionary tasks requires members of high quality and dedication, strong discipline, and tactical flexibility. Only the opportunity for revolution is inevitably presented by history; the revolution itself is a free act of the proletariat and its vanguard. To develop crises into revolution, the proletariat must win the support or at least the neutrality of nonproletarian oppressed classes. Thus the problem of alliances is a key tactical problem:

> Since the proletariat can free itself only through the destruction of class society, it is forced to fight its struggle for liberation on behalf of all oppressed, exploited groups. But whether in individual battles these [other groups] will be on its side or on the side of the enemy is more or less "accidental" because of their unclear class consciousness. It depends . . . very much on the correct tactics of the revolutionary Party of the proletariat.[110]

The themes of practical, dialectical orientation, flexibility, and the importance of alliances are close to Mao's view of the party. Where he and Lukacs begin to diverge significantly is with Lukacs' belief that the party's practical mission will preserve it from error and with Lukacs' related complacency about the party's leading role.[111] Karl Korsch, one of the most prominent Cassandra figures of European Marxism,[112] viewed the correctness of the party's leadership of the proletariat as more problematic and therefore placed greater emphasis than Lukacs on democratic mechanisms of leadership. Korsch's lifelong interest in workers' councils sprang from this concern for the vitality of the party's representative role. For Korsch, as for Mao, the question of the relationship of theory and practice was not an internal, tactical problem for the party. His concern for the real connection between the proletariat and the party led first to a split with Stalinism and later to serious strains in his commitment to Marxism. Underlying Korsch's critique was a very empirical approach to the needs of the proletariat and to the economic and historical roots of developments in Marxist theory.

Antonio Gramsci's view of the party's role and temptations is considerably more political than either Korsch's or Lukacs', and in this respect he is closer to Mao's position. The title of his main work, *The Modern Prince*,[113] already indicates a respect for the realities and structure of political power. Gramsci analyzes the Communist Party as part of a larger political and cultural situation; as a result, his analysis does not assume that the party is isolated from common political diseases and blindness. He stresses the need for accurate situational analyses and the need to avoid bureaucratic rigidity in the secondary leadership. In conformity with the Italian political context, he recognizes the necessity of an alliance of the northern proletariat and the southern peasantry:

> The proletariat can become the leading and ruling class to the extent to which it succeeds in creating a system of class alliance which enables it to mobilize the majority of the working population against capitalism and the bourgeois State; this means, in Italy, in the actual relations existing in Italy, to the extent to which it succeeds in obtaining the consent of the large peasant masses.[114]

Gramsci's analysis of the contribution of the peasantry differs from Mao's 1926–1927 writings in two significant ways. First, the priority of the proletarian class is not as clear in Mao's analysis. Gramsci was a leader of Turin's industrial proletariat, whereas Mao, as spokesman for the Chinese peasant association movement, could expect his colleagues in the trade union movement to maintain the primacy of the proletariat. Second, and more important, Gramsci's analysis of the peasant question is primarily an analysis of their political leadership. Although he is not proposing an alliance with the southern Italian intellectuals as representatives of the peasantry, he does not seem to assume, as Mao does, that the Communist Party has a natural role as the immediate organizer and leader of the peasantry. Although Gramsci moves beyond the dogmatic scornfulness implied in Lukacs' description of "classes with unclear class consciousness," the peasantry appears to remain an external ally to the revolution.

The basic principle which Mao has in common with these European radical theorists is succinctly expressed by Lukacs: "The question of the organization of a revolutionary party can only be developed organically from a theory of revolution."[115] But whereas this thesis was challenging in the context of European Marxism, it was the unquestioned starting point of Marxism in China. Mao's dissension with the Central Committee in 1926–

1927 centered on what should be the compass for strategic and tactical decisions. On this point the positions of the Europeans are more implicit but still discernible: for Lukacs the objective revolutionary interests of the party; for Korsch the revolutionary will of the proletariat; and for Gramsci a careful analysis of revolutionary potential or proletarian advantage. Mao's stress on the overwhelming numbers of the peasantry and the political potential for their misery seems less Marxist and more primitive than these views, but it was an appropriate response to China's less differentiated political situation. In the great watershed between Leninist and revisionist theories of the party, Mao, like Lukacs, Gramsci, and Korsch, is firmly on the side of revolution. But Mao's populist empiricism demanded that revolutionary legitimacy in China be founded on an inclusive mass revolutionary leadership, and thus the peasant question became central to his idea of party policy.

Just as Mao's earlier political attitudes and the peculiarities of the Chinese political context influenced his appreciation of the party's role, they also shaped his grasp of Marxist ideology. Marxist class analysis provided a powerful new paradigm for Mao's revolutionary viewpoint, but it is a paradigm adopted for mass-oriented activism. Mao's class analyses are not primarily studies of economic or political structures; they specify mass revolutionary potential for the national revolution. To find the types of people *(zhong ren)* who can be mobilized—with the firm expectation that these will build up solidly from the lower classes—implies a basic discontinuity of method with Mao's earlier democratic populism, but it includes an even more fundamental continuity of his ultimate aspiration and motivation in politics. Marxism does not have a simple instrumental relation to Mao's continuing pre-Marxist political goals; rather, it is a framework that shapes his perception of political reality. But it is evident in the process of Mao's discovery of the peasant movement that the motive of his application and development of Marxism is the furthering of mass revolution. Until the failure of CCP participation in the Northern Expedition drove Mao into the mountains, his politics did not require more than a populist focusing of Marxist class analysis. It was the unique problems of political-military survival in the countryside which prompted the development of his own political paradigm.

The magnitude and complexity of the contextual changes from the May Fourth Movement to the Northern Expedition make it very difficult to trace specific developments and continuities in Mao's thought. Contradictions of earlier opinions are rare,[116] and similarities between Mao's Hunan politics of 1919-1922 and his return in 1926-1927 can be superficial. In general, the major developments of Mao's pre-Marxist period were practical-political and those of the following period were theoretical-organizational. Mao's already proven abilities[117] at differentiating complex political situations and appropriate policies led to two major theoretical advances: a theory of alliances and the seminal class analyses of "Peasant Classes" and "Classes in Chinese Society." Perhaps more important, the class viewpoint of Marxism replaced the populist universalism of Mao's earlier political appeals with mass revolutionary struggle. The optimism of the "great shout together" and the organizational weakness of federated unions of the masses are replaced by a political strategy and apparatus designed specifically for prolonged and bitter struggle.

The main characteristic of this period is the strategic notion of the national revolution, and the transformations which this notion undergoes in Mao's writings are quite significant. In Mao's Shanghai writings of 1923, the function of the national revolution is to provide a focus on present tasks. The ideas of mediated revolutionary politics, policy by stages, and present objectives versus ultimate goals lie behind the limited concept of the national revolution as the first step of revolutionary success. In a sense this type of politics is an application of Mao's emphasis on doing what can be done to a prerevolutionary situation. The alliance theory implicit in the "Anti-Feng" article of late 1925 is already a considerable improvement over the mechanical stages of "Merchants and the Peking Coup." The nested alliances of the anti-Feng front are clearly related to a definite goal. More important, this scheme does not allow the interests of long-term allies to be sacrificed to the success of a short-term entente. The most significant transformation of the concept of national revolution occurs in the articles on the peasantry. In these the national revolution undergoes a subtle redefinition from the immediately possible political target to the immediately possible mass revolution. The link between the two is Mao's continuing assumption of the ultimate power of the mobilized masses and its corollary that any government or revolution which neglects the masses lacks an adequate foundation. The lesson of the 1911 revolution, also analyzed in the same context by Mao in 1919, shows the shallowness of merely political revolutions. Within this redefinition (or at least respecification) of the national revolution, Mao also shifts the focus of class politics to the numerically overwhelming rural masses. In "The Peasant Question and the National Revolution" it is clear that the peasantry should no longer be regarded as merely a resource to the national revolution. The struggle in the villages, at the base of feudal and imperialist exploitation, is the central problem. With this theoretical perspective already established, Mao's approbation of the village-level peasant associations in the Hunan Report is readily understandable.

Between the established game of elite struggle being played out by most of the political and military forces of the Northern Expedition and the radicalization of demands threatened by the mobilization of the poor peasants there was a strain that could be neither reconciled nor suppressed. The Northern Expedition eventually succeeded and its victory was consolidated under increasingly anticommunist, anti–mass organization leadership. With the hostility of nearly every political and military force in China, the peasant movement failed as an independent base for a national revolution. This event could be taken in two ways: as a vindication of Mao's thesis of the meaninglessness of victory without active mass support; or as a vindication of the CCP Central Committee's complaints that the relatively defenseless peasant movement should curb its demands until after national victory. In any case, despite its unexpected failure, Mao's peasant politics was more farsighted than other aspects of communist policy. When survival became the dominant concern after the general failure, Mao was again in the forefront of rural policy, but in vastly different circumstances.

3 Rural Revolution: 1927–1931

In the latter half of 1927, the first KMT–CCP united front split apart and the KMT crushed most of the urban strength of the CCP. Correspondingly, Mao's concerns changed from problems of the national revolution's orientation to the difficulties of survival in the rural crevices of a hostile environment. In retrospect, it may have been Mao's chief contribution to the Chinese revolution to turn this disastrous fallback to the starting point of revolutionary power into the beginning of a new type of rural revolution and a style of leadership which was novel and uniquely appropriate for Chinese conditions. Mao's new political paradigm began in the scramble for survival on the mountainous border of Hunan and Jiangxi. The paradigm itself would not be formulated for ten years, but the successful political practice which formed its contents were creative responses to the problems of survival.

The movement which Mao found necessary for survival was an integrated political, economic, and military effort with the effective mobilization of the peasantry as its chief concern and resource. Although related to Marxist and Chinese precedents, Mao's strategy for a protracted, self-sufficient, rural struggle constituted a major innovation within both traditions. The major contribution to Chinese tradition was the transformation of the economic, social, and political structure of the village. This was a social accomplishment equivalent to splitting the atom: the most difficult, most basic, and most energy-releasing task. Mao's most prominent contribution to Marxism was a theory of leadership adequate to this task, one built on the principles of flexible closeness to the masses and maximum effective mobilization.

More than any other location, Mao's first guerrilla base at

Jinggangshan is justly celebrated as the birthplace of the Chinese revolution which culminated twenty-two years later in the establishment of the People's Republic of China. Although the catastrophes of 1934 which led to the Long March were just as disastrous for the CCP as the collapse of the First United Front, the major policy changes of 1935-1942 were not as original or basic as those developed in the 1928-1934 period. Researchers have tended to overstate the originality of the later period (the Yanan period) because it was then that Mao formulated the comprehensive, authoritative statements of his political paradigm. Just as Mao claims in theory, however, in the reality of his own political development innovations in practice preceded conceptualizations in theory. The foundation of Mao Zedong's political thought was his political experience before Yanan.

Mao's politics during the early base area period followed a course of development quite different from that of the preceding First United Front period. In 1923, Mao's exile from Hunan occasioned a shift of horizons to national politics which gave added importance to organizational and ideological concerns. In the course of the First United Front Mao's political thought moved from questions of party politics to the theory and practice of national popular revolution. In 1927, the failure of communist participation in the Northern Expedition forced a reduction of Mao's political horizon to the perimeters of a locality where he and those with him could survive as a revolutionary force. With the success of these early efforts Mao's politics moved from the problems of personal survival to theoretical affirmations of the revolutionary significance of the base areas and the organizational and leadership methods necessary to maintain their strength.

The task of this chapter is to describe Mao's practical initiatives during the early base area period and to analyze their inherent rationale. Although it is important to remember that other communist leaders were facing similar problems in other base areas (among them He Long, Zhang Guotao, Liu Zhidan, and Fang Zhimin), I will not attempt to compare their efforts with Mao's since his policy developments in the early base area period were quite autonomous. A serious comparison of early base areas would, however, be interesting and complex enough to deserve a separate investigation.[1] Focusing on Mao's views of his own base area inevitably distorts the general picture of the CCP during this period, which was one of multiple base area activities and continuing underground urban work. But our focus is the development of Mao's politics, and to pursue it we must accompany him into the relative isolation of guerrilla warfare.

The early base area period has two main subdivisions: Mao's activities in the Jinggangshan base area from 1927 to 1929 and the creation of the Jiangxi base in 1927–1931. With the movement of the Central Committee to the Jiangxi base in 1931 and its redesignation as the Central Soviet Republic of the Chinese Soviet Republic, a new phase of Mao's politics begins, a phase which is the subject of the next chapter.

A Sketch of Political Developments

In the summer of 1927, it became increasingly evident to CCP members that Chen Duxiu's politics of restraint were not preserving the united front with the Wuhan KMT but, rather, were preventing preparation for an inevitable armed struggle. Chen's attempt to discourage the spontaneous radicalization of the peasant movement was particularly upsetting to the more radical rank and file. When Tan Pingshan, one of three CCP members serving as ministers in Wuhan, resigned his government post in July 1927, he expressed regret for his inability "to set the peasant movement right from its excessive demands and illegal deeds."[2] Discontent came to a head with the 7 August Emergency Conference, which placed Qu Qiubai in command of the party, approved a long letter to the party membership castigating the old leadership,[3] and started plans for armed struggle against the KMT. Mao was given the major responsibility of winning Hunan for the communists with a peasant uprising known as the Autumn Harvest Uprising.[4]

Mao's leadership of the Autumn Harvest Uprising was a lesson in the difficulty of insurrectionary military operations and the isolation of the CCP forces. After some initial victories, the uprising turned into an almost total rout. Of Mao's four regiments, composed of Northern Expedition troops who had sided with the communists, Hunanese peasants and miners, and local bandits, three were severely defeated and one defected to the enemy during battle. In late September, Mao gathered his remnant forces of no more than a thousand fighters and offered anyone who wanted to disperse into the villages five dollars for the road.[5] In October, those who decided to stay with him reorganized as the First Regiment of the First Division of the First Army of the Chinese Workers and Peasants Revolutionary Army, reached the Jinggang mountains on the border of Hunan and Jiangxi provinces, and started to build a base area. Fortunately for Mao, the fight over the division of spoils in Hunan distracted the major military forces in the area.[6] Mao reversed his bad luck by capturing Chaling, a county seat in Hunan, and holding it for forty days, but beginning in 1928 his attention had finally turned toward retaining and expanding his Jinggangshan base area. The arrival of other retreating army units under Zhu De, Chen Yi, and Lin Biao (Lin Piao) in April 1928 raised the number of communist troops to at least ten thousand, and in May the first of many anticommunist "Encirclement and Suppression" campaigns was defeated.

The chaotic events of late 1927–1928 were rendered even more complex for Mao by his strained relationship with Qu Qiubai's party leadership. While the criticism of Chen Duxiu by the 7 August Conference was a welcome change from the previous paternalistic suppression of differences, it was soon evident that calling for uprisings and assigning blame were obsessions of the new leadership. Mao was retired from the Politburo for the failure of the Autumn Harvest Uprising and for relying too heavily on military strength rather than on peasant enthusiasm, and in the early days at Jinggangshan he was censured for his concentration on the peasantry at the expense of the proletariat. Qu's own peasant policy was one of "revolutionary terrorism" in order to "turn the petit-bourgeois [peasants] into proletarians and then force them into the revolution."[7] This policy was intended to maximize rural support for Qu's continued attempts at insurrection, but it was necessarily opposed as nonviable by those in the base areas. In the summer of 1928, Jinggangshan was bombarded by contradictory directives from various superiors, and Mao was replaced as leader by an emissary who nearly lost both the base area and the army. Events such as these led to a general antagonism between the base area leadership and the Party Center: the former viewed the latter as dogmatic and misinformed; the latter was frustrated by attempting to control opportunistic and nonproletarian subordinates.

The situation was eased considerably by the resolutions of the Sixth Party Congress, held in Moscow in July 1928. The congress upheld Qu's condemnation of Chen's earlier opportunism, but it dismissed Qu's understanding of the rural revolution as "far from penetrating."[8] It declared that China was still at the stage of democratic revolution *(minquan geming)*, a judgment which allowed Mao's experiments in distributive land policy. Although the congress still emphasized armed insurrection and predicted that the contradictions of the reactionaries would soon reach a new, vulnerable crisis point, its more realistic view of the rural situation and its replacement of Qu by Li Lisan promised a better relationship between the base areas and the center.

But closer coordination with the Party Center was frustrated by military developments in 1929 and by Li Lisan himself, who turned out to be even more domineering and insurrection-oriented than his predecessor. In December 1928, the fifteen counties of the Jinggangshan base were threatened by a large KMT force, and it was decided that Mao and Zhu De should cross Jiangxi and set up a new base area on the Jiangxi–Fujian border. Mao spent most of 1929 in constant warfare in these two provinces, getting sufficiently out of touch with the center to be declared dead by the Comintern.[9] Unfortunately this low profile did not protect him from Li Lisan's imperious attentions. As Mao grew more confident of his own approach to guerrilla warfare and base area policy, his struggle on the ideological front with inappropriate central directives grew more intense. He opposed Li's pessimistic demands to disperse the Red Army in 1929. In 1930, when the establishment of some fifteen base areas in China changed Li's mood,[10] Mao took part in Li's last great attempt at urban insurrection, but he had already developed a fundamentally different strategy which he described in a letter to Lin Biao some months before the insurrection.

The struggle to take the big cities of Changsha, Nanchang, and Wuhan lasted from July to mid-September 1930, and with the costly failure of the second attack on Changsha, Li Lisan lost his hold on the Central Committee, Mao and his army returned to their base in Jiangxi, and the attention of all parties interested in the fate of communism in China—the Party Center, the Comintern, and Chiang Kai-shek—turned finally to the countryside. Mao's struggle against Li's agrarian policy, which favored rich peasants, continued in Jiangxi, culminating in the bloody Futian Incident of 8 December 1930. As the revolutionary situation in the cities continued to deteriorate, the CCP Central Committee decided to move to the Jiangxi base, and it was transformed into the Central Soviet Area of the Chinese Soviet Republic in late 1931. The arrival of the Central Committee caused a fundamental change in Mao's leadership role as well as a redefinition of the base area. As chairman of the Chinese Soviet Republic, Mao was charged with almost exclusively civil administrative tasks, leading to important developments in his theory and techniques of revolutionary government, which in turn engendered new conflicts with the party leadership.

The Spatial Dimension of Survival

The general effect of the reorientation toward survival on Mao's political thought can be understood most simply as a transformation of its spatial dimension. Mao's temporal perspective on the revolution also received a severe shock as he went from the conviction in the Hunan Report that a social revolution was imminent to the necessity of preventing the total extinction of organized revolutionary forces. But by far the most important development occurred in Mao's spatial perspective. In an environment of armed hostility, the base area defined the perimeter of direct revolutionary activity. Politics in this context was the mobilization of existing resources in order to extend the perimeter and establish other base areas. Mao had worked within spatial limitations in his Hunan activities of 1920–1923, but that constraint had been merely a recognized horizon of possible political influence rather than a defensive perimeter with control inside and hostile armies outside. After examining the spatial dimension of Mao's rural politics as it was first presented in two works from 1928, we will analyze it more abstractly in terms of its center–periphery logic and interstitial tactics. Finally we will return to Mao's self-confident restatement of his base area strategy in 1930.

Mao's 1928 writings

Mao addresses the question of survival with customary directness in two works written in October and November 1928. Although they concern the same theme, the works differ significantly in their emphases because of different audiences. The purpose of the first work, "Draft Resolution of the Second Congress of County Party Representatives of the Xiang-Gan [Hunan–Jiangxi] Border Area," known in the *Selected Works* as "Why Is It That Red Political Power Can Exist in China?",[11] is to explain the revolutionary significance of their survival to the cadres at Jinggangshan. The ostensive purpose of the second, "Report of the Jinggangshan Front Committee to the Center," called "The Struggle in the Chingkang [Jinggang] Mountains" in the *Selected Works*, is to report and explain this survival to the party leadership in Shanghai.[12] A secondary, political purpose of the report is to argue for the correctness of Mao's policies and against earlier attempts of the Party Center to dominate base area leadership.

Although the "Resolution" was written at a time of victory for the Jinggangshan base, there were sufficient grounds for sobriety in estimating chances of survival. Many communist-controlled areas which had sprung up in late 1927 had already been thoroughly defeated, including Peng Pai's peasant soviet at Hailufeng. The Jinggangshan base itself had been overrun by White forces twice in 1928 (and would be overrun again in 1929 after Mao's departure). A blockade was in effect at the time of writing, and forces were beginning to mount for a third encirclement campaign against the base. Cadres cognizant of the relative weakness of the Red Army and the unpredictable chaos of warlord and KMT politics might well have wondered how long the red flag could be kept flying.

In explaining the significance of communist survival in the base area, Mao betrays his own uneasiness at this time about the shift of the revolution to the countryside. The basic paradox was that on the one hand survival was possible in the base areas because of a peculiarity in China's political superstructure—namely the chronic rivalry and warfare between the various localized elements of her ruling class. On the other hand, Mao's Marxist framework of analysis stressed the unity of economic conditions and hence political situations throughout China (and, more abstractly, throughout the world)—the same classes of oppressed struggling against the same classes of oppressors. Mao's rural strategy was a military necessity, but the localism necessary for Red survival, manifested by an almost exclusive dependence on the most localized class, the peasantry, must be seen as historically regressive from an orthodox standpoint. Mao was diffident about this reorientation, but he did not have the fear of peasant corruption of the revolution evident in the center directives of Qu Qiubai and later of Li Lisan.

One of the specific advantages of the fissured condition of the ruling class, the possibility of advantageous alliances, plays a much smaller part in this article than it did in 1925-1926. Mao's openness to principled alliance is still evident, however. It is of course impossible to ally with imperialism, warlords, or the "new warlords" of the KMT, but the progress of Wang Jingwei's "antiimperialist, antiwarlord, anticomprador" reorganization efforts is reported sympathetically and separately from the KMT's other factional problems. By January 1930, the Comintern had forbidden alliances with any KMT factions,[13] but a consistent notion of principled alliance seems to run from Mao's earlier writings to this article. It is again indicated in the "three conditions for a united front against Japan" (January 1933) and is finally enunciated explicitly in the Zunyi Resolution of January 1935.

Mao's purpose in the "Resolution" is to reconcile the 1927 goal of national revolution with a new starting point. This reorientation demanded much less theoretical adjustment from Mao than it did from his colleagues; as we have seen in the previous chapter, from 1926 he had been insisting that the revolution against warlords and imperialism must be carried out at the rural base of the exploitive system. What is novel in the article vis-à-vis the development of Mao's thought is the practical experience of survival which it summarizes and the strategic reformulation which this new experience required.

The centerpiece of the "Resolution" is Mao's general analysis of the conditions which allow the emergence and survival of Red power. Of the five conditions, the first and most basic specifies the necessary general environment, the second and third are more specific locational conditions, and the last two are organizational prerequisites for the survivors.

How can a small revolutionary force hostile to the common interests of China's ruling class survive? Mao answers that China's localized and divided political economy makes it impossible for the ruling class to sustain unified action. The natural fractiousness of the warlords is encouraged by the indirect colonialism and competitiveness of the imperialist powers.[14] The tension between the inability of the ruling class to unite and their common interest in suppressing the communists produces a strategic situation which oscillates between times of relative cohesion of the ruling class (and therefore coordinated aggression against the Red areas) and times of dissension among the elite in which no coordinated White attack or defense can be arranged. At the time Mao wrote, his Chinese audience had had ample experience of the chronic contention among various powerholders to which he referred. Since the overthrow of Manchu rule almost twenty years earlier, Chinese politics had been characterized by an unending series of factional struggles. They were a sort of national lottery played by local powerholders, the imperialist powers, and politicians. Though the winners varied, particularly at the intermediate and lower levels,[15] the system—or antisystem—endured. Disintegration would stimulate a new alliance motivated to unify the country; and the success of the alliance would induce its own disintegration into a new alignment of friends and enemies. In keeping with his 1926 analysis of the village-level foundations of warlord power, Mao attributes this permanent fracturing of the ruling class's power to China's localized agricultural economy and the imperialist policy of marking off spheres of influence.

The next two conditions which Mao discusses specify where and when a viable revolutionary group can establish itself. It must be situated where the masses have already participated in the bourgeois-democratic revolution. It is necessary to have a modicum of mass revolutionary consciousness and organization. This does not imply an economically advanced area, however. The reasons which Mao later gives to Lin Biao for preferring Jiangxi as a base area are tied to its relatively isolated and feudal political economy. Moreover, the base area must be part of the continued development of the national revolutionary situation. It is evident in this condition that Mao's evaluation of base area success is immediately tied to its contribution to a national communist victory. Both these factors emphasize the dependence of base areas on a larger revolutionary context. Their spatial location depends on their revolutionary exposure; the timing of their emergence depends on a general revolutionary trend. Mao's viewpoint in this matter is quite analogous to Lenin's original view of the Bolshevik revolution—namely, that the October Revolution was a great success toward a larger (world) revolution but could not sustain itself without victories in the industrialized countries. At this time Mao viewed the base areas not as the seat of a protracted revolution but as a way station to a national revolutionary high tide. For both Lenin and Mao, the problem was that their initial revolutionary paradigms were formulated from a perspective which did not correspond to their actual revolutionary situation. In both cases the discord was eventually resolved in favor of reality.

The fourth and fifth conditions—the existence of an adequate Red Army and "the strength of the Communist Party's organization and the correctness of its policies"—are respectively the conditions of adequate military and political organization and leadership. The emphasis on the correct policies of the party is one of Mao's most frequent tropes, and sometimes criticism of past or present party policy seems to be implied.

The practical significance of these last two conditions is more fully developed in the "Report of the Jinggangshan Front Committee to the Center," written one month after the "Resolution." This comprehensive report to the Central Committee in Shanghai falls into two main parts: a narrative account of the fortunes of the Jinggangshan base and a survey of the major issues facing the base area. While the "Resolution" sets forth the revolutionary context of the Red areas, the "Report" provides a thorough analysis of the first year of work in this new setting.

The historical narrative is an essential part of the report because the many changes of leadership during 1928 and the corresponding success or failure of the communists amply substantiate Mao's thesis of his and Zhu De's correct leadership. To use Mao's formulation, this history comprises the "lesson of objective actuality" *(keguan shishi di jiaoxun)*,[16] which led to the base's present policy and leadership. Mao must have enjoyed telling this story. Upon the assumption of leadership by two different party emissaries the Red Army suffered almost annihilating defeats and both times Mao resumed leadership under straightened circumstances and led the army to victory and base area expansion.

The theoretical framework for Mao's historical analysis is a recast version of his five conditions and two strategic periods. The five conditions presented here are: good masses; good party; strong Red Army; good geographical setting; adequate economic base. The difference between this listing and the previous one can be explained by a difference in audience. The primary purpose of the "Resolution" was to formulate and unify the strategic thinking of the cadres at Jinggangshan. The most urgent problem in the context of relatively consolidated local leadership was the overall significance of their mission. The fissured condition of the ruling class was assurance that their survival had not been accidental. Moreover, the essential link with the continued development of the national revolutionary situation was a reminder of the necessity for strategic subordination to national revolutionary planning. The Central Committee did not need such reminders. It needed to be informed of the practical conditions of the base. Most of the restated conditions can be seen as implicit criticism of central party policies: good masses (one of the reasons given in the "Report" for the failure of the southern Hunan uprising was the failure of the masses there to participate); good party (the chief counterexamples were party emissaries); strong Red Army (part of the incorrect leadership of the party emissaries was leaving too small a force to guard the base); and good geographical location (an argument against the constant tendency of the Central Committee to transfer the military power nurtured at Jinggangshan to some place considered more effective). The oscillating strategic periods of enemy cohesiveness and discord play a greater role in the "Report" because these were completely misinterpreted (or ignored) by the Central Committee's emissaries with disastrous consequences.

The Dialectic of Center and Periphery

Mao's tactics and situational analyses are so shrewd in their practical politics that it is easy to overlook their significance for the development of his thought. The spatial dimension they add to his politics is complex and multilayered. Mao's rural revolutionary strategy was not simply the localization of the revolution, but location was an essential moment in a military, political, and economic dialectic.

The spatial aspect of Mao's thinking began as a military necessity. Without allies and unable to achieve national revolution, the question of where and how to survive became urgent. The basic solution was to find an area (Jinggangshan) where the remaining strength of the army plus local support would be stronger than local White forces, and then to expand the perimeter of local revolutionary control until the balance of power made possible a final, national challenge to KMT rule. Although Mao did not use them, the concepts of center and periphery are useful for analyzing the logic of this strategy.[17] These terms can be taken in two senses: in the first they contrast China's established urban center of power with the rural hinterland; in the second they refer to any relationship between a dominating organizational focus and a dispersed area of control.

Mao's base area strategy differed fundamentally from the territorial politics of the warlords. With the disintegration of the Qing dynasty and the failure of attempts to revive the dominant position of Peking, various political-military forces in China realized the autonomy of their own power, becoming subcenters hostile to the reestablishment of an effective central regime. Their "self-government"[18] was an attempt of local elites to avoid subservience to a central elite. Mao's base area was not a subcenter; it was an anticenter. Within its borders it overturned the social relationships which were the basis of both warlord and KMT regimes. Externally it threatened its warlord neighbors most immediately, but its chief target was the KMT. Mao built his anticenter by challenging the fringes of regime control with his military power; then, through local social revolution and political education, he won a constituency which would support further military and political expansion. The constituency upon which Mao relied, the masses of middle and poor peasants, were the true periphery of Chinese politics, the productive but passive objects of rural social structure. Their mobilization created a new political force in China which turned the fringes of central control into a battlefront. The most primitive rural protest was the prohibition of the export of grain from rural districts, and this was common in 1926–1927. But this Luddite response was now replaced by a rural revolutionary strategy which turned the regime's indifference to the peasantry into a source of strength for the peasant movement. The "encirclement of the cities by the countryside" had of course always existed as a geographic fact. But to reverse the direction of domination was a historic achievement.

The center–periphery relationship is also useful for analyzing other aspects of Mao's political situation. Although Mao was busy creating revolutionary centers in the countryside, vis-à-vis the party leadership he was on the periphery, and they in turn were subordinated to the Comintern. The centrality of hierarchical authority seems to share some traits regardless of whether established centers, revolutionary centers, or subcenters are involved. A center is the organizational identity of a system, but the system's success depends on its relationship to its environment. If a center is too energetic in safeguarding a particular idea of its system, its directives become rigid, inappropriate, and only partially informed. Moreover, it is easy for comprehensive leadership to exaggerate the importance of the system's internal regulation. The unique advantage of their position lies in being able to view the entire operation of the system, but they are furthest from its working edges. The converse of the center's tendency to overcontrol is the subordinate's reluctance to yield his discretion. He can always tendentiously interpret orders, but he is in turn subject to the center's personnel sanctions. The contradiction between the center's authority and the periphery's experience can lead to policy struggles, to factions, and to organizational disintegration.

Mao's obedient but strained relation to Central Committee leadership is evident in almost all of his early base area writing. It is clearest in his "Report," which begins with a narration of the catastrophes caused by outside interference and ends with a request somewhere between a plea and a challenge:

> In the future when issuing directives pertaining to matters in this report please be sure to study this report. By no means should you simply rely on the one-sided reports of traveling inspectors.[19]

The center's improper evaluation of base area communications is matched by the inappropriate style of its directives to the base area:

> Also when you give directives relating to military actions, absolutely avoid being too rigid. It would be most suitable if letters from the center allowed us to make determinations according to the circumstances and left us room to maneuver.[20]

After the first year at Jinggangshan, Mao usually made his own room to maneuver as he deemed necessary. Sometimes he made creative applications of center directives which must have seemed perverse to their authors—as when he accepted a criticism of "ultrademocracy" and went on to explain that its cure was better central leadership.[21] Realizing their lack of control, Li Lisan's Central Committee twice gave urgent commands that Mao come to Shanghai, but Mao valued his distance and the orders went unheeded.[22]

Mao's Interstitial Tactics

Mao's method of exploiting hostilities among warlords was as important as his logic of the periphery in determining his locational strategy in 1927–1930. The basic premise was that although the base areas were a threat to all warlords, their rivalry for power among themselves limited the utilization of their greater military strength against a common enemy. Mao exploited this situation by the tactic of locating at the interstices of warlord domains. The rough terrain of Jinggangshan was useful militarily, but its location on the border of Hunan and Jiangxi provinces was just as important. Mao's forces would encroach upon the heartland of neighboring warlords only when the base had become powerful. A warlord's campaign against a border area was limited by two considerations: complete extermination of the border area would involve invasion of another warlord's territory, and if a warlord were significantly weakened by his battles with the communists he could expect to lose in the continuing power struggle with other warlords. These considerations usually led to local alliances against the base, but these were possible only in the absence of greater struggles among the warlords. Coordinating an effort involving several warlords was difficult in any case—and if victory appeared to be in sight or a loss of troops appeared likely, the effort often proved too fragile to be sustained. By analyzing contradictions among the warlords, Mao could estimate the opportunities for expansion and the weaknesses of ententes against him.

Mao's interstitial tactics had an important effect on his locational strategy. On the one hand, they determined the location of the base areas. On the other, that location depended on the circumstances of surrounding powers. Thus Mao's commitment to territory was also relative, although the cost of abandoning an entire base area was very great.

Mao's guerrilla tactics of this period were a reflection of both center–periphery and interstitial logic. The fullest statement of his tactical principles occurs in a letter of 5 April 1929 to the center:

> The tactics we have derived from the struggle of the past three years are indeed different from any other tactics, ancient or modern, Chinese or foreign. With our tactics, the masses can be aroused for struggle on an ever-broadening scale, and no enemy, however powerful, can cope with us. Ours are guerrilla tactics. They consist mainly of the following points:
>
> Divide our forces to arouse the masses; concentrate our forces to deal with the enemy.
>
> The enemy advances, we retreat; the enemy camps, we harass; the enemy tires, we attack; the enemy retreats, we pursue.
>
> To extend stable base areas, employ the policy of advancing in waves; when pursued by a powerful enemy, employ the policy of circling around.
>
> Arouse the largest numbers of the masses in the shortest possible time and by the best possible methods.
>
> These tactics are just like casting a net; at any moment we

should be able to cast it or draw it in. We cast it wide to win over the masses and draw it in to deal with the enemy. Such are the tactics we have used for the past three years.[23]

The weakness of the urban center's control over the peasant periphery allowed the communists to expand by arousing the masses to revolution. But the relative weakness of communist military forces required their mobility in order to exploit advantages of location and time—and mobility required concentration of professional military forces. The premise of these tactics is that territory can be sacrificed for military advantage. It is thus not surprising that Mao advises a commander in a newly won area to pay special attention to the establishment of independent guerrilla units because these could be expected to become permanent assets of the revolutionary movement, whereas civil institutions depended on the protection of the Red Army.[24] In using both interstitial and center–periphery spatial logic, Mao was using location for larger purposes.

As the KMT consolidated its power in the early thirties, interstitial politics became less important for determining location and center–periphery thinking became more prominent. Nevertheless, since a major method of KMT consolidation was the cooptation of local warlords, contradictions did not entirely disappear. Interstitial tactics were important for determining the course of the Long March, and contradictions within the national power structure were spectacularly demonstrated in the Xi'an (Sian) Incident of 1936.

The Experience of Survival

The subject of Mao's 1930 letter to Lin Biao (known in the *Selected Works* as "A Single Spark Can Start a Prairie Fire") is "correctly appraising the current situation and the attendant question of what action to take."[25] On this topic, the ultimate nexus of theory and practice, Mao brings to bear the accumulated experience and convictions of his three years of guerrilla life. The letter is more than a summary of the past. Its reformulation gives a new significance to base areas which sets the theoretical context for Mao's concentration on problems of soviet policy and administration after the failure of the attacks on Changsha and Nanchang later in the summer of 1930.

The letter is basically an argument for the policies and strategies which Mao had found successful and for the essential significance of their *sine qua non*, the base areas, for the Chinese revolution. In it Mao develops for the first time his thesis that the base areas are the legitimate seat of a protracted, rural-centered revolution. This argument is necessary because of the pessimistic attitude about the future of communist-controlled areas which Lin Biao shared with much of the party leadership. Mao's letter was a direct challenge to Li Lisan's rural policy and provoked a strong, hostile reaction from Li. Mao's willingness to confront the center on base area policy is an indication of his self-confidence and also his relative autonomy.[26] The pessimists favored a "relatively more comfortable" strategy of mobile guerrilla warfare not burdened with permanent base areas or the establishment of local political power. Their lack of confidence in the utility of base areas can be explained partly by the defeat of Jinggangshan and partly by the continuing adherence of the party leadership to the Russian model of urban revolution—with their consequent suspicion of the rural, nonproletarian character of the Red Army and even more so of its bases. Mao's argument against this viewpoint is first directed at its theoretical assumption of an urban proletarian revolution and then at its underestimate of the objective conditions for revolution. The first argument is based on a restatement of the strategic implications of China's semicolonial status. The second is based on Mao's successful experience with estimating objective strength, which he documents with lengthy quotations from earlier letters to the Central Committee.

Mao's first argument is a serious attempt to "Sinify" the strategic thinking of the Chinese Communist Party by presenting once again the coherent point of view which he first developed in the "Resolution" of 1928. He accuses Lin of having forgotten China's unique semicolonial status, and he proceeds to develop a complete strategic line from the contentiousness of the ruling class which this implies. Mao expands on his thesis of ruling class fissures by saying that their intensity and scope always increase. He then restates the matrix of principles he had implemented in Jinggangshan and Jiangxi—the great importance of the peasantry and the relationship of the Red Army and guerrilla warfare to the base area. Mao concludes:

> Only thus is it possible to build the confidence of the revolutionary masses throughout the country, as Soviet Russia has built it

throughout the world. Only thus is it possible to create tremendous problems for the ruling classes, shake their foundations and hasten their internal disintegration. Only thus is it really possible to create a Red Army which will become an important weapon for the great revolution of the future. In short, only thus is it possible to hasten the revolutionary high tide.[27]

This summary statement reveals two related advances in Mao's theory of base areas. The more general is the idea that his strategies are essential for the present stage of the revolution. Previously he had argued merely that these conditions were sufficient for the survival of base areas. A more specific innovation is contained in the first "only thus" clause—namely, the function of the base areas as a model of Red power whose success would be valuable propaganda for China's masses. The Mencian notion of propaganda by good example has already shown itself to be an aspect of Mao's political thinking,[28] but this is Mao's first statement that a Red area in China could be a general political model. This is a significant development in Mao's own evaluation of the substantiality of localized communist power. Its effect on his strategic thinking can be seen in his proposal of the conquest of the province of Jiangxi as an immediate revolutionary goal. "Victory in one or several provinces" was a current slogan of Li Lisan's drive toward a new high tide of urban conquests and insurrection, but Mao's attention to Jiangxi proceeded from quite different principles. Jiangxi was not a smaller China but a larger base area. Mao's reasons for proposing Jiangxi are that it is backward, weak, and relatively remote from imperialism.[29] Li argued for seizing heartland: the major cities Changsha, Nanchang, and Wuhan. Mao argues for establishing power on the periphery. Despite Mao's participation in Li's last great "take the cities" campaign a few months after this letter was written, Mao's own thinking had already acquired the foundation for a strategy of protracted struggle centered in communist-governed bases rather than insurrection aimed at cities by whatever means possible.

After arguing for the importance of base areas, Mao begins a second argument against the general pessimism of Lin's outlook. This argument combines Mao's characteristic themes of optimistic activism and the necessity of objective investigation. He diagnoses Lin's depression as a subjective failing caused by the small size of revolutionary forces and defeats due to putschism. According to Mao the objective situation is quite favorable: "A single spark can start a prairie fire."

An important conceptual innovation occurs in Mao's description of the favorable national scene:

> While the imperialist contention over China becomes more intense, both the contradiction *(maodun)* between imperialism and all of China and the contradictions among the imperialists themselves are developing simultaneously in China.[30]

Mao first used the term "contradiction" to indicate opposition between two groups in viewpoint, interest, or policy in the 1928 "Resolution,"[31] but here he elaborates it into the key concept for center–periphery and interstitial analysis. Mao had used *maodun* in a pejorative sense of inconsistent or confused,[32] but in these cases the word described a political group rather than the dynamics of a situation. The usage in this passage is not as sophisticated as Engels' or Stalin's notion of the inherence of opposition (a usage adopted by Mao in "On Contradiction"), but it became an important tool of Mao's political analysis, culminating in "On the Correct Handling of Contradictions among the People (1956)." The term "contradiction" is only a minor aspect of the role of dialectics in Mao's thought, however. In this section Mao's emphasis on the essential interdependence of center and periphery and the connection between local survival and national context reflects an awareness of the interdependence of things which dates back to his earliest writings.

Problems of Revolutionary Leadership

The external conditions of survival in a hostile environment were no more novel and important than its internal prerequisites. With the establishment of base areas, the CCP assumed a whole range of governmental and military responsibilities which were virtually nonexistent before 1928. These problems were new not only to Chinese Communism. No Marxist party had ever faced the political problems of consolidation and construction inherent in governing territory before it resolved the difficulties of tactical weakness and lack of public legitimacy inherent in a struggling revolutionary movement. Mao responded to the practical challenge of the base area by developing policies of mobilization, direction and control, and leadership which were as novel as the problems he faced. Moreover, in his attempt to sustain a Marxist revolutionary movement in a localized, rural setting Mao developed an emphasis on correct leadership which grew into a fundamental contribution to CCP politics and to Marxism. In the previous chapter we discussed Mao's views on revolutionary legitimacy and compared them to the views of Georg Lukacs, Karl Korsch, and Antonio Gramsci. The problem of leadership as it arose in the base areas is a related but far more fundamental problem, and correspondingly our review of its relation to Marxism must go back to Marx and Lenin and their attempts to connect theory and practice through politics. After reviewing Mao's position vis-à-vis Marxism, we will take a closer look at the central problem of base area leadership—that of effective mobilization. Lastly we will consider Mao's critiques of leadership faults, which become "teachers by negative example" of the content of correct leadership.

Mao, Marxism, and Leadership

The claim of Marxism to be scientific socialism rests on its discovery of the direction of history in the contradictions of the present social structure. Orthodox Marxist leadership conceives of itself as the scientific representative of the proletariat—that is, as the knower and hence guide of its revolutionary historical-structural role. As Marx says in the *Manifesto*, "They [the Communists] fight for the achievement of the immediate purposes and interests of the working class, but they also represent within the present movement the future of the movement."[33] As this statement illustrates, Marx's tendency to emphasize the economic determination of history arises not to avoid the burdens of leadership but to borrow the persuasiveness of inexorable development for the revolutionary cause. But this perspective also allows the problems of leadership to be viewed as matters of detail rather than as substantial social-structural problems.

Toward the turn of the century a schism developed in European Marxism between the revisionists who maintained that the vital point was representing the interests of the proletariat, although those interests turned out to be nonrevolutionary, and the radicals who still believed that the party's mission was to bring about the revolution despite the spontaneous opportunism of some workers.[34] Thus Marx's naive notion of a nonproblematic interaction of scientific leadership and worker's interests fell apart into a passive representation of worker's interests on the one hand, and a revolutionary leadership bound to the proletariat mainly through propaganda and agitation on the other. This second, Leninist conception of the vanguard of the proletariat allowed a remarkable degree of leadership flexibility, but correspondingly it relied heavily for its legitimacy as a proletarian party on the scientific correctness of Marx's structural predictions. This organizational commitment of the Bolsheviks to be the true followers of the correct view of society involved them in a reliance on a dogmatic theology of Marxism in the resolution of policy disputes. Problems of leadership were viewed as problems of tactics which could be resolved by analyzing the current stage of the revolution and making the necessary compromises with existing political forces. Incorrect leadership implied a deviation from the correct line.

Although Mao did not repudiate the importance of either the proletariat or Marxist historical materialism, neither of these concepts was useful to him in constructing the base areas. On the microlevel of base area politics, class analysis through investigation of actual conditions was essential to the determination of policy. But for this period of Mao's thinking, Marxist social science was in the service of revolutionary leadership. The Party Center's efforts to reverse this relationship were regarded as inappropriate and dangerous to survival.

Mao's rural strategy involved an even greater isolation of the party from class roots of any species, but at the same time it stressed an active relationship with the oppressed masses. "Proletarian hegemony" and survival were incompatible at JInggangshan, but the peasantry did not replace the proletariat as the class referent of the party, even though it became the party's chief source of support. Despite Mao's plea to the Central Committee in 1928 for more proletarians and a detailed account of Russian policies toward rich peasants, the situation posed leadership problems which could not be solved by economic analysis or by reference to Russian experience. Rather than evade this unique leadership problem, Mao produced a new politics and ethic of party leadership, the theory of which was clearly delineated only in the 1940s. From its base area beginnings, however, it was characterized by uniting leadership flexibility and closeness to the masses through mass mobilization. For Mao, "correct" policy was not simply class policy or a dogmatically faithful policy, but one which was appropriate for the circumstances of its application.

Mao believed that arriving at appropriate policy was difficult but possible. His own labors to achieve this type of correctness and to encourage it in subordinates led to a methodology of leadership which stressed investigation among the masses, objective appraisal of the situation, and avoidance of elitist habits. With these areas of leadership regarded as problematic, Mao, and later Chinese Communism, advanced beyond orthodox Marxism to an awareness of the structural weaknesses of leadership. The "rectification campaigns" which became prominent in the early 1940s were not purges of unsatisfactory cadre but serious attempts to improve their leadership style. The prototype of rectification literature is the Gutian Resolution of December 1929. With his recognition of the situational difficulties of correct leadership, Mao was not vulnerable to the acute embarrassment which European Marxism suffered at the hands of Robert Michels when he demonstrated the oligarchic tendencies of the Marxist parties.[35] Mao was already fighting tendencies of this sort in 1929. On the other hand, Mao's conceptualization of leadership deviance still laid stress on the class origins of the deviations.[36] But political education, or even the hard lessons of experience, could rectify leadership faults. The target was effective leadership, which in most cases was synonymous with effective mass mobilization.

Mobilization and Policy Integration

If mobilization is broadly defined as eliciting cooperation for an end, it is the basic task of social organization. Cooperation can be motivated by identification with the organization and a desire to share in its goal, by rewards for participation, or by sanctions against noncooperation. Each of these motivations—identification, rewards, and sanctions—has its structural implications and limitations. Inducing identification with a public purpose lowers the resource costs of mobilization, but it requires more coordinative effort and also acceptable goals. The organization and its goal must be close to the population; otherwise they would shirk their share of the burden or be indifferent to the outcome. If an organization rewards participation, the resource cost rises, the top leadership acquires greater control of the organization's purpose, and roles become defined. Relying on control by sanctions is also expensive and defines standards of compliance. All these motivations were involved in Mao's mobilization effort, but they were employed differently.

One of the most impressive cases of mobilization through

identity of interests was the Red Army itself, since in the first year most Red Army troops were mercenaries captured in battle. Mao's attempt to transform these erstwhile servants of feudal militarism into a revolutionary army involved an integration of party and army as well as soviets, local forces, and army, but it centered on a democratic structuring of the army itself. This was most important for the absorption and motivation of new elements:

> Especially recently captured soldiers feel that the camp they are in today is a different world from the camp they were in yesterday. Although they feel that the material life of the Red Army is not as good as that of the White armies . . . , they feel spiritually liberated. Therefore they can live with the situation. Also, the same soldier fights more bravely today in the Red Army than he did yesterday in the White army because of the influence of democracy *(minquan zhuyi)*. The Red Army is like a furnace in which all captured soldiers are transmuted the moment they come over. In China not only do the worker and peasant masses need democracy; soldiers need democracy even more urgently.[37]

The content of Red Army democracy (literally, "people's rights-ism") was a whole complex of egalitarian and democratic practices:

> The officers do not hit the men; the officers and men eat and dress in the same way and are treated equally; soldiers are free to hold meetings and to speak out; financial matters are completely open; representatives of the soldiers audit the accounts; soldiers handle the mess arrangements and, out of the daily five cents for cooking oil, salt, firewood, and vegetables, they can even save a little for pocket money, amounting to roughly six or seven coppers per person per day.[38]

The mass politics of the Red Army in 1928 were as interesting as its economic egalitarianism. The soldiers' committees *(shibing [weiyuan] hui)* which were established at company, battalion, and regimental levels had the duties of supervising the officers, representing the soldier's interests, participating in the management of the troops, carrying out political training within the army, and directing mass movements among the population. At this time (and contrary to later practice), Mao thought that with the soldiers' committees there was no need for political departments at these levels in the army. In fact, political departments had proved detrimental: without them, everyone did political work; with them, however, everyone left political work to the specialists.

Mobilization through identification of interest within the villages was accomplished initially by stressing goals which were of obvious benefit to the village masses. Land reform is the basic example. Although land reform depended very much on party direction for its rate and pace, it was of obvious benefit to the poor peasants and hired hands. Not only could the leadership count on active cooperation in implementing such policies, it could use the shared interest established through distributional policies to argue for less immediate projects such as raising troops for the Red Army.

But enthusiasm is most easily evoked for short-range projects with definite results. The problem of maintaining credibility as the leadership of the masses and for the masses was one of establishing channels of mass participation and politics. Since control over local leaders and open political struggle were completely new to the villages, it was easy for the local soviet governments to fall into the feudal patterns of aloofness and arbitrariness. But these superior habits produced the cardinal sin of "estrangement from the masses" *(tuoli qunzhong)*, leading to passivity of the masses and a loss of mobilization potential. The most serious manifestation of estrangement from the masses was "the forcible violation of popular opinion" *(qiangjian minyi)*,[39] the tendency of local government officials to form an exclusive clique and abuse their power.

The middle peasants had less potential for common interests than did the poor peasants because they were more independent economically. After land reform they could not look forward to sharing in any further distributive programs. However, they too were victims of the feudal social structure who welcomed liberation, and, provided that their landholding interests were not threatened by more radical land policies, they had much in common with the base area government. Attempts to increase production and lower marketing costs were especially beneficial, and the defense of the base area meant preservation of their improved status. A major attraction of participation for many middle peasants must have been the local positions of authority and prestige left vacant by the rich peasants and landlords.[40] Insofar as personal opportunism was a motive for assuming village leadership, however, the mobilization requirement of closeness to the masses would inevitably conflict with the imagined privileges of office.

Coercive sanctions were reserved for the remnants of the rich peasant and landlord classes. They were not supposed to be used against poor and middle peasants. Nevertheless, many local soviets availed themselves of coercive measures in meeting their locality's obligations, a habit which was considered both a feudal remnant and a symptom of estrangement.

Since the situation just described remained basically the same into the early years of the People's Republic of China, the problem of mobilization in the base areas is relevant for postliberation campaigns. Skinner and Winckler derive a plausible life cycle for rural mobilization in the 1950s which stresses the succession of ideological, coercive, and remunerative phases.[41] For various reasons—external pressures, changes in leadership, rapid evolution of policy—the rural policy fluctuations of Jinggangshan and Jiangxi cannot be forced into the later cycle of compliance. Since Skinner and Winckler derive their compliance model from Amatai Etzioni's theory of complex organizations rather than from a concrete analysis of rural compliance, they would come away empty-handed from Jiangxi. But the greater interest of the poor peasants in ideological compliance and the more remunerative tendency of middle peasant compliance—as well as the serious tensions between the two—were already important facts of life in Jinggangshan, and the resulting complexities necessitated Mao's rural investigations which are described later in this chapter and in the next. There were rural policy fluctuations before the Long March which were affected by contradictions between poor and middle peasants and between ideological goals and production goals, but no working cycle of compliance emerged. It is my impression that a compliance cycle of mobilization aimed primarily at poor peasants, consolidation aimed at leadership mistakes and stubborn or backward groups, and material welfare aimed at productive individuals and groups developed into an expectation if not a policy during the Yanan period. Skinner and Winckler note differential class responses in their descriptions of individual campaigns,[42] but class is not an integral part of their model. If class appeal were taken into account, the origins and actual workings of the compliance cycle would be more clear.

Mao's chief organizational discovery of the pre-1935 period was popular mobilization, and essential to the maximum effectiveness of mobilization was a strategy which emphasized policy integration. In general, a meaningful task had to be available for every activist whose heart was stirred by a particular campaign. In Jinggangshan the difficulties of survival were apparent to all and demanded a maximum military effort, but if the Red Army were completely in charge of defense, this interest would express itself in a few volunteers and debilitating anxiety. Instead, the party and masses were militarized: all sorts of local military and paramilitary units were organized, and the importance of civil duties for the military effort was emphasized. This policy allowed a pyramid of maximum support for the military effort,[43] and it also allowed other tasks to borrow the urgency of the defense problem to stimulate their own efforts. However, policy integration placed a considerable strain on the leadership capabilities of intermediate and local cadres, because it demanded an active interrelation of their specific tasks with overall policy.

Faults of Leadership

In the second half of the 1928 "Report" and in what is known as the Gutian Resolution of December 1929,[44] Mao provides an extensive critique of leadership faults which gives a concrete picture of correct leadership by specifying its opposite. The report criticizes the nondemocratic ways of local soviets; the Gutian Resolution deals with ideological deviations in the party and army.

In the report, Mao gives a favorable description of conditions in the army but is quite critical of government organs: "Every level of soviet has been set up, but more in name than in reality." Mao's criticism is not that the soviets are not the real organs of power but that they are not what soviets should be. Basically, they lack the new spirit of democratic centralism *(minzhu jizhong zhuyi)* and estrange themselves from the masses. The soviets still act under the feudal principle of power from above:

> Many places do not have councils of workers, peasants, and soldiers *(gong nong bing daibiao dahui)* and the soviet executive committees at township *(xiang)*, district *(qu)*, and even county levels are elected at mass meetings which are called suddenly, preventing the discussion of problems and the conduct of political training. These meetings are easily manipulated by intellectuals and opportunistic elements. All this amounts to a failure to understand what a soviet is. It is a failure to understand that the councils of workers,

peasants, and soldiers are definitely the highest organs of authority, that the executive committee is just an organ for making decisions between meetings. . . . In some localities, there is a council but it is considered to be merely a temporary organ to elect an executive committee.[45]

This basic organizational mistake led to corresponding mistakes in the behavior of the executive committees:

> If there is no representative council or if there isn't a sound one behind the executive committee, its conduct of affairs is often estranged from the views of the masses *(tuoli qunzhong di yijian)*, and there are instances everywhere of hesitation and compromise in the confiscation and redistribution of land, of squandering or embezzling funds, and of recoiling before the White forces or fighting only half-heartedly.[46]

The origin of this evil is evidently the inertia of previous experience with government: "The evil feudal practice of arbitrary dictation is so deeply rooted in the minds of the masses and even of the ordinary Party members that it cannot be swept away at once." The "easy way" is for the highest official to give an order. Thus the executive committee replaces the representative council, the standing committee replaces the executive committee, the paid officers replace the standing committee—and the party replaces the soviet government. By reducing the popular revolutionary character of the soviet, the isolation from the people that this telescoping of discretionary activity entails reduces the effectiveness of the government's military support activities. The reason for the persistence of this old political style is first of all a lack of propaganda and education about the new political system, but there is also a more basic need for democratic centralism to prove itself in struggle:

> Democratic centralism can be widely and effectively practiced in mass organizations only when its efficacy is demonstrated in revolutionary struggle and the masses understand that it is the best means for mobilizing their forces and is of utmost help in their struggle.[47]

Given the rapidity of developments in Jinggangshan, Mao could expect an opportunity for this proof by experience very quickly.

In contrast to later works, Mao does not direct his criticisms of soviet government at hostile class elements in the government—even though he notes that in the beginning the small landlords, rich peasants, and intellectuals took over the soviets, particularly at the township level (the lowest level at that time), and that the oppressed classes, the poor peasants, were not represented.

The leadership problems Mao dealt with in the year between the Jinggangshan Report and the Gutian Resolution were completely different from the problems of local government just described. For almost all of 1929 the Fourth Red Army under Zhu De and Mao was fighting a mobile war against various local powers in southern Jiangxi and western Fujian provinces. The base area which later became the Jiangxi Soviet and then the Central Soviet Republic was not established until August 1929. The Gutian Resolution, a general attempt to identify the ideological problems of the Red Army, was a response to a critical letter from the Central Committee, but it was also an effort to reestablish the army's morale and cohesiveness.

After a year of hard battle and the disorienting effect of leaving Jinggangshan, the founding of the new Jiangxi base demanded a repoliticization of military power, a conscious effort to respond to a different population, and a struggle against the narrow routines and subgroup identities which had accumulated with the army's professionalization through experience. But the problems were not completely novel. Most of them relate to the tasks of mobilization and policy integration within a military framework. Mao's attempt to rectify these "mistaken ideas" by exposing them and suggesting specific remedies is the first example of a Maoist ideological rectification effort. His glossary of faults from this first effort has become an enduring (although incomplete) catalog of ideological defects. These faults—"purely military viewpoint," "ultrademocracy," "disregard of organizational discipline," "Absolute egalitarianism," "individualism"—are worth presenting in some detail both as developments in Mao's theory of leadership and for the historical light they shed on the Red Army's situation.

Mao's analysis of the purely military viewpoint is most notable for his political conception of the Red Army's purpose:

> The Red Army does not fight for fighting's sake but fights in order to conduct propaganda among the masses, organize them, arm them, help them, and set up political power. If it departs from these objectives of mass-oriented propaganda, organization, and armed

political power, then the significance of the fighting is completely lost and the Red Army basically loses the reason for its existence.[48]

The purely military viewpoint is an attitude of estrangement from the masses which leads directly to other distortions: too much importance is attached to winning or losing battles, and the importance and strength of the army are alternately exaggerated, resulting in the opportunism of evading battles in order to conserve strength or the putschism of only wanting to do big things. The cure for these purely military tendencies is political training, but local party and mass organizations are encouraged to voice their criticisms of the Red Army, and the party is urged to be more attentive to military work. Finally a need is expressed for an organic stipulation of Red Army rules and regulations.

Three other mistaken tendencies are most probably pointed out in direct response to Central Committee criticisms: ultrademocracy, absolute egalitarianism, and roving rebel ideology. Ultrademocracy, the desire of the lower levels to decide everything, arises from "the petty-bourgeoisie's aversion to discipline."[49] Mao shows his creativity in applying Party Center criticisms in his suggested methods of correction. The educational methods point out the damage to party organization and fighting ability caused by ultrademocracy and also its petit-bourgeois roots. The organizational methods of correction are aimed mainly, however, at "the leading bodies of the party." There are five organizational solutions. First, the leading bodies must establish themselves as centers of leadership by giving a correct line of guidance and finding solutions when problems arise. Second, they must be familiar with the life of the masses and the situation of the lower levels so as to have an objective base for correct leadership. Third, decision-making and execution should not be too casual. Fourth, all important decisions must be promptly transmitted to lower levels by means of reports at meetings. And fifth, the lower levels must discuss directives in detail in order to understand them and decide on methods of implementation. The actual thrust of this program is to prevent the separation of party levels and estrangement from the masses; as such it is one of Mao's best statements on methods of leadership. In the context of the discussion of ultrademocracy, these organizational correctives imply that the problem is a symptom of isolated and incorrect leadership rather than an independent ideological problem of the lower levels.

Mao's claim that absolute egalitarianism is no longer a serious problem and the relatively trivial examples he lists lead me to suppose that its inclusion as a mistaken tendency originated with the Central Committee. Absolute egalitarianism is simply insisting on equal treatment in everything regardless of the need for concentration of resources. The cure is education to the fact that absolute egalitarianism is an illusion not only under present conditions but even under socialism.

In the section on the ideology of roving rebel bands, Mao not only treats the problem as serious but carefully proves that it is curable. Most of the soldiers in Mao's army were vagrants and mercenaries, and traditionally the outlook of these groups was lawless but not revolutionary. If the army were not used quickly to establish a base for urban proletarian power, it might lose its revolutionary character completely. Mao's approach to the problem is typically frontal: he acknowledges the vagrant majority of the Red Army and goes on to observe the general flourishing of banditry in South China. But he proceeds to show that the traditional roving rebel mentality is no longer a class ideology in China but only the remnant of an ideology:

> But the large-scale roving rebel activities of Hong Chao, Li Zhuang, or Hong Xiuquan are no longer possible in a China which is ruled by imperialism *[sic]*, and particularly in a China of the present period in which advanced weapons (hand grenades, artillery, machine guns, etc.), advanced methods of communication (military telephone and radio), and advanced means of transportation (automotive, steamboat, and railroad) have been introduced. For these reasons the thinking of roving rebels is naturally not able to become the ultimate and powerful view which governs the activities of the Red Army. But its influence . . . is still very great.[50]

As one might expect, the manifestations of the roving rebel mentality are very similar to those of the purely military viewpoint: inattention to political work among the masses and preference for mercenary recruits. The cure is again education and recruitment of more workers and peasants for the army.

Disregard of organizational discipline *(fei zuzhi yishi)* includes two relationships—that of a minority in disagreement with adopted policy and that of individuals in opposition. The general rule on opposition is that objections are encouraged *before* a policy is adopted; they are allowed afterward provided that they are not manifested in work. Criticism should be made within the party and it should not take the form of attacks on individuals. Mao also discusses an extraneous[51] but interesting problem under this heading: the "compartmentalization" *(tesuhua)* of a portion of the party membership. This problem resulted from the party's "big mistake" of separating military and political responsibilities so that military specialists did not attend their branch meetings and regular party members did not discuss military problems. Evidently addressing the military readers, Mao says that their excuse is pressure of business but in reality they fear the masses and do not want to approach them. This leads to their estrangement from the masses and estrangement from the party and constitutes a type of functional elite formation which would make policy integration impossible.

Mao's discussions of the tendencies of idealism (subjectivism) and individualism are related critiques of personal characteristics of some party members which adversely affect party work. Idealism is the lack of a realistic attitude and results in the errors of opportunism or putschism and in the proclivity to take and give criticism too personally. Individualism is the pursuit of personal ends to the detriment of party organization and goals. Examples are retaliation, cliquism, passivity in work, pleasure seeking, and an employee mentality. The method of correction is primarily education, but the conditions which encourage individualism are also noted. Proper conduct of affairs, particularly assignments and discipline, is emphasized, as is improvement of the Red Army's material welfare.

The solution to these leadership flaws is political education of the mistaken individuals and organizational reforms to improve the ideological quality of party life. In political education, Mao continues the predilection of his schoolteaching days by emphasizing practicality and recommending the "mental development method" *(qifa shi)* of education over the "spoonfeeding method" *(zhuru shi)*.[52] Mao attacks organizational laxness in the party, but he also criticizes boring meetings ("going to a meeting is like going to jail") and lazy, self-important chairmen.

The Gutian Resolution and the second part of Mao's 1928 report delineate the basic norms of revolutionary leadership in the base area context. The imperatives derive their strength from a close dialectic of self-interest and public service. Mao describes the necessary behavior for popular mobilization which is the basis of their survival and success. Both true revolutionary identity and survival demand service to the masses. The strenuous attention to the masses which Mao demanded of party, military, and government cadres is both practical and idealistic if Mao's basic assumption of the absolute political power of the mobilized masses is accepted. Any shortcomings which inhibit an intimate relationship between leader and masses reduce one's contribution and stature as a revolutionary and make failure more likely.

By 1930, Mao had developed an ethic of leadership which was to be refined throughout his political career. The chief leadership fault—estrangement from the masses—acquired the subcategories of bureaucratism (complacency of position, reliance on authority to distinguish oneself from the masses) and subjectivism (being too self-centered, not grasping the objective situation), into which many of the specific faults discussed above could be placed. But Mao did not think that a perfect organization would solve every problem; nor was closeness to the masses merely a "human relations" ploy for mobilization. Correct policy was as essential as efficient organization, and closeness to the masses involved a commitment to a popular process of policy formation later formalized as the mass line. The need for the revolutionary organization to learn about objective reality and the needs of the masses was particularly acute after the Red Army's return from the attacks on Nanchang and Changsha in the fall of 1930. The next three sections of this chapter focus on Mao's experience of the objective world of the village.

Revolutionary Fact-Finding

Mao and his army arrived back in Jiangxi in October 1930. The new importance of the base area was indicated by the immediate founding of the Jiangxi Provincial Soviet Government, and a new degree of soviet-centeredness can be seen in Mao's writings. His major concern became rural policy and he devoted much time to systematic investigations of life in soviet villages. The most important element in his village-level concern was land redistribution, but his careful investigations of scattered localities showed that this policy and its execution were inextricably enmeshed in the complexities of local political life. In this section we will concentrate on Mao's process of investigation; later in the chapter we will examine the results of the investigations and the problems they posed for rural policy.

Jiangxi Investigations

We can surmise that three factors influenced Mao to undertake systematic land investigations in the Jiangxi base. The first factor is that Jiangxi is more fertile and more heavily populated than Jinggangshan. This made the land problem more acute than it had been. The second factor is that after the failure of Li Lisan's urban seizure policy, Mao undoubtedly was expecting a protracted struggle in the existing soviets. Jiangxi could not be consolidated nor could its population be mobilized without an effective land policy. Since he was relatively unfamiliar with the area, Mao had to conduct serious investigations before he could design the cornerstone of soviet policy.

The third factor, whose importance is impossible to estimate, is that the party organs in southern Jiangxi were in large part opposed to land redistribution and opposed to Mao. From December 1930 until the summer of 1931 there was what John Rue has termed a civil war between the pro-Mao and anti-Mao forces in the Jiangxi Soviet (or, from Mao's point of view, between the communists and the Anti-Bolshevik League rebels).[53] As Philip Huang has shown in a study of Xingguo county in Jiangxi,[54] this conflict was also related to the infiltration of local soviet and party organs by the Three Dot secret society. Without a systematic survey of local conditions it would be difficult for Mao to be certain of the reliability of local reports and even the nature of his opposition. For instance, the rebels objected to land redistribution but were in favor of collectivization, claiming in this to represent the interests of the laborers against Mao's emphasis on the peasants.[55] Whether their objection represented an attempt to leap over the bourgeois-democratic stage to the socialist revolution, or whether it was merely a counterattack against serious land redistribution mounted by rich peasants in control of local party organizations, was a question which could only be settled by accurate, firsthand knowledge.

Mao's early investigations alternate between careful notes taken on the reports of local cadres and his own research made during pauses in military operations. The utility of personal investigation is evident from the introduction to his first set of investigative reports:

> Doing the Lijiafang investigation enabled me to understand the circumstances of the organization and activities of the two soviet levels of township *(xiang)* and village *(cun)* during the land struggle. Before this investigation, my notion of these circumstances was vague. This investigation allowed me to discover the seriousness of dividing land with the village as the unit. In south Jiangxi nine or ten counties distributed land, and the land law announced by the higher governmental levels said that distribution should have the townships as units. Of the workers in high-level organs, most believe that the distribution was carried out by township, and none realized that the actual *(shiji)* situation is a completely different matter. Generally division was done by village, and very few were done by township. Using the village as the unit is to the advantage of the rich peasant and to the disadvantage of the poor peasant.[56]

This investigation was a help to Mao on an important policy matter in various ways: in his personal development as a correct and effective soviet leader; in confirming an existing policy direction, in checking the effectiveness of existing policy; and in highlighting a problem that might call for redistribution in the future. But the Lijiafang survey is not a thrilling piece of investigative reporting; it is one of four very objective, mostly statistical descriptions of location, government, and land distribution in various townships.[57] Among the four townships, Lijiafang is distinguished by its large and expensive township government, very uneven land distribution among its villages (highest is 400 percent of lowest), some coercion in Red Army recruitment, and mild treatment of former White militia soldiers and officers.

The careful notes which Mao took on reports by local leaders have the advantage of covering many more localities than Mao could have investigated personally; the concomitant disadvantage is reliance on responsible persons as reporters. In "The Situation of Land Distribution in Western Jiangxi"—Mao's notes at an enlarged conference of the West Jiangxi Action Committee and the Jiangxi Action Committee, held 12 to 15 November 1930—this problem is illustrated when one of the reporters singles out for commendation a village which Mao had personally investigated a few days earlier, and Mao appends a question mark to his note.[58] The three major meetings of this conference included a survey of the ragged development of land reform, reports on the extent of rich peasant and landlord infiltration of local party, governmental, and guerrilla units, and examples of the unpredictable complexities of land policy. With the combination of reporting sessions and personal investigation, Mao acquired an experience of the structure and dynamics of rural politics which was difficult to convey to his superiors in Shanghai. It was, however, as good an objective base as could be had for his own discretion in leading the soviet.

Mao's best and most detailed rural survey resulted from an intensive, week-log discussion with eight Red Army soldiers from a certain border district, Yongfeng, in Xingguo county. The result of this investigative session, the "Xingguo Investigation,"[59] was written up in January 1931 and might be called the Hunan Report of the Jiangxi period. Mao applies the same practical-investigative thrust of his earlier classic to the postliberation concerns of the first soviets and arrives at a correspondingly vivid presentation of the party's rural environment, containing policy-relevant information as well as an ethical imperative for each party member to engage himself in similar studies.

One important difference between the Hunan Report and the Xingguo Investigation is that the party no longer needs to be convinced of the importance of the rural movement or the correctness of its apparently extreme actions. Mao's target in the Xingguo Investigation is the basic ignorance of rural conditions caused by the dogmatic style of the CCP's rural leadership. He supports his stress on the importance of local studies by voicing a strong opinion on methods of leadership in the preface:

> The determination of practical policies should certainly be based on concrete conditions. Things fantasized in one's room or things read in carelessly written reports are definitely not concrete conditions. It would be dangerous to determine policy on the basis of plausibility or on reports which don't correspond to reality. The many mistakes formerly made in the Red areas all stem from a lack of correspondence between Party leadership and reality. Therefore careful, scientific, practical investigation is extremely necessary.[60]

Mao's own investigation is a model of what he is suggesting, although military necessities caused him to abandon his investigation prematurely. Mao reports on seven major topics and lists four which were not reached. The seven sections of the report are (1) a survey of eight families (of the eight informants); (2) old land-related relationships in the district; (3) the various classes in struggle; (4) the present status of land distribution; (5) land tax; (6) the soviet; and (7) rural militarization. The topics Mao would have liked to include were the situation of youth and women, commercial activity and price levels, agricultural productivity after land division, and the cultural situation. Mao's method was to propose an investigation outline and discuss matters until everyone had agreed on what should be written down. He suggests the earnestness of his attempt to find out what is really going on at the local level by mentioning that the sessions were lively and interesting, that sometimes his conclusions were ridiculed, and that most of the eight informants were not party members. This one-location, in-depth approach has the endemic methodological problem that its general applicability remains unproved, but Mao addresses this difficulty with a characteristic Chinese logic: "This district [Yongfeng] is at the conjunction of Xingguo, Ganxian, and Wanan counties. If this district is understood, then understanding Ganxian and Wanan counties is not far off, and the situation of the land revolution in all of southern Jiangxi would be approximately the same."[61]

The difference in texture between the Hunan Report and the Xingguo Investigation comes from the latter's concrete, even personal, detail. The Xingguo Investigation begins with fifteen pages of the personal fortunes of Mao's eight informants during land reform. He also discusses the activities and fates of the twelve landlords and thirty-two rich peasants in the district and presents the class background for each district-level official and those of one township. Mao maintains a corresponding level of detail when he describes economic conditions in the district before the revolution and every aspect of land reform. In all, the Xingguo Investigation is the most unrestrained display of Mao's love for the idiosyncracies of real life, a love which few decision-makers or theorists can afford to share. It is also a basic type of cognitive experience of local politics in the soviet; one may presume that other localities would have a mix of similarities and idiosyncracies like Yongfeng, and one careful investigation broadens the horizons of expectation.

Mao as Social Scientist

Both the factual content and the methodology of investigation exemplified in the Xingguo Investigation are extremely important for Mao's later activities. Besides the investigations already discussed, four other articles are important for deriving a picture of Mao's investigative methodology and its place in his political thinking: "Oppose Book Worship" (May 1930),[62] his preface and postscript to *Rural Surveys* (March and April 1941),[63] and "No Investigation, No Right to Speak, No Correct Investigation, Still No Right to Speak" (April 1931).[64]

Mao's most emphatic point in all of these works is the inescapable personal obligation of every cadre to investigate his objective social world. The first paragraph of "Oppose Book Worship" makes this point with vigor:

> Unless you have investigated a problem, you will be deprived of the right to speak on it. Isn't that too harsh? Not in the least. When you have not probed into a problem, into the present facts and its past history, and know nothing of its essentials, whatever you say about it will undoubtedly be nonsense. Talking nonsense solves no problems, as everyone knows, so why is it unjust to deprive you of the right to speak? Quite a few comrades always keep their eyes shut and talk nonsense, and for a communist that is disgraceful. How can a communist keep his eyes shut and talk nonsense?
> It won't do!
> It won't do!
> You must investigate!
> You must not talk nonsense![65]

The spirit of this paragraph expresses one of the oldest traits of Mao's writing—namely, conveying to the reader a sense of urgency in doing something *now*. In his earliest published work on physical education, Mao made it clear to the reader that he was condemned to a feeble brain and a vacillating will in a short-lived body if the message to exercise were ignored. In "Oppose Book Worship," Mao makes it clear that one's identity as a good communist demands serious investigation of one's surroundings because a commitment to revolutionary leadership requires study of the objective situation. "Everyone with responsibility for giving leadership . . . must personally undertake investigation into the specific social and economic conditions and not merely rely on reading reports."[66] The point can be made more elegantly with a dictum from the "Preface to *Rural Surveys*": one must be a student of the masses before becoming their leader.

A composite picture of the object of Mao's rage, the "teacher by negative example," can be drawn from Mao's criticisms. One might expect a root problem of laziness, and indeed Mao observes that some comrades "eat their fill and sit dozing in their offices all day long without ever moving a step and going out among the masses to investigate." But the question of energy is not primary. Unnecessary mistakes can be made "not because of failure to make careful plans before taking action but because of failure to study the specific social situation carefully before making the plans."[67] The basic error is not laziness but what Mao calls "idealism"—the belief that one's mental struggle with a problem can solve it. One might criticize subjective idealism in two different ways. One might emphasize that stubbornness of subordinates results in heresy and dysfunctions in the revolutionary organization. Or one might emphasize that the dogmatism of leadership results in losing touch with reality. This second direction is the one taken by Mao. His target is the ineffective cadre rather than the disobedient cadre. The books whose worship one should oppose are Marx and the party directives.

Mao's position of course indicates no antagonism toward communist doctrines or the CCP's authority. Mao's point is that the correctness of theory and authority is immanent in their practical utility, and this utility is vitiated by dogmatism of believers and subordinates.

> When we say Marxism is correct, it is certainly not because Marx was a "prophet" but because his theory has been proved correct in our practice and in our struggle. We need Marxism in our struggle.[68]

Hence the study of Marxism should not be a quest for purity but a quest for utility. In the same manner, organizational obedience is not a quest for exactness, but one for maximum coordinated effect:

> When we say that a directive of a higher organ is correct, that is not just because it comes from "a higher organ of leadership" but because its contents conform with both the objective and subjective circumstances of the struggle and meet its requirements.[69]

What is considered by the idealist to be the faithful execution of his mission is thus completely redefined:

> To carry out a directive of a higher organization blindly, and seemingly without any disagreement, is not really to carry it out but is the most artful way of opposing or sabotaging it.[70]

This view places a great responsibility on each cadre, because he must make his personal judgment of the applicability of doctrine and directives to his leadership situation. In order to be correct, his decision should be based on an understanding of what needs to be done and what can be done. Investigation is the process of acquiring this understanding of the objective situation.

Mao describes his method of investigation in greatest detail in "Oppose Book Worship." The basic technique is to hold fact-finding meetings of from three to eight persons with concrete experience of the subject of investigation. The investigator should prepare a detailed outline and stimulate discussion on its points, taking notes on the answers. The basic ingredient in a successful investigation is described in "Preface to *Rural Surveys*":

> These cadres, the peasants, the *xiucai* [old-style scholar], the jailer, the merchant and the revenue clerk were all my esteemed teachers, and as their pupil I had to be respectful and comradely in my attitude; otherwise they would have paid no attention to me, and though they knew, would not have spoken or, if they spoke, would not have told all they knew.[71]

The best description of one of Mao's fact-finding meetings is the opening paragraph of the Xingguo Investigation described earlier.

From a different perspective, Mao's justification of investigation as essential to revolutionary pragmatism sets the horizons of "correct" investigation by specifying its utility. An investigation which is not useful for informing the revolutionary movement is a waste of time. Mao is not interested in pursuing "truth"—that is, data (social fact) and laws (regularities of social fact)—for its own sake:

> Of late [1930], the comrades in the Fourth Army of the Red Army have generally given attention to the work of investigation, but the method many of them employ is wrong. The results of their investigations are therefore as trivial as a grocer's accounts, or resemble the many strange tales a country bumpkin hears when he comes to town, or are like a distant view of a populous city from a mountain top. This kind of investigation is of little use and cannot achieve our main purpose.[72]

With the practical goal of a social revolution conceptualized in terms of a Marxist paradigm, the informational goals of investigation are to a great extent predetermined:

> Our chief method of investigation must be to dissect the different social classes, the ultimate purpose being to understand their interrelations, to arrive at a correct appraisal of class forces and then to formulate the correct tactics for struggle, defining which classes constitute the main force in the revolutionary struggle, which classes are to be won over as allies, and which classes are to be overthrown. This is our sole purpose.[73]

The emphasis on fundamental class analysis is particularly strong in "Oppose Book Worship" because in 1930 the basic questions of class alliance, especially what to do with the rich peasants, were a subject of hot debate. Although the context is completely different, this research interest is strongly reminiscent of Mao's 1926 articles on the importance of the peasantry. By the time of the Xingguo Investigation attention had shifted from basic revolutionary strategy to the effects of government policy. What is present in all the Jiangxi investigations (and, less explicitly, in the Hunan Report) is a self-conscious determination of research interest by Mao's immediate problem. But predetermination does not lead, as one might expect, to a debilitating narrowness of perspective in investigation. The necessity of systematic investigation presupposes a social reality which is penetrable but not self-evident. Alert investigation is essential because of its vital informational role in determining concrete revolutionary potential. Thus there is a codetermination of revolutionary purpose (informed by doctrine and authority) and social situation (discovered through investigation). This basic outlook is most explicitly formulated by Mao in "On Practice" (1937).

What has been presented so far is an individual model of the role of social investigation. But beyond the personal need to know one's own objective context there is an organizational need to have coordinated knowledge of a larger objective framework:

> A Communist Party's correct and unswerving tactics of struggle can in no circumstances be created by a few people sitting in an office; they emerge in the course of mass struggle, that is, through actual experience.[74]

As suggested here, the party's own history is a major education in objectivity and correct tactics. But it must also strive to understand its present environment. A grasp of current conditions presupposes a different level of investigation—namely, the gathering of statistics. The article "No Investigation, No Right to Speak, No Correct Investigation, Still No Right to Speak" was written as an explanation for two accompanying questionnaires (on landholdings and population by class) which all cadres were supposed to fill out in their areas. In describing the project Mao shares the perennial dream of practical social science: "If we can now fill in these two questionnaires with correct statistics based on strict attention to reality, then we will be able to solve many of our problems, especially many current practical problems of land distribution."[75] Of course, Mao's desire to clarify policy dilemmas by recourse to "iron reality" (like William James' "brute facts") has many potential pitfalls in its execution, most centering on the pollsters. Mao therefore exhorts the cadres to acquire a deep knowledge of this type of work, to distinguish categories clearly, and to fill in only real quantities. He reminds them: "If every point is not grasped clearly during the investigation and instead you are in a jumble, then this will necessarily lead to a blurring of class distinctions and the statistics will lose their true value."[76] It must be noted, however, that Mao's own definition of rich peasant status is quite vague: "a man for whom exploitation provides a significant portion *(xiangdang bufen)* of income." Only in the second stage of the Land Investigation Movement of 1933, when the success of the movement hinged on the interpretation of "a significant portion," did Mao finally provide an exhaustive distinction between the middle and rich peasant classifications.[77] In this Mao resembles many another social scientist whose project has been weakened by vagueness in a key concept. In any event his attempt to obtain a comprehensive description of the soviet area and to involve every cadre in social investigative work demonstrates a respect for the existing situation which is an important residue of his early base area experience.

The Villages, the Party, and Social Revolution

The general sketch of rural classes and their attitudes toward revolution which Mao proposed in early 1926 remained quite accurate for the basic dynamics of rural politics. The middle peasants, poor peasants, hired hands, and vagrants were the natural mainstays of the revolution; the landlords and rich peasants were its targets and opponents. But to evoke such natural support depended on the party's rural policies, which in turn demanded a fine understanding of village interrelationships and the effects of redistribution in the base area. The arrival of the Red Army and the overthrow of the traditional village elite and its landownership base transformed class relations, sometimes in unexpected ways.

The Peasant Environment

Among environments for revolution, that of revolution among the peasantry was the least understood in 1927. Surely some of the motivation behind Qu Qiubai's directive to proletarianize the peasantry was a desire to force the unfamiliar rural situation into familiar urban relations. Because of his insistence on the centrality of the peasant question for the national revolution and his earlier peasant movement experience, Mao was far better prepared for rural work than most of his colleagues. But the problem of creating a political-military force out of rural conditions was very different from that of inducing peasant participation in a movement which had already shifted the provincial and regional balance of power.

The peasantry had long been a source of frustration to revolutionaries. Despite its numbers and degree of oppression, it is prone to a conservatism which allows it to remain immobile or to be duped by reactionary political forces. To take an illustration from Zhejiang province in 1926:

> [Due to the depredation of warlord wars] people can't make a living, and therefore the peasants are very suspicious of and even curse the republican form of government. All the evils caused by the warlords and the bureaucrats are seen as republican evils. Thus although common opinion is not for restoring the Manchu emperor, it does generally hope for the emperor with the true mandate to emerge and put the situation in order, and then the empire will attain the great peace. They especially don't understand the significance of our party [the KMT/CCP]; on the other hand they are not hostile to it.[78]

The situation described here is that of a population gravely affected by developments in the national political economy but failing to defend its own interests. It is not the complexity of rural class relations which causes inertia. Although there is more than one type of rural class structure,[79] there is less diversity of economic roles in any of them than there is in a corresponding urban setting. So far as class is concerned, the fundamental difference between rural and urban settings is that economic interdependence in the countryside is far less impersonal. As William Hinton has described in *Fanshen*,[80] the land reform cadres in the late 1940s had to educate the villagers to a consciousness of classes—not that the villagers did not remember and resent every instance of oppression, but hitherto they had blamed it on Mr. Chen (the bad landlord) rather than on the landlord (Mr. Chen). For all their numbers and oppressive conditions, the peasants tend to remain isolated in their personal worlds of exploitation rather than form a politically conscious class. To use Marx's excellent metaphor, the peasantry constitutes the mass of the nation in the same way that potatoes put into a sack constitute a sack of potatoes.[81]

From this general description, it follows that a modern revolutionary movement attempting to use the peasantry as its main force would have their political education as its central task—not the replacement of one ideology by another but an original conceptualization of politics by the villagers. This education can only take place at the local level and through the process of political struggle. Unless village affairs are integrated into the world of national politics, the village will remain as external to the new society as it was to the old. To nationalize peasant politics, there must be a localization of modern political leadership.

The village orientation of rural revolution implies that the liberation of each village is an individual event, and the success of deepening social revolution in the villages relies on the participation of each village's inhabitants. Although by defeating the armed forces of the landlords the Red Army also overthrew landlord power in the villages, this in itself did not usually produce a social transformation in the villages. The village poor were still intimidated by the prestige of the remaining rich peasants and landlords—and by the possibility of the return of the White forces. Only with the encouragement of the persistently egalitarian land policy of the base area did the poor and middle peasants emerge to struggle with the remnants of the old hierarchy and the opportunists. To proceed from this basic achievement of rural mass power to the development of a mass political system took even model villages the entire life span of the Jiangxi Soviet.

Village Social Structure

In both Jinggangshan and Jiangxi, there were social entities of some significance which cut across class lines. Both places had strong clan organizations, and at least Jinggangshan had an ethnic problem. As Philip Huang has shown,[82] secret society members involved in smuggling Xingguo chickens for Guangdong salt were a major force in Xingguo after landlord power had been weakened. Moreover, in many cases class membership was difficult to determine, and some individuals did not act according to their class background. Nevertheless, it is evident particularly in the Xingguo Investigation that rural class structure was by far the most important determinant of rural social structure. Thus the most appropriate description of base area social structure is by class, comprising a sort of composite update of Mao's 1926 "Analysis of Various Peasant Classes."

Landlords. Mao reports extreme concentration of landownership in Jinggangshan (60–80 percent) and considerable concentration in Xingguo (40 percent), and the major presence of landlords in Mao's 1928–1930 writings is as leaders of antirevolutionary local forces. In the four townships of Yongfeng district in Xingguo, most of the men of the twelve landlord families escaped or were killed, although two joined the revolution and became government officials. The major form of landlord exploitation was rent, which ranged from 50 to 60 percent (the lower rent being for fields subject to drought and flood). As a group the landlords were not directly involved in usury, although some lent large sums of money to rich peasants at 15 to 18 percent interest and these in turn parceled it out to poor peasants at 30 percent.[83] Moreover, three-fifths of the clan-owned temple lands, which comprised 10 percent of all land in Yongfeng, were managed by "bad gentry" *(liesheng)* whose own rental fields were insufficient to make a living. In all these occupations, the landlords were targets of the revolution. Their land and temple lands were confiscated and debts were canceled. The landlords disappeared as a class with the revolution.

Rich Peasants. This class posed the most complex problems for the base areas. Rich peasants were defined as those who depended significantly on both their own labor and on exploitation in the form of hiring, rental, or loans.[84] Their landholdings were 30 percent of the land in Yongfeng, although they comprised only 5 percent of the population. But their most conspicuous form of exploitation was moneylending. Eighty percent of all money loans were made by rich peasants to poor peasants. Grain loans were handled by the temples and relief granaries at a lower interest rate, but these loans were difficult to obtain in the spring shortage period. The rich peasants preferred to sell almost all their surplus grain and make cash loans for its purchase. Unlike the temples, relief granaries, and pawnbrokers, they were willing to let interest mount on a delinquent debtor rather than foreclose.[85]

As the Red Army approached, most of the rich peasants sided with the landlords. In Yongfeng, twenty-three of thirty-two rich peasants were counterrevolutionary. But the greater presence of the rich peasants in the village, their entrepreneurial habits, and their intimate involvement with village affairs made them a much more potent political adversary of land reform within the village than the landlords. In the power vacuum immediately following the Red Army's arrival, many could use their connections, prestige, and qualifications to secure important offices in the revolutionary government and the party.[86]

Middle Peasants. Since the middle peasants were independent farmers, their oppression by the feudal system was only indirect. Their economic advantages from the revolution were in general not vital. Most increased their land, debts were canceled, oxen cost less, and there were no more marriage, death, or perfumed paper expenses.[87] But their political advances were more important. From a prerevolutionary position outside the basic power structure of the village, they came to occupy 40 percent of local government positions in Yongfeng.

The reaction of the middle peasants to the Red Army was completely different in Jinggangshan and Xingguo due to a basic difference in land policy. The early land policy (prescribed by the Central Committee) was to confiscate all land, including that of the middle peasants, and redistributed shares were not really owned by the peasants who received them. This policy led to a village division between landowners and nonowners, and as a result all the "intermediate classes" (which Mao at this time described as small landlords and owner-peasants) obstructed soviet work and went over to the Whites. In new areas in Jinggangshan owner-peasant land was not confiscated, and there the owner-peasants and poor peasants struggled together against the "local bullies and evil gentry."[88] In Yongfeng this policy had been maintained from the start and thus the middle peasants participated just as well as the poor peasants in the revolution.

Poor Peasants. Before the revolution, the poor peasants depended on rented fields and loans for survival and were in no position to be active in the social and political life of the village. They were the most generally benefited class in the revolution. Not only did they receive land and have debts canceled, but their shortage of grain was made up by a division of the stores of the landlords and counterrevolutionary rich peasants. Moreover, the price of grain went down after the revolution. Having been rescued from an existence which was marginal in every respect, it is not surprising that the poor peasants eventually became the principal pillar of rural governmental power and the leading class in the countryside.[89] But attaining this central position involved struggle against the upper class and vagrant elements who became important elements in the local organs which were set up immediately after the revolution.

Farm Laborers. The hired farm workers, the village proletariat, were so poor and despised before the revolution that in the first year they had improved but not transformed their condition. Mao uses marriage as an index of prosperity. Rich peasants all had at least one wife. Ninety percent of middle peasants were married, as were 70 percent of the poor peasants and 10 percent of the vagrants. But only 1 percent of the farm laborers had wives—and even after a soviet decree that everyone should get married they had a difficult time finding wives.[90] But this was an incidental problem. With the revolution, hired laborers got land, but they had to borrow tools and oxen from better-off relatives. Long-term work disappeared after the revolution, and it is a sign of the low bargaining power of the hired laborers that they did not demand a raise even with a 30 percent decline in part-time work. They were still outside the political structure of the village. There was not a single hired hand in a position of governmental authority in Yongfeng district, a fact explained by their social disabilities. According to the middle and poor peasants, they "can't read, can't talk, aren't enlightened, and aren't familiar with public affairs."

Artisans. Trades which catered to the conspicuous consumption of the wealthy classes were ruined by the revolution, and those artisans either became peasants or left the soviet area. Even traditional crafts like carpentry were disrupted seriously. The demand of underemployed artisans for a share in the land distribution was met with some hostility by the peasants. In one case two hundred artisans in a town were denied land by surrounding peasants.[91] Even in a completely rural district like Yongfeng, eighteen crafts were represented and there was a confrontation over whether artisans should receive land. It was decided that they could receive land, but if they worked over a hundred days a year, half the land would be returned to the soviet. The artisans were cognizant of their more or less proletarian status and had organized trade union branches in rural areas.

Vagrants. This colorful group of bandits, gamblers, beggars, fortune-tellers, Daoists, and others, sometimes designated "lumpenproletarians,"[92] had an importance completely out of proportion to their numbers in the early base area years. In the first year at Jinggangshan, they made up the majority of the Red Army. In Yongfeng, a little over 1 percent of the population were vagrants, but they held ten local government posts. The most plausible reason for the early prominence of vagrants is that in contrast to the rest of the rural population they were risk-takers. Mao optimistically reported that since vagrants received land, their previous occupations thereupon ceased. Their loose ways were sometimes transferred to local party and government operations, however, where for instance only good-looking women were recruited for government work.[93]

The Party

It would be unhistorical and unrealistic to ask the question, "Faced with such an array of economic situations and political attitudes, what was the party to do?" The party had first to commit itself to the task of armed survival and rural revolutionary leadership; only then could it discover the social structure and potential of the villages through a difficult process of policy experimentation. This was a prolonged and painful identity crisis for the cosmopolitan, proletarian-oriented CCP, and the threats of militarization, ruralization, and localization which the center perceived were real. What should be surprising to historians is not that the Central Committee balked at accepting this new starting point for the revolution, but that Mao was so quick to perceive the revolutionary legitimacy and essential requirements of a protracted base area struggle. He was helped in this transition not as much by his Marxism as by the objective necessities of survival and his basic revolutionary-populist approach.

Although praetorianism has never really been a problem for the Chinese Communists,[94] the shift in 1927 to a primary reliance on military strength for survival and expansion was a challenge to many aspects of the party's identity. Qu Qiubai's directive to Mao in September 1927 that "troops and bandits are merely a subsidiary force for agrarian revolution"[95] is not simply indicative of a traditional Chinese (and CCP) distaste for the military. The KMT's subservience to the military forces of the Northern Expedition had led it to blunt and finally abandon its social revolutionary program. That the Red Army remained politically reliable and submissive despite the centrality of military matters was a considerable accomplishment. The major reasons for this success I think are two: the political and social transformation within the army, and the unity between the army's political tasks in the villages and the development of its own military support structures. The principles of political education, equality, and democracy tended to create a revolutionary army rather than an army in service to the revolution. Moreover, the army's support of village revolution was not a political obligation extraneous to its own welfare; it was, simultaneously, the establishment of its own logistical, paramilitary, and recruitment resources. Both these factors were strained by the year of mobile fighting in 1929, and in the Gutian Resolution Mao explicitly brought the army back to its internal and external political-military integration. Mao's political conception of the military was part of his reason for rejecting Li Lisan's and Lin Biao's roving guerrilla strategy in 1930.

The party leadership had another qualm with Mao's rural efforts: the influx of peasants into the party organization and the resulting dilution of its proletarian character. At the Sixth Party Congress in Moscow in the summer of 1928, the complaint was made that "now the party organization is in danger of being separated from the proletariat" and the first item of evidence was "peasants now outnumber worker comrades at a ratio of over seven to one."[96] Proletarian hegemony—the scientific forecast of Marx and the path to power of Lenin—seemed unlikely in a rural setting. In what sense could the party remain the vanguard of the proletariat? This question was never directly addressed by Mao, who thus avoided a major debate on party theory, but at the expense of clarity in a basic concept. The CCP's stress on the industrial proletariat was eliminated not by Mao but by the successive failures of policies derived from it. Mao himself stressed the petit-bourgeois and sometimes even feudal origins of the ideological problems of the base area and the Red Army, and while at Jinggangshan he requested that workers be sent to him to strengthen the proletarian element there. But Mao's operative class orientation was toward the oppressed. He expected the continuation of the political struggle after the petit-bourgeois revolution of land division to come basically from the poor peasants and to be directed at opportunists misdirecting local policy.[97] He expected leadership to serve this continuing struggle and the interests of the party by remaining close to the masses. A mass-line flexibility thus eased out faithfulness to directives or knowledge of historical materialism as the final determiner of policy. Leadership became more important for Mao than discipleship.

The specific task of the party in the land revolution was to provide correct policies and to facilitate the deepening of the revolution. The party was not supposed to dominate the soviets or supplant them as decision-making bodies. Besides promoting the correct line in all matters, the party was to avoid harmful conflicts such as clan wars and the localism endemic to governments.[98] After the general pattern of rural dynamics was known, the party could facilitate the quick movement from one stage of the revolutionary process to the next. But the obligation of closeness to the masses, both in order to avoid dogmatic mistakes and as an ethically correct orientation, remained the basic premise of leadership.

Social Revolution

One argument for flexibility and pragmatism in leadership was the unexpected character of social revolution in the countryside. Three problems in particular demanded innovative leadership from Mao: directing the role of the Red Army as midwife of the rural revolution, balancing protection of the "intermediate classes" with the redistributive needs of the village poor, and guiding the development of rural revolution from initial insurrection to a functioning democratic centralism.

The role of the Red Army in establishing the Jinggangshan and Jiangxi base areas belies both orthodox Marxist and more recent theories of rural revolutionary dynamics. The principle of the reversal of exploitation behind the theory of class struggle would lead us to expect that the most oppressed classes would be the most revolutionary. Arthur Stinchcombe applies this principle to rural areas by predicting that family-size tenants (in China's case the poor peasants) would be rebellious because of the clear sacrifice of most of their income in rent, the unequal distribution of farming risks, and the remoteness and apparent superfluity of the landlord.[99] But the initial role of the rural proletariat (the farm workers) was insignificant, and even the poor peasants, who comprised 60 percent of the population, were not originally in control of the revolution. More recently the thesis has been proposed that middle peasants are most likely to lead a rural revolution precisely because their relative independence from direct exploitation gives them more freedom of action.[100] But the early base area insurrections were not predominantly middle peasant revolutions. In the first insurrections at Jinggangshan, the middle peasants were allied with the rich peasants and small landlords against the revolution.[101] In November 1930, Mao heard reports that 80 percent of the party of Ruijin county were landlords and rich peasants, as were 38 percent of the Shangyou CCP, including a White militia captain.[102] Evidently the necessary condition for the establishment of a base area was the Red Army.

But the Red Army was not a sufficient condition for rural revolution. As Alavi has observed, "The land reform was implemented by peasant committees and not by a communist bureaucracy."[103] The Red Army's destruction of the military power of the landlords and the initial wariness and confusion of the classes most benefited by their overthrow led to a power vacuum which was filled by opportunists and not yet discredited members of the old power structure. Presumably the Red Army's effectiveness in propaganda could make its job of midwifing local insurrections more effective, but it lacked the personnel and the detailed knowledge of local conditions which would have been necessary to supply outside leadership for the first stages of land distribution. But the insurrection was only the beginning of the social revolution in the village.

The most urgent practical task of base area leadership was designing policy which was appropriate for the village social structure, consonant with the party's ideological goals, and efficient for maximizing village support. As early as the Jinggangshan Report, Mao explicitly preferred a comprehensive, mobilizational approach to more radical but less effective majoritarian approach.

It was obvious that successful revolutionary policy must take into account the needs and desires of the masses. If the Red Army relied solely on its military superiority to require compliance, it would greatly raise its cost of administration and reduce its level of village support. But there were alternative criteria for determining the popularity of policy: one stressed the amount of effective popular support which the policy could mobilize; the other stressed its congruence with the preferences of the majority of "citizens." In many cases these criteria do not diverge; a policy preferred by the majority can usually generate considerable active support. But with the issue of land distribution in Jinggangshan, the distinction between Mao's mobilized masses democracy and a more formalistic majoritarian democracy resulted in a major policy divergence. The issue was whether all land should be confiscated for redistribution. Since the majority were poor peasants, their preference could be assumed to be the majority preference. But majority rule did not turn out to be the most feasible land policy because it would have alienated the intermediate classes. The most obvious problem occurred when communist control waned:

> In a revolutionary low tide the most difficult problem of the base area is keeping a firm hold on the intermediate class. The main reason for betrayal by this class is that it has received too heavy a blow from the revolution.[104]

When a region was retaken by the White armies, even the small landowners would lead the troops to the houses of the revolutionary peasants. Hence, as Mao put it, in bad times the poor peasant class became isolated troops *(gu jun)*.

The effect of an anti–middle peasant land policy in normal times was hardly less serious, for it drove the owner-peasants into a powerful collusion with the small landlords which frustrated the mobilization of even the poor peasants. This anti-communist alliance was effected through the clan system, which was dominated more by the intermediate classes than by the big reactionaries. In short, a land policy that was too radical (although in the interests of the majority) produced an opposition too large to be overcome in good times and a tool for the thorough eradication of communist influence in bad times.

This experience led Mao to a nonmajoritarian, although not undemocratic, criterion for policy. If there is a force present which could, if alienated, prevent the mobilization of popular power, their nonalienation becomes a decisive policy guideline. This remained for Mao a fundamental principle, the domestic counterpart of his alliance politics. For Mao, the phrase "overwhelming majority" is not a mere figure of speech or a quantitative proportion: it is the plurality which is needed to overwhelm. The masses should never become isolated troops; the enemy should always be "a handful." The party leadership from 1932 to 1934 did not heed this lesson, but it reappears as a basic principle of Mao's politics in the Anti-Japanese War.

The problem of guiding the social revolution in the villages out of the initial stages to a truly mass government was not finally solved until 1933–1934. The contradiction between an extreme suspicion of local officials and a desire to rely on the masses was quite frustrating. Mao first applied the criterion of class background to purge local party membership in 1928, and this standard increasingly became his chief "quality control." But class background was determined at the local level, and as the disadvantages of being a landlord or rich peasant increased, many of them were redesignated by willing officials. Well over 13,000 disguised landlord and rich peasant families were uncovered during three months of the Land Investigation Movement of 1933.[105] Other methods of control involved general meetings to investigate progress (like the one Mao attended in November 1930), deadlines for implementing various policies, and inspections. The basic problem was to encourage the poor peasants and farm laborers to struggle for a deepening of the revolution. But this was a difficult mobilizational task because the existing local leadership was directly in control of the village. Although Xingguo later became a model county, Philip Huang reports that when the KMT reoccupied Xingguo in April 1931 during their Second Encirclement Campaign against Jiangxi, substantial numbers of poor villagers aided the counterrevolutionary forces.[106] It is likely that in most localities the political struggle evolved in a zigzag pattern with little effective central coordination until 1933.

Land Policy

The central policy concern for base area leadership, and a major policy concern for party leadership in general, was land policy. Land policy remained in flux from 1927 until the Soviet Land Law was proclaimed in December 1931. In part this flux was caused by power shifts and conflicting interpretations of the rural revolution, but even Mao's land policy underwent considerable development as base area experience required the modification of some preconceptions and as its complexity required a corresponding level of detail in application.

Conflicting Land Policies

Especially in 1927-1928, there was a cacophony of land policy suggestions, reflecting the chaos of the times and the novelty of the issue for the party. True to his earlier moderation in the pursuit of rural interests, Chen Duxiu suggested in November 1927 that Sun Yat-sen's slogan of "land to the tillers" was "too profound for the masses to understand."[107] He suggested the "four nots": not to pay rent, not to pay taxes, not to hand over grain to the government, not to pay debts. The policy of the Central Committee under Qu Qiubai was more radical but confused:

> In order to carry out thoroughly the agrarian revolution, the insurrection must undertake to confiscate the landholdings of all the big and medium landlords (total confiscation is the factual outcome), slaughter all village bosses and the evil gentry and reactionaries, and confiscate their properties.[108]

Qu quickly moved to a more consistent policy of total confiscation and revolutionary terrorism, a policy which created the problem, discussed earlier, of a hostile intermediate class in Jinggangshan.

The peasant policy adopted by the Sixth Party Congress in Moscow in 1928 was considerably more realistic.[109] It stipulated that "equal distribution of land should not be applied forcibly in areas where the middle peasants constitute a majority." Although this policy was not as liberal as the one Mao was already applying to the new areas of Jinggangshan, its prudent tone and emphasis on alliance with the middle peasants was a welcome relief from Qu's strident radicalism. As with Qu, the Sixth Congress did not have a clear position on handling rich peasants. It expected them to be hostile, but it suggested that when possible "the CCP should endeavor to absorb rich peasants into the struggle against warlords, landlords, and gentry."

While the Sixth Congress's more prudent view of the rural revolution was welcomed by Mao, its openness to collaboration with rich peasants was exploited by Li Lisan in order to maximize support for his urban insurrections. In his "Land Law" of June 1930,[110] Li made only the rental lands of the rich peasants liable for confiscation and allowed redistribution of land according to labor power. Like Qu and the Sixth Congress, he considered the redistribution a temporary measure and forbade the sale of land while encouraging collective farms. These measures caused a rich peasant, pro-Li party faction to flourish in Jiangxi.

Li's policies met with strong opposition on two fronts: from the Comintern, which had since the Sixth Congress decided on an anti-rich peasant policy that allowed the sale of land,[111] and from Mao, whose experience in running base areas had also brought him to a stronger stand against the rich peasants. The Comintern had already expressed a change of viewpoint in a letter of 7 June 1929.[112] This turn against the rich peasants coincided with Stalin's decision to liquidate the *kulak* (rich peasant) class in the Soviet Union. By September 1930, three months after Li's policy was proposed, the Comintern had already engineered changes which gave up the idea of state cooperatives, permitted the confiscation of all rich peasant land, and also allowed the purchase and sale of land.

Mao's reaction to Li Lisan's land policy was even prompter than that of the Comintern. A resolution adopted by groups under Mao's influence in June 1930 opposed Li's just-published land law with a thorough analysis of the counterrevolutionary nature of the rich peasants and the necessity for a vigorous policy in dealing with them.[113] Although this document was obviously not written by Mao, it is in line with the direction his land policy was taking and with the results of his investigations later in the fall. The Futian Incident of 8 December 1930 dramatized the antagonism which had developed between the pro-Li, pro–rich peasant faction of the Jiangxi Provincial Action Committee and the pro–Red Army, anti–rich peasant forces led by Mao. Eventually, when the Stalinist faction of Russian Returned Students (the "Twenty-eight Bolsheviks") developed their Chinese version of radical antikulakism, even Mao's policy was condemned as pro–rich peasant. By following a fairly constant course, Mao managed to be to the right of Qu Qiubai, to the right and left of the Sixth Congress, to the left of Li Lisan (in land policy only), and then to the right of the Twenty-eight Bolsheviks.

The Development of Mao's Land Policy

Mao's own land policy in Jinggangshan and later in Jiangxi shows the tension between his accumulating experience with land policy and his obligation to implement that of the Party Center. The basic principle of his land policy was distributive equality, and policy developments were by and large attempts to make this equalization more effective.

The primary documents for the study of Mao's Jinggangshan land policy are the report of 25 November 1928 and a "Jinggangshan Land Law" dated December 1928. As we have seen, in the report Mao discusses the alienating effect on the intermediate classes of confiscating all land; he had already changed that policy, presumably from September 1928 when new areas began to be acquired. But the land law, dated after the report, still stipulates that all land be confiscated. Since the law is claimed by Mao, we must assume that it is misdated.

The land law has some traits which are characteristic of Mao's approach to policymaking. The two most striking traits are the amount of discretion allowed to the local units in applying it and the equality of distribution. Almost every important stipulation lists one principal *(zhuti)* method or standard and one or more alternatives which could be used in special circumstances. The principal standard for land distribution was according to population with everyone counted equally. The justification for this standard (printed in the law) is that all need to live. Few families were without young or old, and those unable to do fieldwork were nevertheless still doing valuable work for the soviet. The alternative of giving those able to work twice as much land is also allowed. Another stipulation to be noted is that soldiers and officers in the Red Army and Red Guard, as well as workers in public organs, received shares of land and the government hired people to work it for them. The land law applied in Xingguo county in April 1929 differs from the Jinggangshan law in only one item: the restriction of confiscation to public and landlord land. True to current Party Center policy, neither law allowed the sale of distributed land.

The Xingguo version of the Jinggangshan land law was most probably the formal model for rural work until a new and much more detailed land law was promulgated in early 1930.[114] The new law provided for the confiscation of rich peasant land. Land and many other productive resources were to be distributed equally to all regardless of age or sex, including the dependents of reactionaries who remained in the village. All debts were canceled and a system of progressive taxation was established. The most innovative feature of this law is its principles of redistribution. The first principle of "taking from those who have much and adding to those who have little" *(chou duo bu shao)* is the basic adjustment for quantitative equality. The second principle, "taking from the fertile and adding to the infertile" *(chou fei bu shou)*, adjusts for a qualitative equality of holdings. With only the first principle, rich peasants were inclined to give away their worst fields and retain their best ones as their redistribution share. As Mao noted in his Xingguo Investigation, rich peasants have very good fields, buy only very good fields, and take only good fields as pawn. With the second principle in effect, there was real equality in landholdings. The major remaining inequalities were in farming abilities, labor power, and farm tools.

The two principles of redistribution both reflected and shaped a tendency of land reform to develop in three stages.[115] The first redistribution, done just after the insurrection, was usually characterized by irregularities caused by the initial village leadership. The second division usually attained quantitative equality. The third and most difficult division aimed at qualitative equality. Not all villages followed this three-stage pattern. Often qualitative equality was not achieved despite several divisions, but in one case the first division was qualitative. Sometimes land redistribution was completely outside this framework: the first land division in one locality gave young and old one and a half units, a policy which was criticized because it was based on traditional notions of filial piety.

Complications of Land Policy

Setting the guidelines for confiscation and redistribution of land did not by any means solve all land policy problems or exhaust Mao's leadership responsibilities in this regard. Important complications involving land policy developed from two sources: the inherent complexity of rural conditions and, more important, the disruption caused by land distribution itself.

The first complication resulted from the discovery that village productive resources were not simply fields. Thus the question of how to divide mountains from which cooking oil could be obtained, firewood sources, ponds (large and small), tea plantations, mulberry trees, and so forth was much more complex than any Party Central directive had imagined. Mao's principle was that all things which could be divided should be; but the specification of this principle led to many complicated sections of land laws and extra distribution committees in the villages. Moreover, the economic situations of individual villagers were more complex than the class designations in the laws suggested. This problem is especially evident in the family histories of Mao's eight informants in the Xingguo Investigation. The land reform was not an unmixed blessing for any of them, although they all profited more than they lost.

Not only did land redistribution sharpen the class struggle in the villages, but its complications created unexpected areas of contention. The major complication was caused by the intersection of the agricultural cycle by land redistribution. When a redistribution occurred at a time other than the winter months between fall harvest and spring fertilization, the question arose whether compensation should be given by the new owners to the previous owners for the work they had already invested in the current harvest. Those who lost land in the redistribution, generally the landlords and rich peasants, sought to mitigate their losses by demanding a share of the crop as compensation for their investment. The official policy was "No reimbursement: divide fields, divide shoots," but it is a symptom of the village-level power of the rich peasants that most villages actually gave a discounted reimbursement.

The question of how to divide planted fields was the greatest of the policy issues polarizing rich and poor peasants after redistribution was completed, but it was not the only one. The basic conflict was between the desire of the poor peasants to equalize all property and the relatively successful counterdrive of the rich peasants to limit the rural revolution to the more or less conceded matter of landownership.[116] The expressions of this conflict were not always obvious. For instance, after the land redistribution the rich peasants were opposed to allowing rental of land and the poor peasants were in favor of it. This reversal of traditional attitudes was caused by the following situation. After land was divided, many poor peasants and hired hands in particular did not have sufficient implements or manpower to work their expanded holdings. With their surplus productive power (tools and labor),[117] the rich peasants controlled an urgent seller's market, and they used the antirent propaganda of the communists against their newly land-rich, labor-poor, and tool-poor neighbors. If rent were allowed, the rich peasants preferred a sharecropping arrangement to a set rent, since their profit would not depend so much on intensive cultivation and more land could be rented and worked. The policy which Mao suggested as appropriate for this situation comes down squarely on the side of the poor peasant: first, arrange for the use of the surplus tools of the rich peasants by the poor; second, when land is rented to rich peasants, there is a set rent of not less than 50 percent of the normal harvest; third, no refusal to rent. The village government could forcibly distribute lands to be rented. This last item is a symptom of a serious difficulty in maintaining production. In the Jiangxi Soviet, prerevolutionary levels of production were not regained until 1933, and in November 1930 Mao notes the widespread problem of abandoned fields.[118] Certainly military devastation caused by the many shifts of the Red-White battlefront accounted for some of the lost production, but this experience helps explain Mao's policies after the Long March, which protect the rich peasant economy.

In general, complications necessitated a greater specification of Mao's land policy, but no new principles were added to the economic standard of thorough equalization of holdings and the political standard of reliance on mass struggle combined with a suspicion of rich peasants. This relative stability in land policy was soon upset by the arrival in Jiangxi of the Central Committee under the new leadership of the Twenty-eight Bolsheviks and the reconstitution of the Jiangxi Soviet as the Chinese Soviet Republic in 1931–1932. These developments left Mao still in charge of administering land policy—but a land policy formulated by party leadership and based on principles significantly different from those he had already evolved in base area work.

Conclusion

From 1927 to 1931, the development of Mao Zedong's political thought accompanied the development of his practical success as leader of a localized political-military force. Mao's first theoretical task was to explain the survival of his group after the disasters of 1927. As Mao developed the political-military strategy of base areas from his guerrilla experience, he produced more general norms for correct leadership. Finally, in the large and unfamiliar territory of the Jiangxi Provincial Soviet he faced more involved problems of revolutionary administration. Mao's leadership role during this period was unique: he was subordinated to central party leadership and at times his command was superseded by their plenipotentiaries, but usually his base area and military command were sufficiently remote from Shanghai to allow the comprehensive discretion necessary to the integrated guerrilla policies he developed.

It seems paradoxical that the period of greatest creativity in the development of Mao's politics should come at a time when he was most isolated from international and national politics and from the leadership of the CCP and Comintern. But the feeling of paradox stems mainly from the viewer's expectation of an intellectual source for an intellectual change. Mao's development of a rural revolutionary strategy was perfectly natural within the practical context of survival. Since Mao's political innovations were worked out as solutions to the practical problems at hand, he did not self-consciously assert their originality within communist theory. Indeed, given his subordinate position in the dogmatic hierarchy, it was to his advantage to avoid the appearance of originality. Mao claimed to be dealing with the actual problems of the base areas from an objective vantage point informed by experience and investigation. Thus, he argued, he had arrived at correct policies.

Mao's strategic innovations during this period were based on continuities in his political values. In the mobilization politics of the base areas one finds the same conviction of the supremacy of mass power which was first expressed in his May Fourth writings. In the 1928 "Report to the Central Committee" one finds the same concern for aggregating popular enthusiasm which underlies the 1919 "great union of the popular masses" proposal. Moreover, Mao's emphasis on practical effectiveness is very much in evidence during this period, the most obvious instances being his criticisms of idealist high-level leaders who were unconcerned about the effectiveness of their directives. The attention to revolutionary organization and ideology which was the basic development of the national revolutionary period of Mao's thought is also very much in evidence. Mao's moral demands on party members are classically expressed in the first part of the Gutian Resolution, and Marxist class analysis structures his investigations and policy. Despite the remoteness of the base areas, Mao was still operating within the framework of national and international party leadership. The two new organizations of the base area period, the Red Army and the soviet governments, were not organized with the same ideological and organizational discipline as the party, but with their more popular character they were expected to serve the same ends and observe the same principles.

The basic contribution of the early base area period to the development of Mao's thought is the practical combination of revolutionary populism and organization in a context of localized political-military hegemony. This combination led to the development of a rural revolutionary strategy outside the expectations of Marxist theory or CCP leadership. The apprehensiveness of Party Central leadership concerning Mao's activities in the countryside had some foundation: Mao's new strategy was not simply an application of existing theories to a new environment. His approach to policy and its correlative values constituted a new but latent paradigm for Chinese Communist politics.

Only Mao's success at developing a peasant movement out of his Jinggangshan beginnings has obscured the unique circumstances of base area construction. It was not the mixture of radical urban intellectuals and peasants of all classes which had produced the wildfire growth of the peasant associations in 1926–1927; the naivete of the first and the trust of the second were finally destroyed by the 1927 failures of the Autumn Harvest Uprising and the Canton Commune. Nor was it the smooth infiltration of the villages under the banner of national defense which characterized the Anti-Japanese War. In Jinggangshan and Jiangxi, military advantages of location, the partial politicization of the peasantry and the army through the Northern Expedition, and the exploitive structure of village life were all necessary elements of base area creation. Exclusive attention to any one of these factors would not have produced a viable base. Correspondingly, Mao's solution to the problem of survival in his protracted rural revolution was an undifferentiated emphasis on guerrilla warfare, political education, and egalitarian redistribution.

Not only was the Red Army necessary to the establishment of the base areas, but the militarization of politics within the base area was necessary for the survival of both the army and its base. Abstracting one-sidedly from this aspect of the base area situation, it is not too dissimilar from that of any major bandit or minor warlord, and Mao's chief innovation would appear to be the militarization of Chinese Communism.[119] Such an interpretation overlooks the equally esential role of political education in the base area. Not only the politicization of the military, but also the encouragement of the struggle of the lower classes in the villages, gave a specific political content to communist military power. The Red Army had political functions, and the enthusiasm of its erstwhile captives and the valor of peasant recruits depended on political motives. Particularly in the villages political education was the central task, because a consciousness of the structure of exploitation was necessary in order to move from the personal vendettas of the initial insurrection to a mass-participant system for continuing the revolution. Mao's approach to local political education was neither completely tutelary nor completely formal-democratic. Self-education through struggle was a more important vehicle than central administrative guidance. But Mao was not majoritarian in either an elective or a polling sense: elective assemblies were too malleable by opportunists,[120] and paying sole attention to the desires of the village majority of poor peasants could prove self-defeating. The aim of Mao's mass politics in the early base area period was not legitimacy but mobilized effectiveness. The legitimacy of his mass politics was guaranteed by his mobilization from the bottom of the social ladder in building his "overwhelming majority." Although this approach means that politics is determined by the interests of the last member of the coalition rather than by its core, it does not contravene the interests of the masses but attempts to realize their opportunities. The mobilization criterion for policy expresses a shift of attention in Mao's communism from problems of revolutionary legitimacy to those of mass leadership. His methodology of objective leadership through mobilization and his ethic of avoiding estrangement from the masses developed in conjunction with the new focus.

Political education and economic redistribution were intimately linked in the base area. We have seen that egalitarianism played a significant role in the army, but its most important arena was in land policy. The ultraegalitarianism of the primitive anarchists described by Eric Hobsbawm seems to have been absent, probably because of the army's role in the insurrections.[121] In Jiangxi, land division started out unequal and moved toward quantitative and qualitative equality. Presumably this equalizing process would involve a struggle between the land-losers and the land-gainers, but equal division should not produce a class war to the death since it provides for everyone. Although the early Jiangxi period was too short and unstable to bring to a head the conflict between the leveling tendency of distributive politics and the concentrating tendency of production economics, we can suppose on the example of Yanan and the People's Republic of China (and even of some later Jiangxi models described in the next chapter) that egalitarian distribution would have eventually required the formation of cooperatives in order to regain productivity. In Mao's view, egalitarian redistribution was the real end of oppression within the village. From this base the political-military revolution could continue.

4 Governing the Chinese Soviet Republic: 1931–1934

The transfer of CCP Central Committee leadership from its threatened headquarters in Shanghai to Mao's domain in southern Jiangxi so obviously affected the balance of power in the Jiangxi base that an equally important change in the basis of revolutionary strategy is usually neglected. This change is associated with the proclamation of the Chinese Soviet Republic (CSR) on 7 November 1931, the fourteenth anniversary of the Russian October Revolution. The rechristening of the Jiangxi Provincial Soviet elevated it to the status of a second sovereign power within China, an existing alternative to the KMT-controlled Republic of China. On a less implausible, but also unsuccessful level, it claimed to coordinate the efforts of the various dispersed soviets,[1] of which Jiangxi (or, more precisely, the Central Soviet) was the largest. In fact it was the government of an area centered in southern Jiangxi and including the border counties of western Fujian and perhaps a contiguous area of Guangdong.[2]

The peculiar character of the power relationships between Mao and the party leadership, and in particular between Mao and the disciples of Pavel Mif from Sun Yat-sen University in Moscow, who were known as the "Russian Returned Students"[3] or the "Twenty-eight (or 28½) Bolsheviks," is an important aspect of the political environment of the CSR. The idea of an open factional confrontation suggested by the term "power struggle" is incorrect.[4] Mao's critics were his party superiors whom he had to obey, and they in turn usually avoided denouncing Mao by name while they flailed his policies and friends. Mao had always been a faithful, if distant, subordinate of the Central Committee since 1927, and this relationship did not change with their arrival in Jiangxi. Moreover, the Twenty-eight Bolsheviks espoused the principle of collective leadership and division of responsibilities, rejecting explicitly the patriarchal style of Chen Duxiu and the personal hegemony of Li Lisan. Since both the Comintern and the Central Committee were eager to maintain some continuity in Jiangxi leadership, Mao was a natural choice as administrative head of the new soviet government. Nevertheless, the arrival of the party leadership in Jiangxi had transformed and restricted Mao's leadership role, and throughout the short history of the Chinese Soviet Republic there persisted basic divergences of style and politics between Mao and the Twenty-eight Bolsheviks, although these were not articulated by Mao into an explicit confrontation until the Zunyi Conference of January 1935, when he was elected chairman of the Politburo.

The Twenty-eight Bolsheviks gained ascendancy in Shanghai at the Fourth Plenum of the Sixth Central Committee in January 1931 on the strength of their opposition to Li Lisan and their Comintern connections. However, the situation in Shanghai began to deteriorate rapidly. Later in January, twenty experienced party cadres were arrested by the KMT,[5] and in April the KMT secret police scored a pivotal victory by capturing Gu Shunzhang, chief of security and liaison for the Central Committee. Gu divulged his vast knowledge of CCP personnel and operations to the KMT, thereby shattering the Central Committee's communications network. But the Central Committee had already decided to disperse itself to the soviet areas.[6] The Comintern adjusted to the shift away from the cities by declaring in July 1931 that the Chinese revolution ranked first among colonial movements because of the presence of the Chinese soviets and the Red Army.[7]

In Jiangxi, Mao's receptivity to the Central Committee's new attentions in 1931 must have been aided by their relatively mild reaction to the Futian Incident and by the recognition finally accorded to the importance of base areas. At first the transition went rather smoothly. Mao and Zhu De were members of the initial center control group, the Central Bureau. Most of 1931 was spent in defeating the Second and Third Encirclement and Suppression Campaigns. But in September the Central Committee issued a general critique of army and civil leadership in Jiangxi. The target, as this example makes clear, was obviously Mao:

> Narrow empiricism in the Red Army has had a profound influence on practical work. It negates Marxist-Leninist revolutionary theory

altogether, prompting one to view all questions from one's narrow, nearsighted experience. This is nothing but the backward ideology of the peasantry which will lead to the confusion of a nonclass line.[8]

This critical attitude toward the indigenous leadership was officially adopted by the First Party Congress of the Central Soviet Area in November 1931. The declaration of loyalty by the party in Jiangxi was part of the refounding of the Jiangxi base as the Chinese Soviet Republic. With the arrival of members of the Central Committee throughout 1932, criticism of the earlier leadership grew harsher.

The founding of the Chinese Soviet Republic was the result of optimism about the power of the soviets created by victories in the summer of 1931 and by the sudden availability of leaders of national and international stature. The pretensions of the CSR corresponded very well with the Stalinist background and proclivities of the Twenty-eight Bolsheviks. The political status of the CSR mirrored in the Chinese microcosm the relationship of the Soviet Union to the rest of the world. As was the Soviet Union under Stalin's "socialism in one country" formula, the CSR was simultaneously the government of a specific territory defending its people, the presumed leader of the oppressed masses throughout China, and China's model of the socialist future. As implausible as this self-understanding was, its ideological transformation of the Jiangxi Soviet from the perimeter of revolutionary politics to the showcase of properly communist policy set the ideological environment of Jiangxi politics. The strategy of survival which Mao had already developed was criticized as peasant opportunism and storybook military tactics.

The effect of the arrival of the Central Committee and the establishment of the CSR on Mao's leadership role in Jiangxi was enormous. From autumn 1931 to autumn 1932, Mao's responsibilities changed from comprehensive military and political leadership of a base area to the chairmanship of the CSR government. The functions of ideological, party, and military leadership of Jiangxi were successively assumed by the Central Committee leadership. This was not simply a reduction of scope of Mao's role. In the first place, his integrated approach was incompatible with the division of authority; moreover, the CSR as an administrative entity was quite different from the previous base area leadership.

The First National Soviet Congress held in Ruijin (capital of the CSR) in November 1931 passed a whole body of comprehensive legislation, and it was Mao's new task to implement the soviet law. The effect of the First Congress is well summarized in a pamphlet, *Soviet Political Power*, written in January 1932:

> The great achievement of this Congress has an exceptionally important significance in the history of the Chinese soviet movement. The Congress summarized the soviet's struggles, experience, and lessons over the past three or four years, pointed out earlier weaknesses and mistakes in the soviet movement, passed the constitution of the soviet as well as various laws, for instance the Labor Law, Land Law, Economic Policy, etc., and established the Chinese Soviet Republic. It set up the National Soviet Provisional Central Government, unified the leadership of the various soviet areas, and in this way encouraged the even more rapid forward development of the Chinese soviet movement.[9]

It is evident in this statement that although base area experience was not irrelevant, policy tasks would be defined by the new laws and administrative framework set up by the First Congress. As the chief administrator of this regime, Mao was charged with new duties of implementation. No longer was Mao's goal simply to maximize popular mobilization, and in fact there was a serious tension between the new administrative responsibilities and his previous ideal. The establishment of the CSR brought on a campaign to differentiate clearly at every level between the organization of the soviet government and that of the CCP.[10] The high expectations of the comprehensive legislation adopted by the First Congress placed an unbearable strain on Mao's government apparatus, a strain which inevitably led to the mortal sin of Jinggangshan—a systemic estrangement of officials from the masses.

In coping with the resulting leadership crisis, Mao began to develop mass-oriented leadership techniques which were extensions of his earlier political principles to the problems of permanent and large-scale government. His new approach of reinforcing and utilizing an active and integrated political climate at the local level by means of carefully guided mobilizational campaigns was attempted for the first and only time during the Land Investigation Movement of 1933. The reemergence of distinctively Maoist politics in the Land Investigation Movement was seen by the

Twenty-eight Bolsheviks as a challenge and as a derailment of their proletarian politics. Mao's position eroded rapidly in the first half of 1934, but with the loss of the CSR in July–October (which could hardly be blamed on Mao) and the beginning of the Long March, Mao launched an extensive critique of the military tactics of the Jiangxi leadership which was adopted by the party at the Zunyi Conference of January 1935. In 1936, at the other end of the Long March in Northwest China, Mao extended his critique of military tactics into a comprehensive attack on the politics of the Twenty-eight Bolsheviks.

In sum, Mao's political thought made major advances in the complex political situation of the CSR particularly in the areas of government and administration. But the political situation after 1931 prevented continuity in his base area politics. In fact, it changed Mao's leadership role from that of a distant subordinate with comprehensive discretion to that of a functionary under ideological supervision. Mao's theoretical development consequently was repressed and not on a par with practical policy advances. As chairman of the Politburo from 1935 Mao was expected to provide comprehensive leadership, and in great contrast to the CSR period he produced many theoretical overviews. But the Yanan writings were the triumph of Mao's political paradigm, not its creation.

Socialism in One Soviet: The Policies of the CSR

As chairman of the Central Executive Committee of the Chinese Soviet Republic, Mao was legal head of the Jiangxi government. All of its laws and pronouncements went out under his name and those of his cochairmen, Xiang Ying and Zhang Guotao. It is apparent, however, that Mao's personal responsibility for drafting many of these laws was negligible. Still, his was the job of realizing the policies promulgated under his name, and so they form the context of his activities from 1932 to 1934 and are of particular importance for the first year and a half after the First National Soviet Congress.

Internal Policies

The internal policies of the Jiangxi Soviet were first aimed at creating a model socialist government for the area under communist control—both for that area's sake and for the propaganda value such a model government would have for the rest of China. This self-conscious attitude of being a microcosm for China led those in charge of the First National Soviet Congress to formulate a whole battery of basic laws, a labor law, an election law, a land law, a statement on economic policies, and the like—all of which were disproportionate to the actual legal needs of the area administered. Moreover, the extreme ideological tension of Russia in the early 1930s was forcefully present in Jiangxi in the collective person of the Twenty-eight Bolsheviks, who both asserted and defended themselves in policymaking by a tendency toward doctrinaire formalism.[11] As a result, and with the aid of the active interest of the Comintern, the Russian-educated party leaders can be considered the principal authors of the organic laws of the CSR.

Unlike the slow evolution through practice of Mao's land law, many parts of the soviet laws sprang full-blown from the collective head of the party and remained to be tested and modified in practice. This process of "legislation first, then experience" could also be contrasted with the policymaking process which resulted in what Mark Selden calls the Yanan Way. This involved the collation and evaluation of the diverse practices of various anti-Japanese bases, the sifted experience of which was formulated into general procedures.[12]

Since others provide reasonably thorough descriptions of these major laws,[13] I will not duplicate their efforts here. However, several aspects of Mao's relationship to these laws are important matters for discussion. Despite the pretentiousness and inappropriateness of these laws in many respects, they were not merely for propaganda. In contrast to major sets of model legislation passed but mostly ignored by the KMT during the early 1930s,[14] these organic laws were, for better or worse, the effective policy guidelines. Even the Labor Law, a monument to the rights of the industrial worker written from Comintern stipulations, was effective enough in its inappropriateness to merit a significantly revised new law in October 1933 and an addendum on temporary labor on 20 February 1934. This was true of the other major laws and also of the soviet administrative structure, which underwent at least four major organizational changes in 1932 and 1933.

An extremely important aspect of the Land Law is that the basic principle of land distribution (and hence of local politics) changes from Mao's consistent target of equal distribution to one of elimination of the landlords, oppression of the rich peasants (that is, special distribution laws and only poor lands allotted), and equal distribution among the rest (or the middle peasants could elect as a group to abstain from distribution). Mao's ultimate egalitarian principle of the qualitative equalization of landholdings *(chou fei bu shou)* was attacked as a rich-peasant policy. The Stalinist inspiration of the antikulakism of the new land policy is obvious. Rather than viewing land policy as the key to rural mobilization, it is viewed primarily as an expression of class enmity[15] and class alliance. The penalization of the former oppressors did not stop with the new principles of distribution; they were constant targets of exceptional and vindictive treatment in the CSR. Rich peasants were for instance required to buy state bonds, and in late 1932 all able-bodied rich peasants were to be pressed into hard labor brigades. This harsh treatment made class identity an exceptionally important matter. Since there could be little effective central control over the appropriateness of classification, it is reasonable to speculate that classification gave lower-level soviet officials an awesome power over their neighbors which was debilitating for popular activism and for public criticism of officials. It also strengthened the desire of rich peasants to be classified as something else, and the numbers of "class alien elements" *(jieji yiji fenzi)* who hid among the ranks of the masses is attested to by the 13,526 landlord and rich peasant families who were discovered in July, August, and September 1933 during the Land Investigation Movement.[16] In general, the harsh treatment of rich peasants and landlords must have led to all manner of sub rosa personal politics and arrangements which had the effect of rendering the affairs of the base-level soviets opaque to the leadership. This is the type of separation of government levels and consequent loss of realism and mobilizational potential which Mao had sought to prevent at Jinggangshan with his more moderate land and class policy.

The divergence between Mao's preferred policy directions and the official ones formulated by the party leadership which he had to administer derived from a basic difference of political principle between himself and the Twenty-eight Bolsheviks. The latter position is well described by Mao in a work from December 1935:

> The advocates of closed-door tactics [the Twenty-eight Bolsheviks] say the above arguments for united front tactics are all wrong. The forces of the revolution must be pure, absolutely pure, and the road of the revolution must be straight, absolutely straight. Nothing is

correct except what is literally recorded in the Holy Writ. The national bourgeoisie is entirely and eternally counterrevolutionary. Not an inch must be conceded to the rich peasants. The yellow trade unions must be fought tooth and nail. If we shake hands with Cai Tingkai [leader of the Fujian Rebellion against Chiang Kaishek in 1933–1934], we must call him a counterrevolutionary at the same moment.[17]

Of course, during the CSR period Mao was neither so articulate in his opposition to the "leftist" line nor was he so convinced of its incorrectness. On the other hand, he was not its author, and the development of his administration during the CSR period tended to depart from the doctrinaire bureaucratic model supplied by the First National Congress and return to a locally based politics of mobilization. The undercurrent of conflict between Mao's mobilizational politics with its proclivity toward alliances and the ideology of regime purity guarded by the Twenty-eight Bolsheviks was, I think, the foundation for the political tension between the two.

The close relationship between the purity line and current Russian problems and Stalinist politics is clear. Stalin was interested in achieving a directed mobilization (industrialization) of a society where ideological and political control had been allowed to go to seed in the previous policy stage (the New Economic Policy). Within the Communist Party, Stalin wanted to consolidate a series of factional victories in order to establish personal hegemony. This dominant current in the Soviet Union affected Chinese soviet politics in many ways. Despite the vast difference in political situations between the USSR and China, the purity line seemed plausible. Not only was it necessary for the soviets to preserve their revolutionary identity in an unlikely and hostile environment, but there was now the opportunity to exercise local sovereignty provided by the first prolonged control of a fairly extensive base area. In retrospect, however, this line systematically tended to overemphasize or even absolutize the importance of the existing areas under communist control. The purity line thus led to an isolation of the soviets from their political and social surroundings, a tendency to overestimate the strength and potential of the soviets, and the overly defensive military posture which Mao devastatingly criticized in the Zunyi Resolution of January 1935.[18] The watershed between the class purity and the alliance lines is evidently the Zunyi Conference of January 1935.

External Policies

The basic determinant of external policies was the Chinese Soviet Republic's view of itself:

> From this day forth [1 December 1931] there will be two absolutely different states *(guojia)* within Chinese territory. One is the so-called Republic of China. It is the tool of imperialism, a government of the warlord, bureaucrat, and landlord classes used to oppress the laboring and miserable masses of workers, peasants, and soldiers. . . . The other is the Chinese Soviet Republic, a state of the broad masses of exploited and oppressed masses of workers, peasants, and soldiers. Its banners are: smash imperialism, destroy the landlord class, overthrow the KMT warlord government, set up a soviet government for all of China, fight for the interests of the several hundred million oppressed and exploited masses of workers, peasants, and soldiers and other exploited masses, fight for a genuine peace and the unity of the whole country.[19]

From this self-understanding it can correctly be assumed that the external policies of the Jiangxi Soviet were a peculiar type of "foreign policy." Its desired audience was the population under KMT control; its target was KMT foreign affairs; and the issues were matters which it could have little direct influence on, primarily China–Japan relations. In contrast to the conciliatory policies of the KMT, the communists maintained a constant and vociferous opposition to Japanese encroachments from the fall of 1931 (the "Mukden Incident") until the exit from Jiangxi in late 1934 as the "march north to fight Japan."

There were two major developments in the attitude of the Chinese Soviet Republic toward Japan. The first was its declaration of war against Japan on 15 April 1932. This bore no immediate relationship to armed hostilities. In fact, in the declaration Chinese soviet troops are cautioned to attack first "KMT troops in collusion with imperialism."[20] The declaration encourages spontaneous anti-Japanese mobilization within the soviets. The second development was a proposal of three conditions for a united front in January 1933. The three conditions were: cease invading the soviet; guarantee people's democratic rights; arm the masses and create volunteer troops to fight Japan. The proposal, which was addressed to "the citizens and soldiers of China," was a significantly greater external policy commitment on the part of Jiangxi.

Events were to prove that it was not completely in earnest. On 26 October 1933, a secret united front alliance was concluded between the communists and the Nineteenth Route Army of Cai Tingkai, which had defended Shanghai against the Japanese and was afterward given control over Fujian as part of a political deal to remove it from the sensitive areas around Shanghai. On 20 November, a revolt against Chiang Kai-shek was proclaimed by the Nineteenth Route Army, but within two weeks the Central Committee of the CCP had denounced the Fujian rebels for failing to undertake political reforms. No military action was undertaken by the Red Army to attack the flank and rear of Chiang's forces or to assist the Nineteenth Route Army directly. Instead, the main forces of the Red Army were transferred westward away from that battlefront. For various reasons the revolt was short-lived. There was probably a submerged difference of opinion on the handling of the Fujian Incident; Mao most likely favored a more cooperative attitude.[21] Fifteen days after the Central Committee's thorough denunciation, he sent a much more mildly critical telegram to Fujian. In the middle of January he sent a much more strongly worded directive (still not a denunciation), but by that time the end was near. After the defeat of the Nineteenth Route Army, Mao joined in the official denunciations. In the Zunyi Resolution, Mao observed that of course the rebels were not revolutionary, but cooperation with them would have been very useful in the Fifth Encirclement and Suppression Campaign.[22] However, a serious alliance policy would have been incongruous with the politics of the Jiangxi leaders.

Problems of Leadership

Although Mao was not responsible for the laws of the Chinese Soviet Republic, the individuality of his political thinking is shown in his letters and directives implementing them. Mao's administrative powers were evidently wide-ranging (one Central Executive Committee resolution summarily revises some sentences handed down by the Provisional Supreme Court)[23] and problems of implementation were enormous, so there was a broad field for the exercise and development of his leadership style. The chronic problem with administering the CSR's laws was that they postulated an extremely high level of political dedication for both cadres and masses. Some of Mao's directives deal with bringing the masses up to the level of the laws; others demand that cadres fulfill their responsibilities. Under the pressure of the Fourth and Fifth Encirclement and Suppression Campaigns, these rather ineffective methods were set aside and Mao initiated a series of mass campaigns and movements at the local level.

Mao elaborates his ideas on policy implementation in two letters dealing with the sovietization of new areas: one to Yuan Guoping on 6 March 1932 and another to western Fujian on how to administer the newly captured counties of Shanghang and Wuping.[24] The first letter is most interesting for its analysis of the rural situation; the second gives Mao's ideas on the implementation of soviet law in the cities. Although different in content, the messages are analogous.

Yuan Guoping was in despair over the backward state of the masses in the area under his control. Mao stresses that Yuan cannot abandon the general responsibility of winning over the masses, but he suggests that the work can be split into several steps in order to proceed more realistically. First the masses must be aroused against big landlords; then Yuan should quickly progress to the small landlords (and divide property and fields and abolish debts). "Once the relative majority of the poor masses have arisen" they should drive out the opportunist remnant of small landlords and rich peasants in the peasant association, setting up an organ of mass political authority (the village soviet) and a mass class group (the poor peasant association). Mao notes in the western Fujian letter that the rural revolutionary process should be prolonged only when necessary; this option does not permit cadre laxness (or rich peasant control) in the initial stages. Mao aptly abstracts the process:

> You need to proceed very realistically to understand the local situation and, on the basis of the local masses' sentiments and desires, determine an even more realistic strategy and method—then you can achieve even greater practical results.[25]

In the latter part of his letter to Yuan, Mao insists that the only local work which cannot be turned into a waste of time by the return of White forces is the organization of guerrilla units independent of production. With an even broader perspective in mind, Mao reminds Yuan to take into account the possibility that the enemy will advance before the landlords' power is destroyed.

In discussing the implementation of the Labor Law in the newly captured cities of Shanghang and Wuping, Mao notes three mistaken tendencies which have occurred elsewhere: the passive attitude of simply announcing the law and not checking on its implementation; working through coercive government orders against capitalists instead of through mass struggle, a method which leaves the masses passive and uncomprehending; and forcing measures which exceed local limits so that capitalists go bankrupt and economic policy is ruined instead of designing an appropriate method of implementation based on an investigation of local economic conditions and workers' livelihood. With this last problem, there resulted much unemployment and some workers began to collude with the capitalists. On the other hand, workers' interests should not be suppressed or ignored with the excuse of economic policy:

> In summary, the Labor Law should be implemented with the firm principles of protecting the workers' interests and not harming economic policy. In particular it should strengthen the workers' activism in class war and their support of soviet political power.[26]

It is evident that an alert cadre who investigates and is dedicated to mobilizing the masses would more naturally tend to avoid these mistakes than a Weberian functionary, no matter how dedicated. The point emphasized by the summary statement is the discretionary responsibility of the cadre for maximum achievement of the program as an integrated whole within the area of his leadership. Since achievement is realized through the strength of the mobilized masses, the "sentiments and desires" of the masses must codetermine (through investigation) the content of policy and the course of implementation.

In two general directives issued to provincial congresses in the first half of 1932,[27] Mao reiterates his view of implementation of soviet law, defines mistaken tendencies, and indicates several aids for correcting them. The relationship of law and mobilization is well stated in the first directive:

> Your congress should make developing revolutionary war the heart of all your work. First, you should discuss all sorts of concrete policies for actually mobilizing the masses. The most important aspect of this mobilizational work is to develop struggle and to deepen

struggle. In order to raise the struggle activism of the worker and peasant masses, you need to effectively implement the Labor Law, Land Law, etc. The congress must propose very concrete programs for implementing the Labor Law and Land Law.[28]

The mistakes previously found in these provinces were separation from the masses *(toli qunzhong)*, formalism, bureaucratism, corruption, and passive resistance. The means of preventing or correcting these mistakes are a work review at the congresses with merciless *(wuqing di)* criticism of mistakes, the establishment of inspection teams under experienced and reliable party members (working with the broad masses and mass organizations), and most importantly the consolidation of a truly representative system in local government organizations.

Basically, Mao was demanding that his subordinates in the soviet government maintain the mobilizational ideals of closeness to the masses, policy integration, and flexible leadership despite the government's bureaucratic structure and their official function of implementation. Correct cadre behavior still meant for Mao situational aptness—a standard which requires flexibility and revolutionary commitment and which produces an undifferentiated objective result. The organizational givens of an implementational bureaucracy necessarily lead to a different definition of correct cadre behavior—namely, the successful application of the laws one is charged to enforce within one's administrative sphere. Administrative discipline and control require that areas of official competence be simplified through specialization, and with a specified organizational position it is difficult to maintain an active sense of a larger revolutionary responsibility. Mao's general task in these documents of the first half of 1932 is to show his cadres how mobilizational goals could and should be achieved within the CSR framework. His growing frustration with government cadres stemmed from the fact that achieving both kinds of correctness simultaneously demanded exceptional talent and dedication.

Crisis in Leadership

Mao's dissatisfaction with personnel and behavior in the soviet governments occurred in a context of rapidly intensifying demands on governmental performance. The vitality and military successes of the various soviets, most notably the Jiangxi Soviet and the Eyuwan Soviet under Zhang Guotao, had the effect of sharpening the struggle between the KMT and the communists. Chiang Kai-shek decided to invest a major part of his military strength in extirpating the major communist bases. The Fourth Encirclement and Suppression Campaign—which began in June 1932, defeated the Eyuwan Soviet in November 1932, and was stopped in March 1933—was, viewed positively, an opportunity for a much more significant communist victory. Viewed negatively, it was an unprecedented resource-consuming threat to the existence of the CSR. Even if the institutional governmental structure had been functioning effectively in normal times, these new and to some extent reorienting demands would have necessitated extraordinary measures. As it was, the new obligations seem to have exacerbated the constitutional weaknesses of the lower levels of government, leading to two important campaign failures in the fall of 1932: local elections and urgent mobilization for war. Mao's analyses of these failures led to a major respecification of his mass-line, mobilizational politics.

Mao's call on 20 September 1932 for new elections at all levels of local government was a frontal attempt to correct the insufficiencies of soviet administration.[29] After almost a year of laws and directives, Mao states that "there have appeared many leadership weaknesses and mistakes in leading and developing the central responsibility of revolutionary war." Mao lists military mistakes (lack of rear-area support) and political mistakes—the presence of cadres who are alien class elements and follow a "non-class line" *(fei jieji luxian)*, bureaucratic corruption, a command style *(mingling fangshi)*, forcing the masses, and passivity on special treatment to Red Army dependents and women's rights. Mao's solution is that local governments should have constant renewal through elections which would "wash out" bad cadres and "absorb and attract" new activists.[30] It is expressly stipulated that the old methods of peaceful elections and avoidance of struggle are to be discarded. Elections were ordered for all levels in eleven counties and for certain levels in nine more.

The "Urgent Mobilization for War"[31] issued two weeks later was not critical of local performance, but it demanded a whole range of war-related activities from government officials. The call was for a presumably short-term "total mobilization," since the KMT's fourth attack was pictured as their last-ditch effort. The first point of the mobilization was the holding of local meetings to explain to the workers and peasants what mobilization meant to their own futures. Certain immediate measures were then to build upon the enthusiasm awakened by this understanding: expansion of the Red Army, preparing cadres to send to new areas, immediate collection of the land tax, preparing for effective mass struggle against invading White armies, and destroying city walls. At the end is a statement reminiscent of Jinggangshan that "all life and activity should be militarized." Mao's exhortations fell on deaf ears. The 5 December 1932 issue of the major Jiangxi newspaper, *Red China*, contained long statements by Mao on the election and mobilization campaigns, announcing that each had been a complete failure, analyzing mistakes, and giving new directions for work.

In "On the Inspection of the Election Movement at All Levels," dated 1 December 1932, Mao declared the elections a total failure, noting that not one county had completed its elections, there was no struggle, and the election code had not been followed.[32] The basic problem was that "there was no reform of consciousness through politics,"[33] and this failure made the existing bureaucratism even more apparent. It was therefore determined that all incorrect elections were void and should be held again. To prevent a repetition of the failure, Mao gave detailed instructions for making the reelection a "broad mass political mobilization." This mobilization was to be achieved by emphasizing to the masses that only if they are active will they get an effective government and by going beyond the election code and utilizing assemblies to criticize former representatives and government work. The masses should criticize rich peasants and class alien elements and elect oppressed elements, but only those with ability and the confidence of the masses. These new directives were supposed to be carried out strictly, with the help of work teams and inspectors.

Mao's report on the failure of the urgent mobilization, "On Mobilization for War and Work Styles" (29 November 1932), is similar to the call for reelections, although it pays less attention to specific failures than to the general bad effects of bureaucracy.[34] The basic mistakes of the mobilization were a disregard for the seriousness of the enemy's attack and a bureaucratic style in all types and levels of soviet work. Mao criticizes bureaucratism at length:

Bureaucratism is estrangement from the masses. It destroys the relationship between the soviet and the masses. It is a great danger to the success and development of the soviet. The major symptoms of bureaucratism are perfunctoriness and coercion through issuing orders. This absolutely cannot be permitted to exist within the soviet government.[35]

Bureaucratism expresses itself in the organizational faults of not understanding mobilization (and hence an inability to mobilize successfully), of giving orders to lower levels without facing the problem of implementation, of coercing the masses because of the absence of explanatory assemblies, and of avoiding mobilization because it is unpleasant. To this bureaucratic style Mao opposed a "new Soviet work style" in fourteen points, which is one of the most thorough operationalizations of his mobilization politics of the Jiangxi period. The main points are these:

1. All work should be built on the foundation of mobilizing the masses. Whoever rejects the work of mobilizing the masses necessarily estranges himself from the masses.

2. In executing laws and resolutions one shouldn't simply rely on orders. One must still rely primarily on raising mass consciousness and ardor to support the execution of the law....

4. In mobilizing the masses, use various kinds of soviet organizations and all mass organizations....

6. In executing orders, pay attention to methods of mobilizing the masses, but at the same time attention should also be paid to opinions among the masses in order to have a referent for determining practical measures....

10. Guidance given to lower levels should be practical and concrete....

11. Organize work teams *(gongzuotuan)* to directly aid lower levels. The responsibility of the work team is to do good work in the locality, not to make empty criticisms of people while the work team itself does no work.....[36]

It is remarkable that Mao's suggestions for war mobilization are concerned not with the supply of men and material for defense purposes but with the behavior of government officials. That he is serious about reshaping this behavior is indicated in the concluding sentence, in which he orders every level of soviet "to call a meeting immediately upon receiving this resolution to review its own work using the spirit of criticism and self-criticism *(ziwo piping)*, to oppose all mistakes in work, and to concretely determine ways of implementation. The results of the discussion should be reported to the center."[37]

The inadequacies of the local election and war mobilization campaigns constituted a peculiar kind of leadership crisis for Mao as chairman of the Chinese Soviet Republic. They are important failures stemming from basic dysfunctional behavior of government officials, and yet the appropriate solutions are familiar principles of Mao's Jinggangshan politics. Mao's criticisms of the feudal, authoritarian habits of officials in "The Struggle in the Jinggang Mountains" and his description of the relationships between government levels in the Gutian Resolution are evidently confronting the same phenomena. The root problem of estrangement from the masses, which cuts the revolutionaries off from the source of their vitality, seems to have become a characteristic of government activity in the CSR. To say that Mao "allowed this to happen" is unfair to the continuity of his personal political values, and yet the failures of Autumn 1932 were his responsibility.

The most plausible conceptualization of this leadership crisis is that it was predominantly an organizational role failure rather than a personal one. Mao was in charge of a bureaucracy with an overly ambitious battery of orders, a diffuse recruiting system, and inadequate training and control. The Twenty-eight Bolsheviks faced similar Weberian hells by attempting to impose order, discipline, and scientific division of labor.[38] But throughout the CSR documents we have considered, Mao takes the very different approach of exhorting and commanding officials to balance legal demands and concrete situations in a framework of mobilizational activity.[39] The discord between these behavioral expectations and the prescribed organization made Mao's commands unrealistic. Government cadres tended to become bureaucrats in the hierarchical system even though the directives they were supposed to implement were written to counter that tendency. Mao's demands reached an ultimate point in the election movement when he insisted, in effect, that people who were chronically bad leaders administer an election whose effectiveness would be judged by their self-elimination.[40] The miserable failure of the elections can be said to have resulted from a type of "commandism" on Mao's part. That is, the formalities of organization—the cadres' responsibility and his own authority—blinded him to the impossibility of a successful implementation of his order. If mass mobilization was to be the basis of the regime (and Mao's criticisms are based on this assumption), then the regime itself would have to approach the masses organizationally and adopt an issue-centered political process of campaigns with minimal centralization of authority. This strategy was tried on a large scale for the first time (and only time in Jiangxi) in the Land Investigation Movement.

The Land Investigation Movement

Throughout fall, winter, and spring of 1932–1933, there were a myriad of campaigns in the soviet area—hygienic campaigns, attempts to get government agencies to save for the war effort,[41] continual exhortations to buy government bonds, constant appeals to join the Red Army. The main campaigns focused on the three most basic needs of the CSR in its hard-pressed situation: direct support of the military effort (chiefly Red Army recruitment and improvement of local militia), fund-raising (chiefly through a series of three government bond drives), and agricultural production and its distribution. Despite the importance of the first two campaign foci, we will devote our attention to the third. After the "urgent mobilization for war," problems of military support remain in the forefront (particularly during the Red May recruitment drive of 1933), but Mao does not seem to have been directly responsible for this effort. The bond campaign was more directly in his area, but it is well described by Trygve Lötveit in his study and its complexity exceeds its significance for our purposes. The concern with agriculture, however, led to new attentiveness to local politics which culminated in a comprehensive local-level political mobilization led by Mao: the Land Investigation Movement *(cha tian yundong)*.

Since agriculture provided the only renewable resource available to the Jiangxi government, there was considerable pressure to make the harvest as good as humanly possible. The most ambitious attempt in this direction was a "plant early" movement announced by Mao on 28 December 1932.[42] The idea of this effort was to advance the entire agricultural calendar by one month to enable double-cropping. Judging from discussions of a severe food problem in the summer of 1933, this campaign was a failure.[43] The more general movement was for a "Bolshevik spring planting," which included a field investigation *(cha tian)*, propaganda about the individual as well as the general benefit of increased production, encouragement of production competitions and "attack teams" *(tuji dui)*, establishment of all sorts of cooperative efforts, and productive use of spare time by party units in agricultural pursuits.[44] The "field investigation" segment was supposed to be undertaken in old soviet districts to make sure that all the benefit of the land revolution went to the masses in order to increase their productive spirit.[45] Despite publicity throughout the spring—including one optimistic report on a locality entitled forebodingly "Who Will Compete with Them?"—the movement was given a quite critical evaluation by Bo Gu on 8 April.[46] Although there was praise for the army's efforts, party and government organs were criticized for not doing enough. The cooperative movement was just starting and the unions were not yet functioning. Evidently this mid-movement report failed to change its course, for problems related to agricultural production continued. In late May, Mao and Hu Hai made a report on the failure of the Land Investigation Movement to the Central Bureau (Zhongyang Ju) which induced the party leadership to announce a new and thorough Land Investigation Movement to be executed by the Central Government (Zhongyang Zhengfu) under Mao's leadership.[47] The lengthy and specific resolution by the Central Bureau did not, however, give Mao a free hand with the direction and content of the movement.[48]

Many of the hallmarks of the movement as it was developed by Mao are already included in the Central Bureau document.[49] First, it is a movement to develop village class war, thoroughly solve the land problem, clean out feudal and semifeudal elements (destroying landlords but not rich peasants), and raise hired hand and poor peasant consciousness, activism, and organizational strength. It is also emphasized that the masses be mobilized as broadly as possible through all popular organizations, particularly the labor unions and poor peasant associations. It should involve active, critical elections where mass views are expressed freely. Finally, it should be closely linked with the complete reform of party and soviet work. This resolution differs from Mao's statements at several points. First is its emphasis on earlier policy mistakes of the party as a cause of the inadequacy of land reform, pointedly mentioning Mao's "trim the fat and add to the lean" *(chou fei bu sou)* policy. More important, it emphasizes the leadership role of the hired hands through their unions, whereas Mao placed primary emphasis on the poor peasant associations. But the most pervasive difference is Mao's concentration on the process of implementation.

Mao's general statement on the movement, "Execute a Broad and Deep Land Investigation Movement,"[50] was written on 1 June, the day before the Central Bureau's resolution, but it was not published in *Red China* until 20 June. This delay in itself shows considerable finesse on Mao's part, because it was appropriate for this document to emphasize the general need for thorough land reform (judged inadequate in 80 percent of the Jiangxi Soviet, inhabited by more than 20 million people, including fifteen whole counties and parts of nine others). However, Mao first wanted to develop the movement intensively in an eight-county area. It was thus better for the movement's dynamics to publish it in the midst of reports on the eight-county effort rather than before the Eight-County Conference was announced. Many of the movement's organizational peculiarities are specified in the document of 1 June. First, the centrality of the Land Investigation Movement is guaranteed by giving the chairman of each level's soviet overall responsibility for the movement. Not only are various land, legal, and security organs told to exert their whole strength for the movement, but less directly related organs (for instance the People's Military Committee, with responsibility for local defense and Red Army recruitment) are told to build their efforts on the momentum of the movement. Despite governmental involvement in the movement, one of its functions is "washing out" bad officials and admitting new activists. Second, the poor peasant associations are specified as the most important mass organization in the movement.[51] Mao does not mention the unions, although he does call on "workers' groups" *(gongren xiaozu)* to be active leaders in the poor peasant associations. Third and most interesting is the attention paid to phasing and coordination. The most important aspect of this emphasis has been mentioned already—namely, the general phasing of the movement by starting with only eight counties. On a local level, it is recommended that the movement commence with the most backward locality. Coordination is to be achieved through short training sessions given by model districts; it is to be maintained by periodic work review meetings, monthly at the county level and every ten days at the district level.

From 18 June to 21 June 1933, Mao held a meeting of responsible persons of district rank and above from eight selected counties to discuss the Land Investigation Movement. Mao delivered a report and concluding remarks at this conference, both of which specified in greater detail the expected course of the movement. These were immediately reprinted in *Red China*, as were other documents and news (not all favorable) relating to the eight-county effort throughout the summer.[52]

Mao's report is divided into three sections: the first on why and where the movement is necessary, the second on large-scale mobilization as the first step in the movement, and the third on basing the development of the movement on differences in class struggle among localities. In the first section Mao presents categories for classifying soviet territory in terms of success in land revolution and also gives a plausible explanation of why so many long-held areas are still "relatively backward" in this respect. The three types of areas are new, relatively backward, and deeply penetrated; the respective land strategies are confiscation and distribution, inspection, and reconstruction (concentration on production).[53] The reason Mao gives for so much soviet territory remaining relatively backward is that during the first land revolution many rich peasants became revolutionaries and gained control of the movement because they could read and write. They were well rewarded (or rewarded themselves well) in the first division, but as the revolution was consolidated and more systematic divisions were carried out, the purpose of the soviets clearly diverged from their class interests and they became hidden reactionary and even counterrevolutionary elements. Mao claims that if these elements were not rooted out by land and class investigation, the masses would lose their revolutionary activism. In the second section, Mao gives everyone a concrete place to begin their own contribution to the movement by stressing popular mobilization. He then discusses cadre education—an important point for his audience of intermediate-level officials, since one of their chief tasks is to inform and inspire base-level cadres. The first aspect of education is proper and sufficient information; the second is short classes on movement problems run by advanced areas; the third (introduced by Mao as "a type of education which should occur during activity") is regular work inspections. The final section of Mao's report deals with the variety of local conditions. Not only are there three categories of counties, but there are relatively backward and relatively advanced districts, townships, villages, and families, which should not all be treated the same way. In general the procedure at each level should be to draw models from the advanced but concentrate work on the backward.

Mao's concluding remarks at the Eight-County Conference are evidently a summary of three days of intensive discussion, but there are few changes in his description of the movement which are not mainly the addition of detail to earlier points. The most significant innovation is that now it is recommended that the county, district, and township levels have a land investigation committee for general leadership. The additional detail supplied in the concluding remarks is interesting and significant (for instance, the importance of getting mass approval before confiscating in order to avoid clan wars). But the major utility of the conference was not in redefining the movement: it was the involvement and education of a great number of intermediate leaders through their experience of discussing the movement in concrete detail.

The sense of creative participation in the Land Investigation Movement which was stimulated by the Eight-County Conference was sustained by Mao's manner of supplying direction in the most delicate aspect of the movement—namely, the standards for determining individual class membership. The definition of classes was extremely important because the Land Investigation Movement was expressly a class war, and the dividing line between enemies and friends was the demarcation between rich peasants and middle peasants. Middle peasants were the protected allies of the masses; rich peasants were semifeudal elements to be weakened but not destroyed. An analysis by Mao entitled "How to Differentiate Classes" was published in *Red China* along with his concluding remarks on 29 June.[54] This analysis was a concise description of each class and its major components, but it did not attempt to supply the detail necessary for complicated judgments. Instead on 23 July the basically good work of Huangsong district in Ruijin county was reviewed, and ten incorrect decisions were described in detail with the original and the correct decision. A fully developed directive on class analysis was not supplied until October 1933.

In August a new phase of the Land Investigation Movement began with Mao's "Preliminary Summary of the Land Investigation Movement," published 29 August.[55] The movement had established its character during the summer. The new phase attempted to consolidate the movement by describing its successes and characteristic faults and abstracting detailed rules for class differentiation from the experience of the movement. This phase lasted until 1934, when Mao was heavily criticized by the party leadership and the movement was entrusted to Zhang Wentian, who promptly radicalized it.[56]

All three aspects of the consolidation phase of the movement —praise of models, criticism of errors, and stipulation of new rules —are present in the "Preliminary Summary." First the general success of the movement is noted:

> With the urging of the Party and the Central Government, the Land Investigation Movement has already developed broadly. If it is said that formerly the Land Investigation Movement was barely at the starting point, now one month's work in July after the June Eight County Land Investigation Conference has already exceeded the results of the half-year of work since winter. In general the Land Investigation Movement took on a new form in the eight participant counties. The Land Investigation Movement has already become a broad mass movement.[57]

After establishing the general context of success, Mao describes in detail a model district, Rentian, which moved from being backward to being "first class" in fifty-five days. In discussing its success, Mao not only details the numbers of landlords and rich peasants discovered, amount of land redistributed, and other direct goals of the movement. He also indicates that the movement spurred the district to success in other campaigns: over seven hundred persons volunteered for the Red Army (without a single desertion), and there was remarkable progress in bond buying, culture, and party membership. The reasons for this general success were first that the district realized the importance of the movement and then three aspects of implementation: its mobilization method of starting with the most backward areas, its correct class line, and its excellent attention to mass work.[58]

After presumably encouraging his audience with stories of successes, Mao proceeds to the deficiencies and mistakes in the movement. He observes that some party units ignore movement directives and that unless the party took it seriously the movement would fail. Most errors in the movement were of two types: rightist excesses, ranging from protective misclassification to actively repressing revolution, and leftist excesses of terrorizing middle peasants and treating rich peasants like landlords. Mao calls for a "thought struggle" *(sixiang douzheng)* within the party against the "left opportunism" of ultraseverity in the movement.[59] Mistakes against middle peasants should be publicly confessed and rectified. Criticism of officials should be neither too passive nor too fierce, and persons with a bad class background should not be removed if their work is good. Mao's discussion of methods of implementation generalizes his praise of Rentian's success. On the one hand, cadres should not be "tailists" *(weiba zhuyi)* but should go after the most backward places. On the other hand, everything should be done through the masses and commandism should be avoided. The poor peasant associations should be true mass organizations rather than enlarged party organizations (for instance, membership should not require an introduction), but the principle of hired hand leadership should not be ignored.

Another aspect of the consolidation of the Land Investigation Movement was the attempt to coordinate its hitherto uneven development. The unevenness of development had been consciously promoted by the initial emphasis on eight counties; this had served the purposes of providing a model, developing experience, and limiting an organizationally demanding experiment to a manageable arena. By September the eight counties were developing their own advanced problems. Experience had already improved the guidance of the movement, and more trained personnel were available.

The document most characteristic of the consolidation phase of the Land Investigation Movement is the lengthy "Resolution on Some Questions in the Land Struggle," issued 10 October 1933.[60] This document was written for problems which were too complex for the relatively simple class definitions of "How to Analyze Classes." Some of these complexities were equivocal cases where rules for adjudication were clearly needed—for instance, how to handle cross-class marriages. However, most of the quality of the resolution derives from its attempt to codify from movement experience a realistic class equity for rural conditions. True to the tendencies of his earliest Jinggangshan land law, Mao avoids categorical distinctions which are easy to legislate but impractical to enforce. He attempts in this document to specify and even quantify the meaning of terms like "significant exploitation," "major occupation," and "well-off middle peasant." This attempt at specification leads inevitably to a depth of detail in the resolution which would have been indigestible at the beginning of the Land Investigation Movement but must have come as a welcome standardization to cadres facing a variety of borderline cases with a set of well-understood but simple definitions. Since the easiest thing to do was to classify an exploiter who worked as a rich peasant[61] and an exploiter who did not as a landlord, many provisions of the resolution are definitions of acceptable amounts of exploitation, work, and related details which were to the advantage of middle peasants threatened by rich peasant classification. Even with the detail provided, considerable latitude is allowed in extenuating circumstances with the consent of the masses. The controlling principle is the effect of a decision on the masses and their allies:

> This type of evaluation of circumstances must be 100% precise. It should not call a well-off middle peasant a rich peasant, because that makes the middle peasants dissatisfied. But at the same time it should not call a rich peasant a well-off middle peasant, because that makes the poor peasants dissatisfied. Therefore it should be a careful evaluation and it should receive mass approval.[62]

The effect of the resolution was a new bias toward litigiousness in favor of middle peasants. This bias evidently dampened the original enthusiasm of the movement and prompted many demands for redress for earlier alleged leftist excesses. At the Fifth Plenum of the CCP Central Committee held in January 1934 in Ruijin, Mao and his resolution were blamed for this state of affairs. The criticism of the resolution was that it replaced the investigation of class *(cha jieji)* with the calculation of class *(suan jieji)*,[63] it diverted cadres from continuing to develop the movement, and it provided opportunities for counterattacks by rich peasants and landlords. Nevertheless, with some significant modifications (no classifications prior to the movement could be changed; no changes could be made unless the masses doubted their earlier verdict) Mao's document remained the standard for correct classification. But in propaganda and spirit, the spring 1934 phase of the Land Investigation Movement under Zhang Wentian achieved a reradicalization with its sweeping slogans and criticisms of Mao's rules. This new radicalization developed to the point that in June Zhang Wentian had to issue new condemnations of left extremism.[64]

The pattern of Mao's guidance of the Land Investigation Movement shows a recognition of the ineffectiveness of the commandist leadership style, which he had shared with other communist leaders, and the adoption of a mass-line leadership style in guiding the movement's cadres. First a clear and simple picture of the movement was given; then, in the Eight-County Conference, the cadres were encouraged to involve themselves in the elaboration of the campaign's purpose. The initial efforts of the cadres were directed at the most backward units, where the greatest rate of progress could be expected and slight mistakes would do the least harm. Individual cases of success and failure and instances of correct and incorrect classification were described in detail. Finally, in August, the consolidation began with the evaluation of results, identification of general errors, and stipulation of standards. The reassertion of central control in consolidation went beyond merely coordinating local efforts, but it also avoided the extreme of taking them over. The October resolution in particular used the general experience of the first phase of the movement to create a unified and detailed scheme of class equity. It represented a significant advance in class policy which would not have been possible without the variety of spontaneous experience which had informed it. Together with "How to Differentiate the Classes," the resolution became a classic of the communist rural revolution; in 1947 and 1948 both statements were republished with commentary as directives for the national land reform.[65]

The Effects of Popular Mobilization

The Land Investigation Movement was by far the most important arena of Mao's renewed politics of popular mobilization, but the resurgence can also be seen in his other writings of 1933. Mao's foreign policy statements began in late 1933 to stress that the CSR was a state where poor people ruled themselves. His writings on the bond campaigns emphasized that not only was commandism in the sale of bonds bad in itself but it was less effective than propaganda and the stimulation of voluntary contributions.[66] In a long report on economic reconstruction in August 1933, the themes of popular mobilization and integrated politics are prominent. Mao identifies Bolshevization with "massification" *(qunzhong hua)* and juxtaposes them to bureaucratism and commandism, noting that commandism looks successful at first but its results cannot be consolidated.⁶⁷ Against those who would postpone serious economic work until after the defeat of the Fifth Encirclement and Suppression Campaign, Mao claims that even war preparations would suffer if everything else were neglected for their sake. He emphasizes instead a self-conscious integration of land investigation, labor law implementation, elections, cultural work, military work, and economics.

It was at the local level that popular mobilization and policy integration were to be combined. In December 1933, Mao investigated two model township governments and reported on them in detail. The description is reminiscent of the Xingguo Investigation in style, but the content is quite different, since this locality is a thoroughly transformed society.

The investigation of Changgang is most like the Xingguo Investigation in its introduction, since it inveighs against cadres at higher levels of soviet government who know nothing about the actual content of local level work and thus "are not able to truly solve the problem of 'making all soviet work serve the needs of revolutionary war.'"⁶⁸ What is new in the introduction is Mao's self-confident formulation of the basic policy problem and process:

> Our tasks have already been put forward; from expanding the Red Army to repairing roads and bridges, many plans have been announced. The problem is how to mobilize the masses to really and completely execute these tasks and plans. An extraordinarily tense revolutionary war demands that we solve this problem quickly and generally. But the solution to this problem is not something to be thought out within our brains. It depends on novel and concrete experience collected in the process of mobilizing the masses for executing all kinds of tasks. This experience should be developed and used to expand our scope *(lingyu)* of mass mobilization so that it corresponds to even higher tasks and plans.
>
> Presently in many local soviet organs duties are discharged in a perfunctory manner, and the serious mistake of coercive directives exists. These are 100% bad for the relationship of soviet to masses and greatly obstruct the fulfillment of soviet responsibilities and plans. On the other hand, there are numberless working comrades in lower-level soviets in various localities who have created many good methods of mobilizing the masses. They are one with the masses, and their work brings great results. One type of responsibility of higher soviet officials is to gather and rationalize *(zhengli)* this good experience and disseminate it over a broad area. This

type of work should be started immediately in every province and in every county. The most effective method of combating bureaucracy is to give them living models.[69]

Changgang is an exceptionally good "living model" because of its proliferation of grass-roots organizations, its mass work style, and its excellent results in most campaigns. Mao describes Changgang in detail—organizations, responses to various campaigns, cooperative activities, and changes in life and prices since the revolution. It is not an example of the Land Investigation Movement's success in exposing class enemies and strengthening proletarian consciousness, since only a modest number (six) of class alien elements were uncovered and Mao notes that only one in ten inhabitants understood what "leadership of the workers" meant. Organizationally, however, Changgang had an exceptionally well-developed and well-run government apparatus. The representative assembly met frequently in well-run meetings; there were work reports every other meeting. Each representative was in charge of fifty inhabitants. The township had fifteen committees which were composed of the heads of corresponding village committees. Special groups like the election committee (for the Second National Congress) and the women's association were also functioning, though a bit too placidly for Mao's tastes. The peculiarity of Changgang's work style was that it was "able to use its whole strength to mobilize the masses and also use the greatest patience in persuading the masses."[70] As a result, Changgang was able to better the lot of its inhabitants, meet all its quotas and campaign responsibilities, and achieve an increase in harvest in 1933 despite a tremendous loss of manpower to the Red Army.

Caixi, the second township discussed, was the best in the CSR in setting up cooperatives and was also exceptional in Red Army recruitment.[71] Eighty-three percent of the men in Caixi were volunteers. Mao attributes this militancy to three aspects of Caixi's military effort: propaganda instead of coercion, special treatment of Red Army families, and solid and well-trained local forces. The district's most impressive accomplishments were in economics, where production, consumer, and food cooperatives made possible substantial improvements despite the drastic reduction in the male work force.[72] Although most fieldwork in 1933 was done by women, production was 10 percent above prerevolutionary output due to active agricultural cooperatives dating back to 1930.

There were fourteen consumers' cooperatives in the district giving dividends to members and 5 percent discounts to Red Army families. The food cooperative, which started in 1930 as a government bureau, was important in stabilizing the price and availability of grain. As a result, a thirty-item price comparison showed indigenous produce mostly at or below prerevolutionary prices. Because of the tightening KMT blockade, however, exports had collapsed and prices of imports, particularly salt, had risen drastically.

These two investigations of December 1933 are worthy additions to Mao's series of rural surveys beginning with the Hunan Report. They originate from the same conviction that the really important policy level is the basic level at which policies are applied, and with rural policies the basic level is the village. They also have the same motive of politics through investigation. Mao's descriptions of rural dynamics make certain policies or policy orientations seem self-evident and necessary rather than debatable alternatives. Objectivity and comprehensiveness—but not detachment—are investigative virtues for Mao. In the Changgang and Caixi cases, the policies demonstrated by description to be correct are numerous tenets concerning mass mobilization and integrated policy. But these investigations are unique in that they are the first studies to show the results of correct and established revolutionary policies. The description is not dominated by the event of the oppressed overthrowing the oppressors; rather it concentrates on effective forms of self-rule of the masses.

Summarizing the Jiangxi Experience

The beginning of 1934 was a watershed for Mao's political status in the CSR. Hostility to some aspects of his leadership had been present since the end of the Fourth Encirclement and Suppression Campaign in the spring of 1933. This is evident in the campaign against the Lo Ming line, in which Mao's brother Zetan was criticized for deriving his military tactics from *The Chronicle of the Three Kingdoms* and recommending to his men that they study that work.[73] Incidentally, it was in the campaign against the Lo Ming line that Deng Xiaoping (Teng Hsiao-ping) suffered his first removal from office as an opportunist.[74] That old scores were not forgotten by the party leadership is indicated by their reference to the earlier incorrect policy of "taking from the fat and adding to the lean" as a cause for the survival of feudal elements.

The growing concentration on the military task of defeating the Fifth Encirclement and Suppression Campaign and the criticism of Mao's management of the Land Investigation Movement led to a diminution of his political influence[75] and a reduction in the importance of the tasks left assigned to him. Of course, this did not remain the situation for long. One year after the Fifth Plenum was the Zunyi Conference, at which Mao assumed a comprehensive leadership position in the party. But by the time of the Zunyi Conference the Long March was already four months old.

Fortunately for our purposes of analyzing Mao's thought, he was in a reflective and summarizing mood in the last year of the CSR. One reason for this disposition is evident in the Changgang and Caixi investigations—namely, that a significant amount of experience had been gathered. Another reason for Mao's summarizing tendencies was the occasion of the Second National Congress held at the end of January. The elections to the congress, which ran through the preceding fall, were supposed to bring a new harvest of activists into the soviet governmental processes, and Mao's speeches which opened the congress are his most eloquent summaries of purpose and experience in Jiangxi.

Mao's New Idea of Local Government

Two basic ideas reach a degree of stability toward the end of the Jiangxi period: Mao's notion of how to run a popular movement and his conception of local-level soviet government as mass self-government. Both rely on the principle of mass activism, but campaigns direct activism toward a specific purpose whereas local revolutionary government is an enduring structure for planning and coordinating local contributions to campaigns, providing services, and handling local problems.

Over the course of Mao's chairmanship of the CSR, the campaigns became more important for the implementation of soviet policy on the local level than the officials. However, it is particularly evident in the Land Investigation Movement that the nature of campaigns had shifted from being an authoritative call for implementation of a directive (the 1932 election campaign) to being a real dialectic of policy implementation and policy creation—that is, a real dialectic of leaders and led. This approach was ill-suited to the formal discipline of Weberian authority with its orientation toward strict implementation (producing bureaucratic and commandist tendencies) and presumptions of universal application. The new campaign style demanded more than compliance from cadres and masses: it sought enthusiasm.

Since the conceptualization of a campaign originates with the leadership, persuasion is the key to mobilization. This fact presents a tremendous challenge to campaign planning and leadership, because effective persuasion demands communication, grounds for persuasion, and finally channels for mass action. The most immediate aspect of communication, that of broad and frequent delivery of the campaign message, was already recognized as a necessity in the first election campaign of 1932 and in the urgent mobilization for war. The need for motivation and structure was not recognized until after the failure of these two movements. In Mao's criticism of the urgent mobilization campaign he observes that the estrangement from the masses involved in bureaucratic behavior prevents success in mobilization. Much progress was made with the problem of motivation in the Eight-County Conference, which attempted to involve a large number of cadres in the definition of the Land Investigation Movement and then gave special attention to their accomplishments. Among the organizational innovations important to communication were the more developed meeting schedule and structure of the basic soviets.

The second element of mobilization, grounds for persuasion, involves the basic identity of interests between leadership and masses. Grounds for persuasion of the masses were not emphasized in the first election campaign; they were prominently mentioned in the urgent mobilization; but they were fully elaborated only in the criticisms of these two campaigns. With the policy of immediate distribution of confiscated goods, the Land Investigation Movement gave central importance to this factor. Basically the grounds for motivation emphasized in late 1932 were the mutual threat of White victory, the real progress that the soviet had brought about (land laws, labor laws, elections), and the personal benefit of active participation (election of competent officials). The persuasive factors remain substantially the same in the Land Investigation Movement, but the contents change considerably. The mutual threat argument, the danger of class enemies and reactionaries, is not as impressive as that of enemy armies. But the personal benefits were more tangible in the form of immediately shared land and confiscated items. Real progress in soviet life was presumably even more marked in 1933, judging from the cases of Changgang and Caixi and from Mao's report at the Second National Congress.

The third element of mobilization, channels of mass action, was for the most part left to the local government and party organs until the Land Investigation Movement, when the poor peasant associations and other mass organizations were emphasized. These associations had no hierarchy above the township level and open (in fact, as large as possible) membership for the lower classes.[76] But with mass response comes the delicate question of popular spontaneity conflicting with the plans of the leadership. This problem can be mitigated by multistage processes of give and take between cadres and masses. For instance, Mao's suggested process of land investigation has four stages: discussion of classes (propaganda); class investigation (only of the bad minority); public approval of classifications (by the poor peasant association and a village mass meeting); confiscation and distribution.[77] Party leadership must prevail in clashes with mass organizations, but it must reform rather than simply dissolve poor peasant associations that are troublesome.

Complementing the effective persuasion of the campaign structure on specific issues is the emphasis on participatory self-government in the township-level soviets. The structure and principles are clear enough in Mao's descriptions of Changgang and Caixi, but they are worked out in detail in a handbook for local government written in March 1934.[78] The growth in significance of township soviets is clearly reflected in the changes in the relevant organic law sections between late 1931 and 1934. The 1931 law does not allow the township soviet to have a presidium *(zhuxi tuan)* or for that matter any standing committees; moreover, it limits townships to three subsidized officials (the basic municipal soviet is allowed fourteen, and a district is allowed thirteen).[79] Villages *(cun)* are not mentioned. In the 1934 document,[80] the presidium is described and twenty-five standing or special committees are specified. Moreover, villages are discussed as necessary subdivisions of the township. Each representative to the township assembly is supposed to have thirty to seventy inhabitants as his responsibility "in order to receive the views of the inhabitants and also for leadership work," and he is up for election every six months.

The main novelty of Mao's township pamphlet in the context of this later law is his emphasis on village-level work, although he does develop township work per se with some characteristic touches. Predictably, Mao emphasizes the need for responsible persons and groups to prepare well for meetings and the need for practical discussion. He adds the new techniques of concentrating on only one major problem at each meeting,[81] and starting the next meeting with a report of work already done on the problem previously discussed. The presidium is encouraged to feel responsible for the investigation and education of representatives. Mass organizations without their own hierarchies are completely the responsibility of the township soviets, and their leadership should be involved in relevant projects. Of greater interest is Mao's claim that "the heart of township work is village work."[82] This is so because much of the township's practical work is carried out at the village level, and it is also the level at which regular mass meetings (every two weeks) are held. Township mass meetings are called only for specific purposes. Township work thus does not diminish in intensity from top to bottom. Both the township representative assembly and the village representatives meet every ten days, and although there are many more committees at the township level, the direct mass work is at the village level. In contrast to Zhang Wentian's rather Weberian and authority-conscious piece on district government,[83] Mao pays little attention to specialization and hierarchy. Mao's model for active township government was never widely applied in Jiangxi, however, because the Fifth Encirclement and Suppression Campaign soon proved to be the last.

The Second National Congress of the CSR

The National Congress was planned as an important event involving internal policy direction and external propaganda. It was to summarize two years of governmental experience, consolidate leadership both within the Central Soviet and among the dispersed soviets, and demonstrate the accomplishments of the "Soviet road" for China.[84] A new election law was announced for the occasion (it included the preferential voting rights for workers which the people of Changgang could not understand), and the campaign led to another detailed statement by Mao on how to run an election.

The first order of business when the congress opened was Mao's "Report to the Second Congress" of the Central Executive Committee and the People's Commisariat. This report began on

24 January and was concluded the following morning. It was then discussed by the 776 delegates in groups until 27 January, when Mao made his concluding statement. The report was then adopted by the congress and it moved on to other business.[85]

Mao's report, which is quite long, is divided into five sections: (1) the present situation, (2) the antiimperialist leadership of the CSR, (3) the struggle against the encirclement and suppression campaigns, (4) basic policies of the soviet during the past two years, and (5) concrete tasks for attaining national unity. The first section observes that although the main problem now is civil war, its struggle is an especially important part of the world revolution. The second section presents the soviet stand against imperialism, particularly its hostility to Japanese incursions. The third section recalls the success of the soviet against the Fourth Encirclement and Suppression Campaign and describes the Fifth Campaign as the concentration of all reactionary forces with the help and leadership of the imperialists.

The fourth and fifth sections of the report, which describe the accomplishments and present tasks of the CSR, are its most detailed parts. Among the ten categories of the "basic soviet policies of the last two years," the most interesting are those dealing with the soviet democratic system, the land revolution, and economic policy.[86]

Mao's discussion of the soviet democratic system begins with his most eloquent statement of the principle of self-rule which had evolved in the CSR:

> The workers' and peasants' democratic dictatorship is the people's own political power. Its relationship with the masses *(minzhong)* should maintain the highest degree of intimacy; only with this can it serve its function. . . . It has already become the organizer and leader of the revolutionary war; in addition it is the organizer and leader of the livelihood of the masses. The greatness of its strength is incomparable to that of any other state form in history. But its strength completely depends on the people; it cannot for an instant be separated from the people. The soviet regime must use force to deal with all class enemies, but with its own class—the poor masses of the workers and peasants—it cannot use any force; its expression can only be the broadest democracy *(minzhu zhuyi)*.[87]

Mao cites four demonstrations of broad democracy in the soviet. In the first, the elections, he notes many improvements. He then cites the municipal and township representative assemblies, giving some details of the Changgang system, and claims at the end:

> Everyone can see that when soviet political power has attained this level of democratic development it will have gone beyond any other governmental system in history. Moreover when the soviet relies on this system and unites with the broad masses, it will make the soviet the organ most able to develop the creative power of the people, it will make the soviet the organ most able to mobilize to meet civil war and revolutionary reconstruction. This is also something not accomplished by any other government in history.[88]

The two other illustrations of soviet democracy are the various freedoms allowed to the revolutionary masses and finally the reduction in size of administrative units.

Mao emphasizes the importance of land revolution by noting that the soviets and the Red Army owe their existence to it. From the experience of the soviet he distills seven principles of land revolution: (1) all struggle should be through the masses and have their approval, (2) confiscated land and items should be distributed among the poor masses, (3) distribution should only occur if the majority wants it, (4) the Land Investigation Movement looks for hidden exploiters, not for a general redetermination of class status, (5) those who oppose land revolution should be attacked, (6) class struggle should be used and landlord-instigated clan and locality struggles should be avoided, (7) soviets should propagandize thoroughly and develop poor peasant associations and hired hand unions.[89]

Mao's statement on soviet economic policy, which is included in his *Selected Works* as "Our Economic Policy," is notable for its description of the dynamics of agricultural production, a responsible state role in the overall economic of the soviet, and the role which cooperatives were beginning to assume in soviet economic life. Agricultural production was generally lower than the traditional output of the area, although it had greatly improved in 1933 and in some places had surpassed old standards. The drop in production which accompanied land revolution was attributed to uncertainties about land distribution. The government's attitude of comprehensive responsibility toward the economic life of the soviet is evidenced by its concern for border commerce, export commodity production, and development of new industries. Evidently the need for regulation was not clearly recognized until the summer of 1933, when the unregulated export of grain in the previous fall was seen as a cause of the food shortage.[90]

Mao balances his promise of more economic intervention with a guarantee of a more stable political environment for private capital in the soviet. Previously the attitude toward nonagricultural wealth had been more or less predatory. This is indicated by the statement in the financial section of Mao's report that "on the basis of past experience, this type of income [confiscations and fines] often has a major role."[91] An analogous type of irresponsibility was the tendency, already criticized by Mao, to ignore and postpone economic reconstruction because of military urgencies. The development of cooperatives according to Mao was extremely rapid. There were now 1,423 cooperatives of various sorts in seventeen CSR counties. These were primarily consumer and grain cooperatives, but there were a significant number of producers' cooperatives.

Despite the various accomplishments listed in Mao's report, the last section on "Concrete Tasks for the Thorough Defeat of the Fifth Encirclement and Suppression Campaign and Attaining National Victory" conveys the feeling of a dangerously difficult task. True to Mao's integrated policy approach, the "concrete tasks involve every area of soviet work, first of all the Red Army, but also economic reconstruction, soviet development, and antiimperialist work in White areas." Many things cited as accomplishments earlier in the report reappear here as problems to be emphasized. This treatment underscores the fact that the salient message of the report is not the degree of success in various areas but the significance of various tasks. Unfortunately for the viability of the report, its assignment of relevance presupposed the continued existence of the CSR.

Mao's concluding remarks on the discussion of the report have a more timeless quality about them because they discuss one basic government problem: the relationship of mass livelihood to revolutionary war.[92] Mao had raised this issue in his report but felt that it was not sufficiently addressed by the delegates. The government's key tasks and their relation through popular mobilization to revolutionary war are eloquently stated:

> If the soviet only mobilizes the people to carry on the war and does nothing else, can it succeed in defeating the enemy? I answer, no it

cannot. If we want to win, we must do a great deal more. In reality, the basic task of the soviet is to guarantee the interests of the broad masses, to lead the economic struggle of the workers, to restrain capitalist exploitation. It must lead the peasants' struggle for land and distribute the land to them, heighten their labor enthusiasm, and increase agricultural production, establish cooperatives, develop trade with outside areas, and solve the problem facing the masses—food, shelter and clothing, fuel, rice, cooking oil and salt, sickness and hygiene, and marriage—in short, all the practical problems in the everyday life of the masses should claim our attention. If the soviet attends to these problems, solves them, and satisfies the needs of the masses, it will really become the organizer of the well-being of the masses, and they will truly rally round the soviet and give it their warm support. Comrades, will the soviet then be able to arouse them to take part in the revolutionary war? My answer is it will, it will certainly be able to.[93]

This is not simply a commitment to serve the people. It expresses the conviction that serving the people is the necessary ground for mass mobilization which in turn is the guarantor of success in revolutionary war. This is basically the same conviction that lay behind the argument of "The Great Union of the Popular Masses" in 1919 and behind Mao's suggestion of a peasant strategy in 1926. He concretizes his point in the concluding remarks by citing a bad example of a city which concentrated only on war aims and turned out to be ineffective even in that; the good models, Changgang and Caixi, achieved good results in everything. The process of popular mobilization implied in this close connection between mass service and task success is put in terms quite similar to those of Mao's first mass-line statement of 1926:

> The soviet should convince the masses that it represents their interests, that its life is intimately bound up with theirs. It should help them proceed from those things to supporting the soviet, to an understanding of the higher tasks we have put forward, the tasks of the revolutionary war, so that they will support the revolution and spread it throughout the country, respond to our political appeals, and fight to the end for victory in the revolution.[94]

This process is not one which renders practical services unnecessary after the masses have understood higher goals. It is a constant dialectic of new tasks in a context of demonstrated identity of interests. Party leadership is the leadership of the masses; it must begin with the actual condition and needs of the masses. Success in leading the masses is sufficient to guarantee success in the revolution, because "the masses are the true bastions of iron which no force can smash." Mao concludes his speech with emphasis on the importance of finding methods of implementation, underscoring his point by contrasting examples of bureaucratic methods and their results with good methods and results.

The central idea of Mao's positive summary of the Jiangxi experience is the growth of beneficial accomplishments and effective methods in the CSR and the revolutionary significance of closeness to the masses. The accomplishments and methods he details are to a great extent innovations of the Jiangxi period and would probably have been the basis of an increasingly popular and powerful regime there had the trajectory which he plotted been allowed to develop. As it was, even in the vastly changed circumstances and strategy of later stages of Chinese Communism the experience of Jiangxi proved to be a valuable experiment. Not only did many specific policies resurface in Yanan or in the national land revolution, but Mao's thesis of the substantiality of self-government became the premise of later periods. The seriousness and comprehensiveness of government operations which Edgar Snow observed in Bao An in 1936 can be viewed as a result of realizations in Jiangxi in 1933. On the other hand, the importance which Mao attaches to popular mobilization is a reappearance of one of the oldest themes of his political thought.

The Zunyi and Wayaobao Conferences

The last issue of *Red Flag*, 12 October 1934, could not be printed. Its mimeographed pages contain heroic but pathetic appeals for continued resistance against the KMT. The Red Army had escaped, but the pretense and real accomplishments of the CSR had collapsed. The necessity of the Long March, which began in October 1934, was a jolting change of context from the long-range problems of socialist China to the most immediate military questions of survival. At the Zunyi Conference of January 1935, Mao resumed his direction of military strategy which had been terminated in late 1932. Appropriate to this resumption and to the military failure of the CSR was a critique of military policy during the Fifth Encirclement and Suppression Campaign, and this is provided in the Zunyi Resolution.[95] At the Zunyi Conference the Twenty-eight Bolsheviks argued, not surprisingly, that the defeat of the Jiangxi Soviet could not have been avoided. Their self-criticism—that the leadership underestimated objective difficulties and overestimated revolutionary strength—led to the face-saving conclusion that victory was impossible. Mao vehemently disagreed with this assessment, saying that defeat was due to the adoption of a purely defensive military line against the Fifth Encirclement and Suppression Campaign. The military leadership was afraid of Chiang's blockhouse system of encirclement, overconfident in the Red Army's strength, and rigid in their principle of not yielding an inch of soviet territory. They had abandoned the flexible military tactics developed earlier by Mao and had adopted a policy of resistance to KMT advances which left the initiative with the KMT. Mao then reiterates the essentials of his guerrilla strategy. He says that the blockhouses should have been ignored rather than attacked. The Red Army, he argues, should have gotten outside the rings of blockhouses, threatened nearby KMT-held cities, and thus rendered the fortifications a liability for the KMT. Moreover, Mao criticizes the leadership and timing of the Long March, which was too late, too secretive, and too panicky.

This set of military errors took place within a larger context of policy mistakes which was not discussed by Mao until the Long March was concluded in December 1935.[96] At that time the Wayaobao Conference was held and "a new stage of Chinese revolutionary history" was inaugurated—that of the anti-Japanese national revolution. A necessary element of the party's political realignment was a critique of its previous errors. The general critique was presented in Mao's report at Wayaobao, and it is evident in the resolution adopted by the conference. It is supplemented in some details by Mao's lectures on military strategy from 1936.[97]

Since the basic policy announced at Wayaobao was the alliance of "different individuals, different organizations, different social classes and levels, and different troops" against Japan, the primary fault of the previous leadership is described as "closed-doorism." This fault is broadly construed as self-satisfaction with the party's propaganda that it was the vanguard of the revolution, a narrow focus on work among the lower classes and among workers, and an unwillingness to form alliances.[98] A large number of specific leadership errors can be grouped as symptoms of these three aspects of closed-doorism.

The Stalinist proclivities of the Twenty-eight Bolsheviks substituted ideological chastity for a strategy appropriate to a localized revolutionary movement. This dogmatic self-image is symbolized by the establishment of the Chinese Soviet Republic. In an actual situation of "strategic defensive" the party leadership pretended that the struggle was between two equal powers. "Our fight against Chiang Kai-shek had become a war between two states, between two great armies."[99] Maintaining and intensifying the socialist identity of the CSR as the Twenty-eight Bolsheviks understood it meant progressively greater isolation of "their" China from the rest of China. Mao's position in 1936 was considerably more realistic:

> We are a state, but today we are not yet a full-fledged state. Today we are still in the period of strategic defensive in the civil war, and are very far removed from being a full-fledged state. Our army is still much inferior to the enemy both in numbers and in technical equipment, our territory is still very small, and our enemy is constantly out to destroy us and will never rest content until he has done so.[100]

Within the political context of the CSR, the adamancy of party leadership regarding the treatment of various classes has already been observed. The harsh stand against the rich peasants led to serious problems of control and mass apathy. The preferential treatment of workers was misunderstood by the majority of the population. In the period of the Second United Front, the anti–rich peasant provisions of the Land Law were stricken and the unity of all classes against Japan was emphasized. When the period of "strategic offensive" finally arrived in 1947, however, Mao's perspective on the class nature of the rural struggle again became current.

The most immediate manifestation of closed-doorism was the party leadership's coldness toward alliances. Particularly in Mao's report the handling of the Fujian Rebellion is castigated, not simply from a military viewpoint but because of the implied refusal to ally with other classes:

> Whose class interests does the 19th Route Army led by Cai Tingkai and others [the force behind the Fujian Rebellion] represent? Those of the national bourgeoisie, the upper petty bourgeoisie, and the rich peasants and small landlords in the countryside. . . . Whatever

course Cai Tingkai and his associates take in the future, and despite their Fujian People's Government's adherence to old practice in failing to arouse the people to struggle, it must be considered beneficial that they turned their guns, originally trained on the Red Army, against the Japanese imperialism and Chiang Kai-shek. It marked a split within the KMT camp.[101]

The alliance policy adopted at the Wayaobao Conference was broad enough to include any anti-Japanese group or class, but it avoided the kind of overcommitment to a specific alliance that exacerbated the disaster of 1927. The united front focused on an issue with very broad appeal: opposition to Japanese imperialism. Since this issue could be expected to be paramount for a number of years, the united front policy could be expected to be relatively stable. The strategic thinking behind the united front strategy was considerably more subtle than that achieved by the purity line of the Twenty-eight Bolsheviks. Rather than have the politics of the revolutionary party be simply an immediate expression of its identity and goals, Mao's politics are immediately determined by what is discerned to be the principal contradiction of the political situation. The Stalinist virtues of dogmatic faithfulness and accuracy in execution are replaced by the more discretionary virtues of flexibility and alertness.

Mao's criticisms of the narrowness and rigidity of the Jiangxi leadership are made with the advantage of hindsight, but his anti–closed-doorism perspective also antedates the failure of the Twenty-eight Bolsheviks' leadership and even their arrival in Jiangxi. The united front strategy of 1935 is the most fitting framework for the political-military strategy of popular mobilization, because both are directed by the same principle of achieving maximum effective mobilization. In the situation of the Long March, Mao could not simply return to his old views or put his once-suppressed opinions in command, because the movement now lacked a base and the national context had been redefined by the growing intensity of Japanese incursions. Mao's already established notions of political and military leadership would have to be transformed by the environment of their new application and by Mao's new role of comprehensive leadership within the party. His theoretical attention turned first to the development of a strategy appropriate to war against Japan and then to the conceptualization of the principles which had already become firm in his experience and applied thought: the dynamic unity of theory and practice and the absolute political power of the mobilized masses.

Conclusion

At this point we can begin to see in general terms how Mao's political thought developed in the CSR period from 1931 to 1934 and why it has been so difficult for researchers to specify his politics during this time. The conundrum of CSR political history is this. The potential for factional struggle was certainly there within one organization: two major groups existed with different experiences, personal loyalties, and policies. Moreover, Mao's side lost; and when it later emerged victorious it claimed that there had indeed been a sharp conflict. Yet there are few signs of a struggle. There are many Central Committee criticisms which certainly have Mao in mind, but they do not attack him by name. More important, there is no evidence that Mao used his tremendous personal prestige to further his differing views or to defend himself. It seems that Mao lost but he never fought. Researchers who noted the loss have presumed a battle; those who found no battle have asserted that the struggle is a later fabrication.[102] This is not the only time in CCP history when later smoke has had a problematic relationship to original fire. Lowell Dittmer evokes this conundrum in a far more productive way than most students of Jiangxi in his study of "two-line struggle" rhetoric in the Cultural Revolution.[103]

The paradigm approach has great utility in studying the CSR period. Above all, it provides an elegant explanation for both the facts and the later significance of the period in which the apparently contradictory components of other approaches each have their place. My interpretation is that in the early base area period, 1927 to 1931, Mao developed his basic rural strategies in order to survive. These were derived primarily from close and anxious attention to the problems of guerrilla leadership and only secondarily harmonized with Marxism and the Central Committee. In retrospect, it was the beginning of Mao's characteristic approach to rural revolution, but at the time it was merely necessary. The explicit tensions between Mao and the Central Committee were center–periphery tensions. The center–periphery problem appeared solved when the center moved to the periphery in 1931, and Mao's policies, which were in fact of peasant origin, seemed out of place among the Stalinist pretensions of the CSR. Within the sphere left to him Mao tried to do his version of a good job, which meant an orientation toward maximum result and the avoidance of estrangement from the masses. This approach led to basic administrative innovations in the CSR which because of their massline character conflicted with the Twenty-eight Bolsheviks' notions of proper policy. In 1934 it became clear to both groups that their approaches were in basic conflict, and Mao was removed from leadership roles. At this time, it was not practical for Mao to develop his policy differences into a challenging, alternative theory of CCP leadership. Mao may have been caricatured as a Sancho Panza by the Central Committee, but he was certainly no Don Quixote. Besides, such general theoretical formulations are incredibly difficult and risky, except for professional philosopher-princes. In 1934 Mao was content to state the principles of good leadership which he saw the Twenty-eight Bolsheviks ignoring. His concluding remarks at the Second National Congress are a concise summary of his approach in an ironic setting: he emphasizes the importance of concern for the well-being of the masses because in three days of discussion the delegates had forgotten to mention it.

There was no fight in the CSR because Mao's practical policy initiatives were too novel to have a ready-made ideological defense. Mao's belief in them was incommunicable, and he bowed to authority and persuasiveness. In 1959 Mao was self-confident enough in dealing with Peng Dehuai to threaten to return to Jinggangshan and fight in his own way; but not in 1931.

Although there was no fight, there was a major and irreconcilable tension between Mao and the party leadership in the CSR. The political approach of the Twenty-eight Bolsheviks presumed a mass base and emphasized discipline. Their policies against bureaucratism were Weberian rationalizations of the bureaucratic structure. Their goal was the efficient and accurate delivery of Party Central directives. The popularity and appropriateness of the content of directives was no problem because they knew the Marxist theory of class struggle, the Leninist theory of imperialism, and the latest directives of the Comintern. Mao emphasized investigation as the source of correct (appropriate) policies, and his goal was maximum effective mobilization. He was opposed to bureaucracy ancient or modern, efficient or inefficient, because its one-way control structure did not encourage interaction with the masses. The mass campaign approach exemplified by the Land Investigation Movement was a partial solution of the problem of maintaining coordination while minimizing hierarchy. The complex of campaigns developed in Yanan in 1942-1945 are a more complete expression of this alternative form of democratic centralism.

What took place in the CSR was a clash of political paradigms, but it was not a battle of two fully articulated paradigms. Mao's was still in embryo, a growing collection of policies that worked and political principles. The Leninist-Stalinist paradigm of the Twenty-eight Bolsheviks was self-confident and it was also in authority. It is inevitable that Mao would be submissive and avoid conflict in such circumstances. It is also inevitable that when he became confident of his mature paradigm in later years, the time of practical development under an ill-fitting leadership would be viewed retrospectively as a more defined struggle, a time when truth was with the minority. Mao's 1945 analysis of CSR politics is an effort at historical self-understanding as well as an official history.

5   The Foundations of Mao Zedong's Political Thought

The general thesis of this study has been that Mao's political thought evolved in a dialectical interaction of theory and practice and became a characteristic political viewpoint by the time of the Long March. More pointedly, my claim is that the interaction of theory and practice with the goal of effective revolutionary action is the basic characteristic of Mao's own pattern of development and the main trait of his political thinking. The novelty of Mao's political paradigm for Chinese and Marxist politics became evident only when it was authoritatively and comprehensively elaborated in the 1936–1945 period. But Mao's emphasis on the primacy of practice should be a warning not to begin the study of his political thought with its formulation. My intention has been not simply to present a prehistory of Mao's political thought but to take the first step toward seriously understanding, evaluating, and using it. The study is not complete because Mao's politics continued to develop, but I hope that it is not partial in the sense of leaving out of consideration an essential aspect of his political thinking.

The previous chapters of this study have presented in detail the development of Mao's thought in its practical political context. This concluding chapter delineates the significance of Mao's experience before the Long March for his later politics and the coherence of his implicit paradigm. After reconsidering Mao's relationship to Marxism and to Chinese political culture, I wish to define the limits of a practical foundation of a political paradigm.

Mao's Political Development

As Chalmers Johnson correctly points out,[1] the Chinese Communist Party entered a new strategic situation with the defeat of the Chinese Soviet Republic and the approach of war with Japan. War with one imperialist power and the threat of direct colonialism replaced the divided and oscillating scenario of 1927. As we would expect from Mao's flexible and investigative approach, he made correspondingly major changes in policy, muting the themes of class struggle and economic redistribution and emphasizing a united front of all patriots against Japan. Mao's new position of party leadership and the reorientation required by the transformed political environment stimulated the most prolific period of Mao's writing.

Despite the novelties of the period after the Long March, it had certain similarities with the previous stages of development in Mao's thought. Like the May Fourth period, although on a much grander scale, Mao's leadership role again became one of first among equals because of his demonstrated capabilities. The most prominent policy horizons again became national, as they were in the first five years of the CCP, and united front politics reemerged. The peasantry remained the basis of political strategy, and an emphasis on survival reminiscent of Jinggangshan replaced the purity line of the Twenty-eight Bolsheviks. It is somewhat more difficult to find a continuing element of basic policy from the Jiangxi period. The anti-Japanese stance of the CSR received new emphasis and development, but the land policy was changed to one of protecting rich peasant interests,[2] military policy reverted to guerrilla tactics, and the Stalinist character of policy preoccupations receded.

The lessons of the CSR period were retained for the more analogous government situation in Yanan after 1940 and in the civil war period, however, when domestic policies again became as salient as the politics of national defense against Japan. Mao's extensive government experience was only beginning to bear fruit in Jiangxi when the CSR was defeated. That experience formed the foundation of his later government activities. In the legal implementation phase of his administration in Jiangxi, he learned critical lessons about estrangement from the masses and its two subsets, bureaucratism and commandism. Through the mass campaigns of 1933, particularly the Land Investigation Movement, Mao grasped the fundamentally positive principle of politics through nonbureaucratic mass campaigns. The structural implications of this leadership method were realized in the model of small-unit soviets stressing mass mobilization and active participation. The principles of popular mobilization, which were almost spontaneous in the threatened intimacy of Jinggangshan, were elaborated into stable axioms and methods of organization. Many policy details—for example, work teams, methods and principles of class analysis,[3] thought struggle—became valuable additions to Mao's arsenal of governmental techniques. More important, the attention to the proper initiation of a major campaign which is clear in the Land Investigation Movement set a pattern of emphasis on cadre motivation and mobilization, self-restraint on the part of top leadership in order to provide encouragement rather than enervating control, and the establishment of authoritative guidelines and regulations only after a considerable body of experience has been gathered.

This model of the policymaking and implementation process allowed the relationship between Yanan and the anti-Japanese base areas to become a productive dialectic of base area creativity and Yanan's authoritative coordination rather than the strained relationship of ideological tribute and real independence which existed between Yanan and the Soviet Union.[4] This process was also essential to the domestic policy processes in Yanan, as is particularly clear in the case of the Zhengfeng (Rectification) Movement. In short, many of the political novelties of the Yanan period are in content developments from earlier Jiangxi innovations. But they are transformed because of Mao's comprehensive leadership, his self-consciousness and self-confidence in application, and the new context of the Anti-Japanese War.

The same claim of continuity in a transformed context can also be made for each earlier period of Mao's thought in relationship to the one succeeding it. The policy innovations of the CSR period can be seen as a return at a higher level of organization to the principles of maximum mobilization evolved in the survival politics of the base area period. Closeness to the masses, self-government, integrated policy—these were principles whose importance and whose methods of implementation had to be rediscovered in the CSR environment, but they were present in his earlier politics. Similarly, Mao's base area politics rested on his analysis of the revolutionary potential of the countryside and the importance of land revolution which had been developed in the pursuit of a truly revolutionary national policy during his Guangdong period. Again, Mao's party and alliance politics of 1923-1926 presupposed the continuity of his May Fourth activism, practicality, and populism. And these have their roots in Mao's earlier experiences. The basic innovations of each period were always essential assumptions of the following one and had undiminished though less distinct importance for the whole of Mao's career. The Zunyi Conference is an excellent synecdoche for the movement of Mao's politics: the introduction of a new stage of his political thought is accomplished by using his tested principles of guerrilla leadership in criticizing the military mistakes of the Twenty-eight Bolsheviks.

It is thus tempting to search for the true origins of "Maoism" in his earliest experiences, but this is an inadequate approach from two points of view. From a theoretical viewpoint, this approach rests on the assumption that the principles of continuity in Mao's political thought retain their whole significance when they are abstracted from the actual course of Mao's politics. This assumption is of course an alternative open to the researcher, but it has the disadvantage of being in disagreement with Mao's theoretical predispositions. Not only does Mao himself insist on the unity of theory and practice; as we have seen, he typically generalizes from experience rather than implementing preconceptions. From a historical viewpoint, an approach which tends to distill the significance of a continuity of thought or action into its first instance presupposes an inaccurate model of Mao's political development. His political thought did not simply accrete through time, each succeeding layer being more determinate and superficial than the last. Each general recasting of his political activities created a new world of significance for his political thought. In each phase studied, the present situation is as important as past experience in determining the shape of his politics. Hence each innovation has historical roots in experience which condition its applicability in different circumstances. For example, the experience that the May Fourth enlightenment did not transform Chinese politics produced a new context of politics which can be seen as an application of Mao's principles of practical activity and revolutionary populism to new circumstances. But it should also be remembered that this application gave a new meaning to practicality and populism for Mao—and his new practicality and populism were unacceptable to some who had been his coworkers in the earlier period. The change in referent transforms the significance of the term.

If the unity of theory and practice is seen as a central element in Mao's thinking, the rootedness of his political thought in the practical tasks at hand ceases to be a frustrating obstacle to interpretation and becomes the key to a precise understanding of Mao's intentions. It is important to study the phases of development chronologically from the beginning because only with this approach is all of the relevant policy experience available to the researcher. Such an approach does not preclude generalizations about Mao's political thought, but I think it can make the difference between naive and responsible generalizations.

The Implicit Paradigm of Mao's Politics

Although Mao himself did not formulate his political paradigm at the end of the CSR period, his political development reached sufficient maturity by that time for us to delineate an implicit paradigm of his politics. This is a useful task because it gathers up the commonalities of his political development thus far into a single picture. Moreover, Mao's later formulation of his political paradigm occurs at a new stage of his development, and in order to separate the true innovations of his post-1935 political thought from his generalizations on earlier experience, we must attempt a 1935 synthesis. In the following paragraphs we will analyze Mao's implicit political paradigm at three levels: the paradigm of personal example, the strategy of revolution, and the paradigm of politics.

In discussing the contribution of the first half of Mao's life, it is important to recall that a paradigmatic model is not only a grand intellectual scheme which subsumes particulars. It is also the textbook case,[5] the repeatable experience which shows how to act properly under the paradigm and at the same time demonstrates its utility. For a political paradigm the exemplar is the correct political actor, in our case the model revolutionary. In Jiangxi the collegiality of the Twenty-eight Bolsheviks did not permit the lionizing of any individual leader, and if it had, Mao would have been an unlikely candidate. But despite a relative lack of publicity, his leadership style undoubtedly had some influence on his comrades, and traits which were much publicized later were already clearly present.

Mao's most remarkable personal characteristic as an activist was his concern for effectiveness. Complemented by extraordinary dedication and energy, Mao's orientation toward concrete results shaped his political participation from the May Fourth period on. Mao was not an opportunist, but he did aim for goals which he thought were attainable and he sought to mobilize broad support for them.

Directly related to Mao's practical orientation was his concern for an accurate, objective grasp of the political situation. This concern is evident in the detail of his May Fourth writings and his early CCP writings, but it develops into an explicit exhortation for personal investigation in 1926-1927, when the CCP began to ignore what Mao perceived as the revolutionary potential of the peasantry. In emphasizing investigation, Mao stresses a basically cognitive concern—how to know correct policy—without allowing the question to become either formalistically methodological or introspectively epistemological. Investigation is a practical activity; its criterion is effectiveness.

Like all forms of policy analysis, Mao's investigations and recommendations involved values, and these are an essential part of his personal paradigm. Mao's chief political value was the importance of serving the interests of the masses. In many of Mao's writings, this principle merges indistinguishably with his emphasis on effectiveness. The bond between these two is Mao's conviction that the mobilized masses will be the prevailing political force. Hence any policy against the interests of the masses will be ineffective. Belief in the power of the masses and commitment to their interests survived the disappointment of May Fourth hopes and the defeat of the 1927 peasant movement, but these failures did lead Mao to depend less directly on the power of mass spontaneity and to pay more attention to revolutionary organization. The interests of the revolutionary organization, party, Red Army, or soviet government do not, however, displace those of the masses. A criticism of legitimacy is implied in Mao's 1926-1927 term "the *really* revolutionary party" and his later obsession with avoiding "estrangement from the masses." Both phrases indicate that professional revolutionaries are not the autonomous purveyors of revolution but are primarily the organizers of mass efforts.

Mao's revolutionary strategy is intimately bound up with his political values. Although his anarchist-utopian expectations in 1919 of a bloodless transformation of society were soon dashed, his conviction that the largest "union of the popular masses" ultimately prevails remained a basic premise of his politics. This is most obvious in Mao's fascination with numbers. In proposing a peasant strategy in 1926, Mao considered that the number of peasants was proof of their political potential. He does not explain why China's history has been a history of elites, but he is confident that the present problem is one of mobilization: "395 million people, organize!"[6]

Class struggle was one of Marxism's major contributions to Mao's idea of revolution. The notion of the class structure of political economy provided a universal and presumably scientific scheme for explaining social grievances and organizing for their elimination. However, it is evident in his 1926 articles on peasant classes that Mao tends to use class analysis for categorizing the misery of different groups and their revolutionary potential. What interests Mao is class struggle rather than the relationships of production.

Mao's revolutionary strategy is centered on popular mobilization, but it had also to cope with the superior power of the counterrevolutionaries. This lesson was learned gradually and painfully. For many of Mao's generation, becoming a communist was a recognition of the necessity of revolutionary organization. The passing of the May Fourth Movement proved that the new China would not be born spontaneously. Professional revolutionaries must operate in a hostile political environment to bring about a revolutionary situation. Individual dedication was not enough; organizational discipline and an orienting ideology were also required for coordinated and effective prerevolutionary work. Alliances were a principal means of reducing resistance by pursuing limited and achievable common goals. But if the revolutionary organization compromised mass interests for the convenience of an alliance, it lost its legitimacy and even if successful it could not achieve a real revolution.

The basic strategic lesson of the 1927 disasters was that "political power grows out of the barrel of a gun." Mao's response to the necessity of a strategy for survival was an integrated combination of guerrilla warfare and revolutionary base areas at the rural fringes of warlord and KMT control. The idea of a rural-based revolution, a remarkable innovation for a Marxist, did not originate as a theoretical innovation but as a practical necessity. Yet Mao's guerrilla strategy was a natural development from his view of revolutionary legitimacy because it was based on the mobilization and politicization of the oppressed peasantry, the overwhelming majority of China's population. This is the basic dimension of a complex of center–periphery logic in Mao's guerrilla strategy: the periphery of established Chinese politics—the middle and poor peasantry in the countryside—became the center of revolutionary politics. Mao's strategic thought underwent considerable development after the Long March, but it retained its rural revolutionary foundation despite reorientation toward national defense against Japan.

In order to sustain and legitimize his rural revolutionary strategy, Mao had to develop a paradigm of base area politics which could mobilize peasant support for the revolution. Originally the important elements of the political paradigm were a policy of egalitarian redistribution of resources, a cadre ethic emphasizing closeness to the masses, and a military-political structure which integrated mass support. With Mao's lengthy and specialized governmental experience as chairman of the CSR, the politics of mobilization became more systematic and institutionalized. Particularly important was the development of the campaign structure for major policy targets and the focus on grass roots politics. By the end of the CSR, Mao had identified the major role of revolutionary government as serving the people. The mass line of policy interaction between leadership and masses lacked only an official formulation.

Competing Foundations of Mao's Politics

I have presented the development of the implicit paradigm of Mao's politics as the result of an ongoing interaction between his political environment and his attempts to improve it. But it is also evident that the theory in this interaction of theory and practice is overtly Marxist theory and that Mao's environment of practice is Chinese. It is thus possible to juxtapose Marxism and Chinese political culture as alternative sources of Maoism or to prefer one as more basic to the other. Cogent arguments can be made for each of these competing foundations. In my opinion, however, both positions are mistaken in their common assumption that Mao can be reduced to his sources, because this assumption implicitly denies that Mao made major innovations within both Chinese and Marxist contexts. Confusion occurs because Mao was content to leave his relation to Marxism and to Chinese political culture an unclear dialectic.

In recent studies relating to Mao, those emphasizing his Chinese roots have been the more interesting. Wolfgang Bauer, for instance, ends his grand examination of Chinese conceptions of happiness with a stimulating analysis of traditional cognates of Mao's ideals.[7] A more culturally limiting thesis about the basis of Mao's politics is Richard Solomon's *Mao's Revolution and the Chinese Political Culture.* His argument is a psychological one that China's political culture encouraged social dependency and therefore Mao's contentious personality made him a natural leader. This claim aroused immediate protest from many China scholars.[8] Some felt that Chinese political behavior was not as homogeneous as Solomon had portrayed it; others believed that a subrational explanation of Mao's thought and its success was unnecessary.

A more plausible explanation of twentieth-century developments through their traditional roots was advanced by Thomas Metzger in his *Escape from Predicament.*[9] He greatly improves on Solomon's psychological thesis by describing the aspects of interdependence and even moral autonomy present in traditional unequal relationships. Metzger does not argue that the Chinese were psychologically bound by behavioral patterns but that they were conceptually bound by their Neo-Confucian intellectual heritage. The bounds of twentieth-century development, including Mao, were set by an optimistic rejection of the personal moral dilemma which Metzger sees as a central assumption of Neo-Confucianism:

> My argument is that, to a large extent, it was the indigenous, intense, centuries-old desire to escape from a metaphysical, psychological, political, and economic predicament which led many Chinese enthusiastically to devote their lives to the overthrow of traditionally revered institutions and the adoption of strange and foreign ways.[10]

Metzger's method of analysis is to concentrate on the clichés of thinkers rather than on their self-conscious innovations. He does this with the shrewd reflection that the bits of common wisdom accepted by a group of thinkers are as much a defining aspect of their intellectual world as the problems they dispute.[11]

The major difficulty with Metzger's methodology and interpretation for our purpose of trying to understand Mao is that it presumes there was no real origination of political ideas in twentieth-century China. It is true that many Chinese held views having elements in common with Mao and the CCP. To take a random example, in the first volume of the *Yenching Journal of Social Studies* (1938) there are articles praising direct field research for social science and a sociocultural theory of knowledge.[12] Moreover, the moral dilemma which Metzger finds in Neo-Confucianism does seem to have faded in its fourth century. Surely it is facile to interpret these similarities as primarily the result of running in the same direction from an inherited predicament. To "escape" into the manic-depressive intellectual milieu of China's last hundred years is rather like curing a cold by catching pneumonia. The fact that twentieth-century Chinese thinkers thought in the twentieth century is probably more important in explaining shared perceptions.

In the new and urgent world of the twentieth century what counted was what people did politically, not common environmental or cultural residuals. To stress what Mao and Taiwanese conservative philosophers have in common is to miss the vastly greater significance of their differences. Escapism may be the key to the philosophy of Tang Junyi, Metzger's favorite conservative philosopher, but Mao's practical political engagement involved him and eventually the People's Republic of China in new intellectual and moral predicaments which constitute new chapters in the development of China's rich tradition of secular ethics. Many clichés of China's new public ideology are drawn from the period covered in this book, but they have originated, as we have seen, in the practical experience of revolutionary politics and the struggle for survival.

As Stuart Schram has pointed out,[13] the discussion of Mao's Marxism has usually been strained to an unnecessary shrillness because it is an issue of personal ideological importance to the scholar. Consequently the tension which one feels in the Wittfogel-Schwartz debate on Mao's Marxism is not completely due to the intellectual excitement of the exchange,[14] and many of the contributions to *Modern China*'s series of articles on the subject seem to shed more heat than light.[15] The two polar facts of the discussion—that "Mao was not Marx" and that "Mao claimed to be a Marxist"—are equally irrefutable. Yet the proponents of each side expand the significance of one pole while denying it to the other. Those most emphatically for Mao's Marxism end up claiming in effect that were Marx Mao, he would be Mao, while those on the other extreme claim that it is quite Maoist, although un-Marxist, to claim that Mao is a Marxist.

Surely it would be more useful to ask the questions "what did Marxism mean for Mao?" and "what does it mean to say that Mao was a Marxist?" I will postpone answering the second question because it is more appropriately asked vis-à-vis Mao's later formulations of his thought. The first question, however, can be answered for the period we have covered. The primary impact of Marxism on Mao's politics was that it provided a theory of social dynamics and a professional revolutionary organization. The Marxist contribution to Mao's thought is most clear in the 1923–1927 period, but despite later developments the theory of class struggle and the importance of the party remain basic aspects of his politics. In comparison to Marx, Mao's idea of class was more immediately centered on the question of political potential. In comparison to Lenin, Mao's idea of the party involved a far greater degree of interdependence with the masses. Interdependence was already evident in Mao's idea of the legitimacy of the really revolutionary party in 1926; during the base area period it developed into the policy interdependence later known as the mass line.

The main source of the conflicting interpretations of the foundations of Mao's thought is the complexity of his intellectual environment,[16] but there was also a theoretical ambiguity in Mao's politics which was sometimes intentional. Mao's practical orientation contributed to his theoretical ambiguity in two ways. First, Mao considered theoretical problems only insofar as the situation demanded. During the period under consideration Mao used theory but he did not attempt to generate a complete theoretical structure consistent with the developing novelty and maturity of his practical politics. The challenge of analyzing Mao's political thought before the Long March is not that of understanding his conceptualizations but conceptualizing the consistencies of his politics. This is not only a problem for the early period of Mao's thought. I think that Mao's politics never received a thorough theoretical formulation. His political thought continued to exist in an unclear dialectic with the political situation and the ideological hegemony of Marxism-Leninism.

A second practical reason for Mao's theoretical ambiguity was that in order to be effective he had to seem obedient to his superiors and diligent in his Marxism no matter how creatively he was applying their respective orders and principles. Early in life

Mao had cited the Confucian classics against his father (a use they were not intended to have),[17] and there are later cases of his clever use of ideology for legitimation. One example is Mao's description of ultrademocracy in the Gutian Resolution of 1929 in which he inverts a complaint of the Party Center against the periphery. Another example is a 1933 attempt to identify "Bolshevization" with "involving the masses" (qunzhonghua).[18] Here Mao attempted to capture the Bolshevik label which had been used by the Twenty-eight Bolsheviks to indicate ideological discipline and efficiency for his new tendency toward mass campaigns and comprehensive local government. Typically, Mao's specious usages are not vague "Fourth of July" statements; he carefully specifies the referent and then uses the label. He stretches the concept to fit a new practical context in what amounts to a subtle process of redefinition. This tendency to develop through new definitions rather than through new concepts requires the researcher to take seriously the practical context of terminology. It also eventually produces a polysemy of basic concepts which frustrates efforts to build a concise ideological structure.

The Limits of Practical Revolution

The historic significance of Mao's revolutionary paradigm is that it broke the bottleneck of modern Chinese history by developing a political program appropriate to Chinese conditions and yet cognizant of the transformative potential evident in the modern West. The foundations for reconstituting China had to be worked out in practice, and Mao's orientation of populist empiricism enabled him to generate many of the policy innovations which later characterized the successful Chinese revolution. Mao was not the lone genius whose formula saved China; it was rather his concern for effectiveness and his willingness to learn from the masses which minted the revolution in his image. But a practical paradigm has its limitations.[19] The effectiveness of such a paradigm results from its appropriateness for existing conditions, but its success changes those conditions and undermines its own appropriateness. This basic limitation can be seen in different areas: in changes in policy, in power relationships, and in political goals. By 1958 the limitations of Mao's original political paradigm had become as important as its strengths, and a new crisis of appropriate political leadership began to emerge.

The first kind of limitation is related to the flux of reality and the necessity of theoretical guidance. The task of policy adjustment must be confronted constantly by practical leadership if it is to retain its effectiveness. The second kind of limitation is caused by the structural problems that emerge when a practical paradigm becomes authoritative, as did Mao's after the Long March. Mao did not confront these problems directly, but their presence can be observed in the course of his leadership. A third kind of limitation emerges with the success of Mao's political paradigm in 1949. Having broken the practical bottleneck created by precocious, isolated intellectualism, a new bottleneck developed—namely, the lack of adequate theoretical guidance for the new forces of Chinese society. The old goals of survival and revolution had been secured, and the constant refrain of Chinese intellectual modernization—*zou nei tiao lu?*, which road to take?— could be asked for the first time as a practical question. From 1957 to 1976, Mao attempted to answer this question with the techniques and values of his successful preliberation experience. Not only was the context of postliberation China different, however, but the role of Mao's political paradigm had changed from that of practical guide to that of ideological standard.

Mao was quite conscious of the first kind of limitation—the transitoriness of any attainment in practical understanding or effectiveness. Two major problems of practical leadership with which Mao had to cope were contextual changes which made experience less relevant and the necessity of a theoretical orientation before action. These problems demanded constant flexibility and attentiveness because they transcended the routine difficulties of leadership.

A basic problem with empirical politics is that present and future developments change the salience of data in unforeseen ways. The apparent solidity of investigation can become seriously misleading if a major shift occurs between the context of observation and the context of application. A major experience of this sort for Mao was the 1926 peasant movement. The optimism of the Hunan Report was based on a month of firsthand investigation into the activities of peasant associations. But the wildfire growth of the associations occurred in a favorable political and military climate; with the change of climate in mid-1927, the "mighty storm" of the peasant movement was disappointingly weak.

Mao was well aware of the problem of contextual invalidation of experience, and his treatment of it in "On Practice" is penetrating. Without flexible alertness to changing circumstances, experience can become narrow empiricism, as subjective and misleading as its opposite, dogmatism. Since prediction involves the assumption that contexts will be similar, Mao was usually cautious in his expectations. Consciousness of the limits of experience prevented Mao from being complacent when entering a new strategic stage. A new stage either demanded basic rethinking and reinvestigation, as in 1936–1937, or it required learning from the experience of others, as with the 1949 emphasis on learning from the USSR.

Besides the problem of contextual invalidation, practical political leadership cannot escape the primacy of theory in the process of thinking. Rational action must be based on theoretical orientation. Experience can modify or even challenge a theoretical orientation, but orientation sets important parameters for experience. Broad investigation of the experience of others vastly reduces the problem of orientation, but investigation itself is an action and has its own interpretive framework. Mao's cognizance of this problem can best be seen in the Xingguo Investigation, in which he emphasizes the importance of personal investigative work and notes that most of his informants were not party members. But a comparison of Philip Huang's research on Xingguo with Mao's study shows certain limits of Mao's investigative interest, and a close reading of Mao's exhortations to investigate also reveals an emphasis on revolutionary effectiveness rather than on investigation for investigation's sake.

Mao was particularly eloquent on the larger problem of the essential but not absolute role of theory in "Oppose Book Worship." His basic principle was that the justification of theory is its usefulness. The slogan "No investigation, no right to speak" captures Mao's contempt for abstract ideology, and it was understandably set upon by the Twenty-eight Bolsheviks as an example of Mao's peasant empiricism. But Mao's critique of the practical pretensions of theory was a critique of dogmatic behavior, not an alternative political paradigm. During the Jiangxi period, Mao remained a practical subordinate of dogmatic leadership and eventually saw his administrative gains lost to the Fifth Encirclement and Suppression Campaign.

The second kind of limitation of a political paradigm is caused by the structural tensions inherent in authoritative leadership. In my opinion Mao was quite aware that this kind of limitation posed constant political problems, but he never confronted it in principle as he had the first kind. There were three major structural problems with the authoritative role which Mao's political paradigm assumed: first, the adjustment from being a subordinate, implementational paradigm to being a directive one; second, the political cross fire in which the intermediate leadership was caught; and third, the tension between the political utility of an image of infallibility and the need for flexibility.

Surely a major reason for the ease with which the Twenty-eight Bolsheviks took command in Jiangxi and an explanation why their influence lingered in Chinese politics until 1941 was that Mao was not anxious to assume the role of general leadership. To solve one's allotted problems is a very different labor from charting the general direction of a movement. Mao made the adjustment brilliantly in the 1936–1942 period, but even in the authoritative formulation of his thought he is loath to move beyond discussion of the task at hand. This reluctance led to the problem of the unclear dialect of Mao's thought and Marxism which I alluded to earlier. Although Mao claimed supreme political authority, his ideological claim was to have correctly applied Marxism. The resulting ambiguities in the ideological role of the Thought of Mao Zedong not only cause headaches to observers of China but confound the ideological dimension of Chinese politics itself.

Another area of painful ambiguities was the role of the cadre, the organizational link between Mao and the masses. On the one hand cadres were enjoined to behave like Mao, to act like "general commanders," flexibly adjusting directives to local conditions. On the other hand, they were subordinates expected to execute orders. Above all, they were expected to act correctly. As in the biblical parable of the talents, Mao granted remarkable discretion to cadres and then held them accountable for their results. Popular mobilization required this approach, and it worked if organizational objectives were clear. The standards for judging effectiveness, however, particularly after 1949, were often ambiguous or conflicting. Certain aspects of Mao's organizational leadership then tended to expose subordinates to uncontrollable personal risk. Until the Cultural Revolution this risk was mitigated by Mao's belief in the inevitability of mistakes and Liu Shaoqi's systematization of inner-party discipline. But the attempt in the Cultural Revolution to solve forcibly the problem of intermediate leadership destroyed the mutual trust which made ambiguous responsibility viable.

Another structural problem of authoritative leadership which became especially acute with the Cultural Revolution was the contradiction between Mao's political image as leader and the necessity to adjust policy according to mistakes. As an individual Mao could experiment, make a mistake, analyze the mistake for subjective weakness and objective misinformation, and correct his action. But Mao was the leader of an organization; to admit a mistake might adversely affect morale and legitimacy and therefore create an additional problem. On the other hand, a false image of infallibility could create cynicism and distrust of official reports. The problem of image versus honesty became serious with the Great Leap Forward. At this time Mao compromised by maintaining a public image of infallibility while admitting his mistakes to cadres.[20] With the factional commitments of the Cultural Revolution and its heavy reliance on his image, however, Mao's mistakes forced him into a more consistent position of infallibility.

The third kind of limitation of Mao's political paradigm was created by its success. After 1949 the old problem of China's theoretical imagination outrunning her political development was replaced by a new one: her political innovations and achievements were outrunning conceptualizations. The immediate solution was to rely on Leninist-Stalinist theories of the socialist state and on Soviet Russia's experience and help with the transition to socialism. But ideological borrowing was no solution to the problem. Chinese conditions were different, Russian experience was not all positive, and twenty-two years of base area government would not be completely irrelevant to the problems of the People's Republic of China. Moreover, it could be expected that China's new stage needed creative policy innovations as well as adjustment of existing models.

As with the other two kinds of limitation, Mao showed awareness of these problems in his politics. The return to Russian tutelage was a recognition of the inadequacy of guerrilla expertise for the problems of socialist construction. Certainly Mao's private comments on the Russians in the 1950s show that he was not surrendering blindly to their advice.[21] Mao's sponsorship of the Hundred Flowers Movement in 1957 and his emphasis on democratic centralism in the early 1960s demonstrate a strong concern for mass creativity and his anxieties about CCP bureaucratism and defensiveness.

Nevertheless, Mao's encouragement of creativity was shaped by his own experience of policy innovation and his conviction that the masses would be educated through struggle. As Mao put it in 1957, "Marxism is a wrangling 'ism,' dealing as it does with contradictions and struggles."[22] Mao's idea of a political forum was not one with guarantees of freedom of speech in the Western sense, but a forum where one had the freedom to risk his political future on the conviction that his contribution would eventually be judged a "fragrant flower" rather than a "poisonous weed." This was a risk Mao himself had often taken, and he heartily recommended it.[23] It was, however, unrealistic to expect this kind of openness to be an adequate encouragement to creativity in a socialist state. Mao had enjoyed the practical freedom to innovate in a chaotic and fragmented China; the political and ideological consolidation of the PRC foreclosed such ventures. Revolutionary effectiveness no longer functioned as a practical criterion of truth. It became an ideological standard of truth—revolutionary effectiveness now meant Mao's idea of revolutionary effectiveness.

The independent course which China took under Mao's helmsmanship from 1957 to 1976 involved many innovations and also wide oscillations in policy, but Mao's active roles in the Great Leap Forward and in the Cultural Revolution constitute in large part the current image of Mao. The link between this image and Mao's early career as described in this book is strong; the values and methods of Mao's later politics were an affirmation of his earlier political experience. But it is important to note that in his last twenty years Mao was active in phases of ideological leadership and passive in more practical phases. The first twenty years of his politics were exactly the reverse. The last limitation of Mao's political paradigm, ironically, was its appropriateness. The practical solution of the problems of one phase could not simply be transmuted into the ideological solution of the problems of the next. The foundations of Mao Zedong's political thought held firm, but the different context produced by its own success changed its significance.

Notes

SOURCES

Chen Cheng, reels 1–21

    A microfilm collection produced by Hoover Institute Microfilms in 1960. It comprises CCP publications captured by the KMT general Chen Cheng when he defeated the Chinese Soviet Republic in Jiangxi (the "Kiangsi Soviet") in 1934. Despite haphazard arrangement it is the most valuable resource for Western studies of the Jiangxi base area from 1930 to 1934.

Keio, reels 1–29

    The Keio microfilm collection was produced at Keio University in 1963 for the Center for Chinese Studies, University of California, Berkeley. It comprises documents on Chinese politics, focusing on the CCP, from 1920 to 1932. The collection includes rare periodicals and monographs, as well as *Gendai Shina no kiroku* [Record of modern China], a Japanese Foreign Office file of articles from Chinese newspapers on domestic politics from 1924 to 1932. The Center for Chinese Studies has prepared an excellent handbook for the materials: *Guide to Early Chinese Historical Materials: The Keio Collection* (Berkeley: Center for Chinese Studies, 1972).

MZJ 1–10

    Mao Zedong Ji [Collected works of Mao Zedong], 10 vols., ed. Takeuchi Minoru et al. (Tokyo: Hokubosha, 1971–1973). Not only an exhaustive collection of Mao's pre-1949 writings, but a variorum edition showing divergences among available texts. The 1920 newspaper articles on Hunan self-government are the only important writings of Mao analyzed here which are not in *MZJ*. For the post-1949 period, see John Starr and Nancy Dyer, comp., *Post Liberation Works of Mao Zedong: A Bibliography and Index* (Berkeley: Center for Chinese Studies, 1976).

SR

    Mao Zedong, *Selected Readings from the Works of Mao Tse-tung* (Beijing: Foreign Languages Press, 1971). Compiled in 1965, *SR* is primarily a collection of highlights from *SW*, but some works, including "Oppose Book Worship" (1930), first appeared here.

SW 1-5
: Mao Zedong, *Selected Works of Mao Tse-tung*, 5 vols. (Beijing: Foreign Languages Press, 1965, 1978). Various collections of Mao's works have been published since the 1940s. The version used here is the official edition of the People's Republic of China. The first four volumes cover the pre-1949 period and were compiled in the early 1950s. The edition was not intended simply to republish old texts. According to the Publication Note, Mao "has read all the articles, made certain verbal changes and, in isolated cases, revised the text." It can be concluded from *MZJ*, though, that the overwhelming majority of emendations are stylistic improvements and simplifications of historical context. *SW* 5, the first of several planned post-1949 volumes, was published very quickly after the downfall of the Gang of Four. In 1979 complaints began to emerge about the quality of editing in *SW* 5.

INTRODUCTION

1. See Stuart Schram, trans. and ed., *Chairman Mao Talks to the People* (New York: Pantheon, 1974), an anthology of Mao's post-1949 writings.
2. Brantly Womack, "Theory and Practice in the Thought of Mao Tse-tung," in James Hsiung, ed., *The Logic of Maoism* (New York: Praeger, 1974), pp. 1-38.
3. See "Communique of the Third Plenum of the Eleventh Central Committee," *Peking Review* 52(20 December 1978):6-16.
4. For a fuller discussion of the 1978 campaign, see Brantly Womack, "Politics and Epistemology in China since Mao," *China Quarterly* 80(December 1979):768-792.
5. Deng's speech at the Army Political Work Conference, *Renmin Ribao*, 3 June 1978, pp. 1-2.
6. Those who are skeptical of the commitment of post-Mao leadership to non-elitist values should read "Bu neng wangji yu shui guanxi" [It is impossible to forget the fish-water relationship], *Renmin Ribao*, 19 August 1978, p. 2. This article discusses the tendency toward party estrangement from the masses since 1949.
7. Song Tianzhang, "Beijing shi fou pi Mao" [Is Beijing really criticizing Mao?], *Zhengming* 11(September 1978):6-7.
8. See Hong Yung Lee, *The Politics of the Chinese Cultural Revolution* (Berkeley: University of California Press, 1978).
9. Attributed to Carlo Schmid, professor and leader of the German Social Democratic Party (SPD), in "Ein Denker in der Politik," *Die Zeit* 50(10 December 1976):6.
10. "Be Concerned with the Well-Being of the Masses" (1934), in *Selected Works of Mao Tse-tung* (Peking: Foreign Languages Press, 1976-1977), vol. 1, p. 150. (Hereafter cited as *SW*.)
11. Schram, *Chairman Mao Talks to the People*, p. 293.
12. Ibid.

CHAPTER 1: MAO BEFORE MARXISM

1. Richard Solomon, *Mao's Revolution and the Chinese Political Culture* (Berkeley: Univeristy of California Press, 1971).
2. Frederic Wakeman, Jr., *History and Will* (Berkeley: University of California Press, 1973).
3. The source for these statements is Mao's autobiographical interview with Edgar Snow in Snow's *Red Star over China* (New York: Grove Press, 1961), pp. 121-188. Although the scholarly studies provide additional information and perspectives, this account remains the most readable and stimulating resource for Mao's early career.
4. Stuart Schram, "From the 'Great Union of the Popular Masses' to the 'Great Alliance,' " *China Quarterly* 49(January 1972):88.
5. Xiao San, *Mao Zedong tongzhi di qing shao nian shidai* [Comrade Mao Zedong's boyhood and youth] (Peking: Renmin Chubanshe, 1949); Li Rui, *Mao Zedong tongzhi di chu qi geming huodong* [Comrade Mao Zedong's early revolutionary activities] (Peking: Renmin Chubanshe, 1957); Li Rui, "Qingnian Mao Zedong di sixiang fangxiang" [The ideological trend of Mao Zedong in his youth], *Lishi Yanjiu* 1(January 1979):33-51.
6. A marginal comment on Friedrich Paulsen's *System der Ethik* recorded by Li Rui, *Mao*, p. 43.
7. The best-known incident is related by Mao: "When I was about thirteen my father invited many guests to his home, and while they were present a dispute arose between the two of us. My father denounced me before the whole group, calling me lazy and useless. This infuriated me. I cursed him and left the house. My mother ran after me and tried to persuade me to return. My father also pursued me, cursing at the same time he demanded me to come back. I reached the edge of a pond and threatened to jump in if he came any nearer. In this situation demands and counter-demands were presented for the cessation of the 'civil war.' My father insisted that I apologize and kowtow as a sign of submission. I agreed to give a one-knee kowtow if he would promise not to beat me. Thus the 'war' ended, and from it I learned that when I defended my rights by open rebellion my father relented, but when I remained meek and submissive he only cursed and beat me the more." See Snow, *Red Star*, p. 126.
8. See Xiao San, *Mao*, pp. 7-10. Incidentally, in this respect Mao was the opposite of Lenin, of whom Maxim Gorky said: "I never met or knew a person who with such intensity and force felt hatred, aversion, and contempt for the misfortunes, grief, and sufferings of the people." M. Gorky, "O Lenine," *Russkii Sovremennik*, 1924/1, quoted in N. Valentinov [N. V. Volski], *The Early Years of Lenin*, trans. Rolf Theen (Ann Arbor: University of Michigan Press, 1969), p. 206.
9. An instance of this is recalled by Mao in Snow, *Red Star*, p. 130.
10. Ibid., p. 125.
11. "Zixiu Daxue changli xuanyan" [Introductory statement of the Hunan Self-Education College], in Takeuchi Minoru et al., eds., *Mao Zedong Ji* [Collected works of Mao Zedong], 10 vols. (Tokyo: Hokubosha, 1971-1973), vol. 1, p. 82. (Hereafter cited as *MZJ*.)

12. I will not attempt to specify in detail the various intellectual influences on Mao because little improvement could be made on Wakeman's treatment of this subject in *History and Will*.
13. Snow, *Red Star*, pp. 129-130.
14. Jerome Chen makes a valiant attempt at narrating the political history of China at the time of Mao's youth in *Mao and the Chinese Revolution* (London: Oxford University Press, 1965).
15. With the exception of Taiwan.
16. *Hunan jinbainian dashi jixu* [A record of major events in Hunan for the past 100 years] (Changsha: Hunan Renmin Chubanshe, 1959), p. 311.
17. In 1920 Mao became involved in a movement for Hunan provincial self-government and wrote some articles on its behalf which are discussed in detail later in this chapter. The Chinese texts of Mao's Hunan self-government articles were published by Angus McDonald in *Hogaku Kenkyu* [Legal research] 2(February 1972):90-107. McDonald later published English translations of these articles in "Mao Tse-tung and the Hunan Self-Government Movement, 1920: An Introduction and Five Translations," *China Quarterly* 68(December 1976):751-777.
18. "*Xiang Jiang Pinglun* quangan xuanyan" [Introductory statement of the *Xiang River Review*] (14 July 1919), *MZJ* 1:55.
19. Snow, *Red Star*, p. 133.
20. From a letter quoted in *Wu-Si shiqi qigan jieshao* [Introduction to periodicals of the May Fourth period] (Peking: Renmin Chubanshe, 1958), vol. 1, p. 154.
21. Snow, *Red Star*, pp. 155-156; Li Weihan, "Huiyi Xinmin Xuehui" [Reminiscence of the New Citizens Study Society], *Lishi Yanjiu* 3(March 1979):3-24.
22. Consider the case of the Sichuan (Szechuan) communists who established a provincial party branch in 1924 not knowing that a Central Committee had existed for three years. See "Wu Yüchiang," in Anne B. Clark and Donald Klein, *Biographical Dictionary of Chinese Communism* (Cambridge: Harvard University Press, 1971), vol. 2, p. 961.
23. There is a tantalizing eleven-page description of this work in *Periodicals of the May Fourth Period*, vol. 1, pp. 151-161.
24. My reference edition of this work is the two-volume third edition (Berlin: Wilhelm Hertz, 1894). Some chapters were retitled in the third edition, and Cai's translation of the titles indicates that he used the later ones. From Li's manner of citation and the pagination given, I suspect that Cai's translation does not include much more than "Book Two: Basic Concepts and Questions of Principle" (vol. 1, pp. 145-429). However, I have not seen the Chinese translation. An overview of Paulsen's philosophy is available in Wakeman's *History and Will*, pp. 195-206, and in Paul Fritsch, *Friedrich Paulsens philosophischer Standpunkt*, vol. 17 of *Abhandlungen zur Philosophie und ihrer Geschichte*, ed. R. Falckenberg (Leipzig: Quelle und Meyer, 1911).
25. Most of the work is available in Stuart Schram's *Political Thought of Mao Tse-tung* (New York: Praeger, 1969). There is a complete, deluxe French

translation by Schram: Mao Zedong, *Une Étude de l'Éducation Physique: Article traduit et presenté par Stuart R. Schram* (Paris: Mouton, 1962).
26. *MZJ* 1:53–55. The *Xiang River Review* published only four regular issues. The fifth was suppressed by Zhang Jingyao, the Hunan warlord.
27. "Minzhong di da lianhe," *MZJ* 1:57–69. Translation by Stuart Schram in *China Quarterly* 49(January 1972):76–87.
28. Li, *Mao*, pp. 38–44; Li, "The Ideological Trend of Mao," p. 45.
29. Paulsen, *Ethik*, vol. 1.
30. A point by Fritsch, *Paulsen*, pp. 14, 30.
31. Mao's marginal comments run to 12,100 words (the book is 100,000 words), and underlining abounds. Mao said in 1950, "At that time we were all a bunch of idealists. Happening upon the idealist theories of books like this, I felt a very deep interest and received a revelation which really caused my mind to incline toward it despite its impurities and idealistic dualism." See Zhou Shizhao, "Di yi shifan shidai di Mao zhuxi" [Chairman Mao at the First Normal School], *Xin Guancha* 2(2) (25 January 1951):12. It might be remembered that Marx indicates a similar respect for idealism in the first "Thesis on Feuerbach."
32. Li, *Mao*, p. 42.
33. Ibid., p. 43.
34. Mao's efforts at physical education were gratified in an appropriate manner: the First Normal won more than sixty medals in the 1917 provincial competitions.
35. The text is reprinted in *MZJ* 1:35–47. A photostat of the original is printed with Stuart Schram's French translation. This photostat is more useful than the *MZJ* version because it preserves Mao's profuse emphases. Professor Schram's English and French translations were of great help in rendering the quotations from this work, and his introduction to the French translation contains much relevant background information.
36. *MZJ* 1:41; Schram, *Political Thought*, p. 158.
37. *MZJ* 1:35.
38. *MZJ* 1:40, 39.
39. *SW* 3:271–274.
40. These activities are described by Xiao San and Li Rui.
41. From Mao's autobiography; Snow, *Red Star*, p. 145.
42. Chang Kuo-t'ao [Zhang Guotao], *The Rise of the Chinese Communist Party, 1921–1927*, vol. 1 of *Autobiography of Chang Kuo-t'ao* (Lawrence: University of Kansas Press, 1971), p. 17.
43. *MZJ* 1:49–51.
44. *MZJ* 1:53.
45. According to *Periodicals of the May Fourth Period* (vol. 1), the review had a tremendous impact on the Hunan revolutionary movement and a significant effect on the whole country. Two thousand copies were printed of the first issue, and it was sold out the same day. Five thousand copies were printed of subsequent issues. Zhang Guotao, never a great admirer of Mao, writes, "This paper, which advocated the precepts of the New Culture Movement, ranked high in prestige among the various little provincial

publications." See Chang [Zhang], *Autobiography*, vol. 1, p. 129. Because Chen Duxiu was impressed with the *Review* he contacted Mao about organizing a Communist Party branch in Hunan; see *Autobiography*, vol. 1, p. 105.

46. Quoted in *Periodicals of the May Fourth Period*, vol. 1, pp. 146–147.
47. The term which is translated "democracy" throughout this chapter is *pingmin zhuyi*, which is more commonly translated as "populism." But Mao's parenthetical equivalences of this term in its first usage are *demokelasi* (a transliteration of "democracy") and *yi zuo min ben zhuyi, min zhu zhuyi, shu min zhuyi* (government of the people, by the people, and for the people). Thus I prefer Mao's translation to the standard one.
48. *MZJ* 1:54.
49. Li, *Mao*, p. 42.
50. *Periodicals from the May Fourth Period*, vol. 1, p. 150.
51. *MZJ* 1:58, 65; Schram, "The Great Union of the Popular Masses," *China Quarterly* 49(January 1972):77, 84.
52. *MZJ* 1:68–69; Schram, "Great Union," pp. 86–87.
53. "Zur Kritik der hegelschen Rechtsphilosophie: Einleitung," in *Marx-Engels Werke* (Berlin: Dietz, 1972), vol. 1, pp. 390–391. Marx reasons from the peculiar misery and backwardness of German society to its potential for radical revolution (p. 387) and concludes that "the *emancipation* of *Germany* is the *emancipation* of *mankind*" (p. 391).
54. *MZJ* 1:57; Schram, "Great Union," p. 76.
55. *MZJ* 1:69; Schram, "Great Union," p. 87.
56. Schram, "From the 'Great Union' to the 'Great Alliance,' " p. 94.
57. McDonald, "Chinese Texts," p. 100; "Translations," p. 769.
58. *MZJ* 1:59–60; Schram, "Great Union," pp. 78–79.
59. Solomon, *Mao's Revolution*, p. 184.
60. See Zhang Guotao's almost humorous story of the difficulty of founding the Peking Communist Party nucleus with a majority of anarchists in *Autobiography*, vol. 1, pp. 110–113; see also Wolfgang Bauer, *China und die Hoffnung auf Glück* (Munich: Carl Hanser, 1971), p. 489.
61. Jiang Qun, "Wuzhengfu zhuyi zhi jiepo" [An analysis of anarchism], *Communist* 4(7 May 1923):14. Keio reel 1.
62. Mao mentions "rich and poor classes" and "powerful and weak classes" (p. 59), but they are not regarded as the basic units of the union of the masses.
63. Snow, *Red Star*, p. 147. I do not mean this to be taken pejoratively—the mixture is coherent and not superficial.
64. Roxanne Witke translates many of these fragments in her article "Mao, Women and Suicide in the May Fourth Era," *China Quarterly* 31(July–September 1967):128–147.
65. "Notes from *Socialist Upsurge in China's Countryside*," *SW* 5:263.
66. McDonald, "Chinese Texts," pp. 90–107; "Translations," pp. 751–777.
67. McDonald, "Chinese Texts," English summary, p. 105.
68. "Zizhi yundong yu shehui geming" [The self-government movement and the social revolution], *Communist* 3(7 April 1921):8. Keio reel 1.

69. Quoted in *Periodicals of the May Fourth Period*, vol. 1, p. 156, from *Collected Correspondence of New Citizens Study Society Members*, vol. 2.
70. Snow, *Red Star*, pp. 154-155.
71. "Wenhua shushe zuzhi dagang" [Outline of the organization of the Cultural Book Society], *MZJ* 1:71.
72. "Wenhua shushe shewu baogao, di er qi" [Report of the affairs of the Cultural Book Society, second period], *MZJ* 1:77. The first-period report concerned the founding of the society. The printing department published the three-volume *Collected Correspondence of the New Citizens Study Society Members* which Mao edited.
73. Robert Owen, *A New View of Society* (London: Everyman, 1963), pp. 7-10.
74. Han Suyin, *The Morning Deluge* (Boston: Little, Brown, 1972), p. 101.
75. *MZJ* 1:81.
76. *MZJ* 1:82-83.
77. *MZJ* 1:84.
78. A counterattack is indicated in Li, *Mao*, p. 154.
79. *MZJ* 1:37, 41, 61-62.
80. The term is also used in "Great Union" (*MZJ* 1:58-59), but only generally.
81. *MZJ* 1:83. The same notion of class an an excluding and oppressing group is echoed in Mao's 1964 reference to a "class of bureaucratic officials." This flexible and noneconomic notion of class became central to the political analysis of the Gang of Four. See Tang Tsou, "Mao Tse-tung Thought, the Last Struggle for Succession, and the Post Mao Era," *China Quarterly* 71(September 1977):498-527, especially pp. 506-510.
82. By "exclusive" I mean defining itself as opposed to a larger group. The closest Mao comes to an exclusive reference group is in the Workers' Night School advertisements. There he explains the motives of "us students" to potential enrollees. However, Mao does his best to identify the project with the workers' idea of their own interests by using a question-answer format. Moreover, the night school was directed at eliminating the main barrier between workers and students—that of literacy.
83. "Physical Education," *MZJ* 1:35; McDonald, "Chinese Texts," p. 99.
84. Quoted in *Periodicals of the May Fourth Period*, vol. 1, p. 152.
85. *MZJ* 1:76. There are similar occurrences in McDonald, "Chinese Texts," pp. 99-100, and "Self-Education College," *MZJ* 1:84.
86. Quoted in *Periodicals of the May Fourth Period*, vol. 1, p. 152.
87. "Introductory Statement of the *Xiang River Review*," *MZJ* 1:54; "Introductory Statement of the Hunan Self-Education College," *MZJ* 1:82-83.
88. McDonald, "Chinese Texts," p. 100; "Translations," p. 772.
89. *MZJ* 1:41; Schram, *Political Thought*, p. 158. Emphasized in the original.

CHAPTER 2: MAO, THE PARTY, AND THE NATIONAL REVOLUTION: 1923-1927

1. "Xin Shidai fagan ci" [An introduction to *New Age*], *MZJ* 1:83.
2. "Wu-si shiqi Hunan renmin fan di fan feng yundong baokan jixu jilu zhi san" [Hunan antiimperialist, antifeudal popular movement periodicals of

the May Fourth period, third collection], *Hunan Lishi Ciliao* 4(1959): 76-77.
3. This was an intentional organizational strategy on Mao's part. See Li Weihan, "Reminiscence of the New Citizens Study Society," p. 14.
4. Ibid., p. 18.
5. For an interesting justification of the founding of a Russian Study Club, see Yin Bo (Peng Huang), "Duiyu faqi Elosi yanjiuhui di ganyan" [Thoughts on the founding of a Russian Study Club], *Hunan Dagong Bao*, 27 August 1920; in *Hunan Historical Materials* 4(1959):87-90.
6. Better known as Siao Yü. In Snow, *Red Star*, p. 144, Mao accused Siao of embezzling from the Peking Palace Museum in 1934; presumably Siao's retaliation is his book, *Mao Tse-tung and I Were Beggars* (New York: Collier, 1959).
7. The longest excerpt is translated by Stuart Schram in *Political Thought*, pp. 296-298. The commentaries are, first, "Hunan May Fourth Periodicals," pp. 74-85, and, second, *Periodicals of the May Fourth Period*, vol. 1, pp. 151-161.
8. "Hunan May Fourth Periodicals," p. 83.
9. Wu Xie, "Wo wei shenma zhujiang Gongchandang zhuyi?" [Why do I recommend communism?], *Communist* 4(7 May 1921):24. Keio reel 1.
10. Sun Duo, "Zhongguo guomin yundong zhi guoqu ji jianglai" [The past and future of China's national movement], *Qianfeng* 1(1 July 1923):8-9. Keio reel 1.
11. This comparison is made in Sun Duo, "Past and Future," p. 2.
12. Symptomatic of a perfunctory grasp of Marxism in the early issues of *Communist* is that "Engels" is spelled in the text "Eongeles" after the characters for his name—incidentally, in the same article "Kropotkin" is spelled correctly (no. 4, p. 14). The current social structure of China is described as capitalist (p. 26).
13. See for instance "Ben bao lubu" [Announcement of this paper], *Vanguard* 1(1 July 1923):1.
14. Zhang Guotao, *Autobiography*, vol. 1.
15. These activities and their significance for Hunan are carefully described in Angus McDonald, *Urban Origins of Rural Revolution* (Berkeley: University of California Press, 1978).
16. See Maurice Meisner, *Li Ta-chao and the Origins of Chinese Marxism* (Cambridge: Harvard University Press, 1967), pp. 180, 188.
17. "Yingguo ren yu Liao Ruhao" [Englishmen and Liao Ruhao], *Guide Weekly* 38(29 August 1923), MZJ 1:93-95; "Shengxian jing yu Zhao Hengdi" [The 'Provincial Constitution Sutra' and Zhao Hengdi], *Guide Weekly* 36(15 August 1923), MZJ 1:91-92.
18. Sun Duo, "Past and Future," p. 4.
19. The expression "language game" comes from the philosophy of Ludwig Wittgenstein and refers to the quasi-institutional unity of word usage, behavior, and understanding of the world involved in living in society. See Karl Otto Apel, *Hermeneutik und Ideologiekritik* (Frankfurt: Suhrkamp, 1973), p. 8n.
20. "Beijing zhengbian yu shangren" [The Beijing coup and the merchants],

MZJ 1:87–90. Every article in this issue of *Guide Weekly* (no. 31) begins "Beijing zhengbian yu . . ." (The Beijing coup and . . .).
21. The mechanism of this enforcement is the subject of another article, "Zhiyan shui" [The cigarette tax], *Guide Weekly* 38(29 August 1923), *MZJ* 1:97–98.
22. *MZJ* 1:88.
23. Ibid.
24. "The Cigarette Tax," *MZJ* 1:97.
25. "Zichan jieji di geming yu geming di zichan jieji" [The capitalist revolution and revolutionary capitalists], *Guide Weekly* 22(25 April 1923). In his book *Guanyu Mao Zedong tongzhi zai di yi ci guonei geming zhanzheng shiqi di liang pian zhuzuo* [On Comrade Mao's two essays from the period of the First Revolutionary Civil War] (Beijing: Renmin Chubanshe, 1953), Zhang Ruxin compares Chen's essay to Mao's "Analysis of the Classes in Chinese Society" and the "Hunan Report" to illustrate the difference between Chen's opportunism and Mao's revolutionary Marxist thinking. This is of course tremendously unfair to Chen since his article was written three years earlier. But compared to Mao's articles on the same question, Chen's style involves a more rigid, compartmental class analysis and the moderation or control of mass activities.
26. As explained in the "Manifesto of the First National Congress of the Kuomintang" (30 January 1924), included in *The Kuomintang: Selected Historical Documents, 1894–1969*, ed. Milton Shieh (Baltimore: St. John's University Press, 1970), pp. 75–86.
27. For instance it was shared by Feng Yuxiang's Guomin Jun (National Army) and by the anticommunist Western Hills group of old KMT members. On the antiimperialism of the Western Hills group see *MZJ* 1:140 and also Tang Leang-li, *The Inner History of the Chinese Revolution* (New York: Dutton, 1930), pp. 230–231.
28. "The Capitalist Revolution and Revolutionary Capitalists," p. 164. What Chen is trying to say here could be much better said in terms of principal and secondary contradictions.
29. See Karl Marx and Friedrich Engels, *Collected Works* (New York: International Publishers, 1975), vol. 3, pp. 294–297.
30. Chen Duxiu, "Zhongguo guomin geming yu shehui ge jieji" [The Chinese national revolution and the various classes of society], *Vanguard* 2(December 1923):1–9.
31. Chen fails to note that because of imperialist penetration the proletariat can grow faster than the native bourgeoisie in a dependent country. The Vietnamese justify the early proletarian leadership of their national revolution with this analysis. See Le Duan, "Hold High the Revolutionary Banner of Creative Marxism" (1963), in *Le Duan Selected Works* (Hanoi: Foreign Languages Press, 1977), pp. 66–67.
32. "Wang Chen lianhe Guo-Gong hezuo dao di" [Joint declaration of Wang and Chen of KMT–CCP cooperation to the end], *Chenbao* (6 April 1927); in *Gendai Shina no kiroku* [Selected items of record on contemporary China], April 1927. Keio reel 13.
33. Mao Zedong, "On New Democracy," *SW* 2:339–384.

34. For a thorough study of Mao's later united front politics see Lyman Van Slyke, *Enemies and Friends: The United Front in Chinese Communist History* (Stanford: Stanford University Press, 1967).
35. See "Zhongguo Lening—Mao Zedong" [China's Lenin—Mao Zedong], in *Zhongguo di hong xing* [China's red star], ed. Lin Yiqing (n.p.: Xin Zhongguo Chubanshe, 1937), pp. 145-152.
36. "*Zhengzhi Zhoubao* fagan zhi liyou" [The reason for publishing *Political Weekly*], *Political Weekly* 1(12 December 1925); *MZJ* 1:111.
37. "Xiang zuo haishi xiang you?" [To the left or to the right?], *Political Weekly* 2(13 December 1925); *MZJ* 1:127-128.
38. A major upsurge of antiimperialist sentiment and organization which originated with the killing of demonstrators by the International Settlement police in Shanghai on 30 May 1925 and culminated in the great Hong Kong strike of 1925-1926.
39. Perhaps the second phase would be a bit more complex, since it could be expected that Wu Peifu and Sun Quanfang would quarrel over the spoils. See "Anti-Feng Propaganda Outline," *MZJ* 1:102.
40. *MZJ* 1:105.
41. "San-san-san-yi zhi" [The 3-3-3-1 policy], *Political Weekly* 1(5 December 1925); *MZJ* 1:113.
42. "You pai di zui da benling" [The greatest ability of the rightist faction], *Political Weekly* 3(20 December 1925); *MZJ* 1:140.
43. *MZJ* 1:139.
44. This overemphasis has recently been enthusiastically corrected by Roy Hofheinz, *The Broken Wave* (Cambridge: Harvard University Press, 1977). The best work on the early peasant movement is Peng Pai's own account of his activities in Hailufeng: *Seeds of Peasant Revolt: Report on the Haifeng County Peasant Movement*, trans. D. Holoch, East Asia Papers no. 1 (Ithaca: Cornell University, 1973).
45. Snow, *Red Star*, p. 160.
46. Wang Shoudao, "Geming di yaolan" [Cradle of the revolution], *Lishi Yanjiu* 4(1977):60-61.
47. Zhang Guotao, *Autobiography*, vol. 1, p. 308.
48. See Peng Pai, *Seeds of Peasant Revolt*; Chen Duxiu, "Zhongguo nongmin wenti" [The Chinese peasant question], *Vanguard* 1(1 July 1923):51-57. Keio reel 1.
49. "Gao Zhongguo di nongmin" [To the Chinese peasants], *Communist* 1(7 April 1921):3-7.
50. Ibid., p. 3.
51. Chen Duxiu, "Chinese Peasant Question," p. 55.
52. James Harrison, *The Long March to Power* (New York: Praeger, 1972), p. 61.
53. "Quanguo nongmin gaiguan" [Overview of the national peasant movement], originally in *Zhongguo nongmin wenti* [The Chinese peasant question]. Included in a rich anthology: *Di yi ci guonei geming zhanzheng shiqi di nongmin yundong* [The peasant movement in the period of the First Revolutionary Civil War] (Beijing: Renmin Chubanshe, 1953), pp. 7-8.

54. *Peasant Movement in the First Civil War*, pp. 20-32. See also Wang Shoudao, "Cradle of the Revolution."
55. "Zhongguo nongmin zhong ge jieji di fenshi ji qi duiyu geming di taidu" [An analysis of the various classes among the Chinese peasantry and their attitudes toward revolution], *Zhongguo nongmin* [The Chinese peasant] 1(January 1926); *MZJ* 1:153-159.
56. *MZJ* 1:156.
57. *MZJ* 1:154.
58. We can assume that the foundation of warlord military power on landlord economic power is a chief theme of a lost Mao pamphlet from this period, *The Class Basis of Zhao Hengti and the Tasks before Us*, referred to in Snow, *Red Star*, p. 161.
59. "Zhongguo shehui ge jieji di fenxi" [An analysis of the classes in Chinese society], *The Chinese Peasant* 1/2(February 1926); *MZJ* 1:161-173. An abbreviated version is the first article in *SW* 1.
60. The relevant passage of this manifesto is as follows: "In China today, from north to south, from the commercial centers to the villages and hamlets, poor peasants and overworked laborers are to be found everywhere. Because of the sufferings which they have undergone and their aspirations for liberation, there is in both of them a powerful will to revolt against imperialism. Therefore the success of the national revolution depends upon the participation of the peasants and the laborers of the whole country. The Kuomintang is now engaged upon a determined struggle against militarism and imperialism, against the classes opposed to the interests of the peasants and laborers. It is a struggle for the peasants and laborers, one in which the peasants and laborers also struggle for themselves." See *KMT Documents*, pp. 81-82.
61. *MZJ* 1:161.
62. *MZJ* 1:162.
63. Ibid.
64. "Guomin geming yu nongmin yundong" [The national revolution and the peasant movement], written as the foreword for *Nongmin wenti* [The peasant question]; also published in *Nongmin yundong* [The peasant movement] 8(21 September 1926); *MZJ* 1:175-179.
65. *MZJ* 1:175.
66. *MZJ* 1:176.
67. The first instance of this pattern of argument is in "A Study of Physical Education," where Mao argues that moral, intellectual, and physical education are interrelated but physical education is basic. The pattern dominates Mao's 1956 speech on "The Ten Major Relationships," *SW* 5:284-307.
68. Originally the scope of the book was to have been even broader, including both the problem of oppression caused by people (imperialism, landlords, and such) and the problem of oppression caused by nature (drought, sickness, insects, and the like). Even though problems of the second sort were eventually excluded, Mao emphasizes that they deserve active attention even before the first type of problem is solved.

69. *MZJ* 1:177.
70. See Martin Rein, *Social Science and Public Policy* (New York: Penguin, 1976), p. 86.
71. *MZJ* 1:177.
72. See *KMT Documents*, pp. 120, 123-124; Zhang Guotao, *Autobiography*, vol. 1, pp. 599-600.
73. According to Tang Leang-li, this measure was introduced in Guangdong as early as 1921 (*Inner History*, p. 139). As late as November 1926, however, the Hunan peasant movement had not suggested election of county magistrates (*MZJ* 1:193).
74. *KMT Documents*, p. 131.
75. From the "Readers' Voices" column of *Guide Weekly* 184(21 January 1927):1957.
76. Ironically, this comment is taken from a short article by Chen on the 1923 setback in Peng Pai's Haifeng efforts: "Guangdong nongmin yu Hunan nongmin" [Guangdong peasants and Hunan peasants], *Guide Weekly* 48(12 December 1923):368.
77. Zhang Guotao, *Autobiography*, vol. 1, p. 598.
78. Zhang's description of Borodin's vacillation regarding peasant policy is instructive in this regard: "The views that Borodin expressed on the peasant land problem generally changed with China's political climate. Early in 1924 he had proposed to Dr. Sun Yat-sen such plans as confiscation of the property of landlords and nationalization of land, but they were not accepted by Sun. In 1925, following establishment of the National Government, Borodin's entire efforts were directed toward close cooperation of the CCP with the KMT leftists to consolidate the revolutionary dictatorship in Guangdong, and so he stopped talking about the land revolution. On May 15, 1926, after the Second Plenum of the KMT, he was no longer optimistic over the future of KMT-CCP cooperation, and so he again stressed the land revolution. The view of the Guangdong District Committee [opposing the CCP agrarian resolution of July 1926 as too mild] . . . had his support. Toward the end of 1926, after his arrival at Wuhan, his attention was devoted to developing the anti-Chiang front, and once more he ceased to attach importance to the peasant land problem." See *Autobiography*, vol. 1, pp. 600-601.
79. "Mao Zedong tongzhi di zhongyang nongmin yundong jiangxi suo" [The Central Peasant Movement Institute run by Comrade Mao Zedong], *Lishi Yanjiu* 5(1977):26-27.
80. The counterattack is described in detail by Shu Jian in "Guangdong nongmin yundong zuijin zhuankang" [The most recent situation of the Guangdong peasant movement], *Guide Weekly* 185(27 January 1927):1972-1974.
81. "Guangdong nongmin yundong gaikuang" [An overview of the Guangdong peasant movement], in *Peasant Movement in the First Civil War*, p. 39.
82. Ibid., pp. 17-19.
83. Shi Feng, *Fang Zhimin* (Shanghai: Shanghai Renmin Chubanshe, 1975), pp. 15-22.

84. Since 21 May is called the "Day of the Horse," this is known as the "Horse Day Incident." See "Da geming shiqi Mao zhuxi zai Wuhan" [Chairman Mao in Wuhan at the time of the great revolution], *Lishi Yanjiu* 5(1977):24.
85. The institute had over 800 students in its first and only class (180 peasants, 40 "responsible persons from peasant militias," 140 experienced movement workers, 40 workers, and 400 students). The class started on 7 March 1927 and graduated on 18 June 1927. See "Central Peasant Movement Institute."
86. *MZJ* 1:201–205; "Central Peasant Movement Institute," p. 31.
87. *MZJ* 1:205.
88. *SW* 1:29.
89. *MZJ* 1:205.
90. "Hunan nongmin yundong kaocha baogao" [Report of an investigation of the Hunan peasant movement]; *MZJ* 1:207–248; *SW* 1:23–59.
91. "Chairman Mao in Wuhan," p. 19.
92. Ibid., p. 19; also Hofheinz, *The Broken Wave*, pp. 310–311.
93. The best discussion of editing in the *Selected Works* is Jerome Chen's essay on "Mao's Literary Style" in Chen, *Mao Papers* (London: Oxford University Press, 1970), pp. xv–xxxi.
94. "*Geming tongzhi,*" *MZJ* 1:208, 212; "*geming dang*" (revolutionary party), p. 233; "*geming pai*" (revolutionary faction), p. 212.
95. *MZJ* 1:207–208. I follow the translation of *SW* as closely as the original text will allow.
96. It should be noted, however, that Mao does not assume omniscience in peasant matters. Although he evidently expects the spread of cooperatives to be a basic part of rural reconstruction, he does no more than indicate their potential because experimentation with them was just beginning.
97. This phrase and the general lack of historical references in the report is an interesting contrast to Li Dazhao's "Tudi yu nongmin" [Land and the peasants] of early 1926. There the emphasis is on the continuity of present unrest with Chinese peasant rebellions and with the Taiping Heavenly Kingdom. See *Selected Works of Li Dazhao*, pp. 523–536.
98. *MZJ* 1:212.
99. *MZJ* 1:213.
100. A "riffraff theory" of the peasant associations is provided by the respected historian and member of the KMT left, Tang Leang-li: "In order to understand the agrarian problem in China, an analysis of the social groupings in the countryside is necessary. As elsewhere, the rural population in China consists, briefly speaking, of landlords, farmers, and vagabonds without any occupation. Owing to the peculiar character of the Chinese family system, both the very rich and the very poor are found in one family, the rich members being landlords and the poor leading a vagrant life. There is an obligation on the part of the richer members of the family to support their poorer brothers, who, however, only get a bare livelihood. It is these poor brothers of the landlords who mainly compose the class of the vagabonds. They have much the same ideas and outlook as their richer brothers. The Communist agrarian policy now [1927–1930] merely works in the inter-

ests of these vagabonds, not of the peasant-cultivators, the farmers. For the latter are on the whole unable to read and to understand the meaning of Communist agitation. The vagabonds, on the other hand, are more literate, being gentry-to-be, and to them the policy of land seizure had a special appeal. Not so to the majority of the bona fide farmers, who cannot gain anything by it but who are bound to suffer on account of the disorganization of the whole system." See *Inner History*, pp. 272-273.
101. *MZJ* 1:219.
102. See Hofheinz, *The Broken Wave*, pp. 34-53.
103. *MZJ* 1:249. "As told by Lin Xiang (77-76 BC) in his *Xin Xu*, Lord She was so fond of dragons that he adorned his whole palace with drawings and carvings of them. But when a real dragon heard of his infatuation and paid him a visit, he was frightened out of his wits." See *SW* 1:59, n. 35.
104. *SW* 1:307.
105. See Peter Lösche, *Der Bolschewismus im Urteil der deutschen Sozialdemokratie* (Berlin: Colloquium Verlag, 1967), particularly pp. 269-270. Another similarity in the German and Chinese receptions was the role played by the Versailles Peace Conference: "[German] intellectuals and literati who lost their confidence in Western parliamentary democracy because of the harsh terms of peace proposed by the Entente at Versailles prepared the ground for the later Bolshevization of the German Communist Party [KPD] through their uncritical, emotional turning toward the Russian Soviets." (Ibid., p. 272)
106. Ibid., pp. 250-257.
107. Georg Lukacs' phrase, quoted approvingly by Karl Korsch in a review of Lukacs' book on Lenin. See K. Korsch, *Die materialistische Geschichtsauffassung* (Frankfurt: Europäische Verlagsanstalt, 1971), p. 149.
108. In Georg Lukacs, *Geschichte und Klassenbewusstsein* (Berlin: Malik, 1923), pp. 298-342.
109. Ibid., p. 335.
110. Ibid., p. 327.
111. "A really thorough centralization of all of the strength of the Party will of itself because of its inner dynamic push the Party forward in the direction of activity and initiative." (Ibid., p. 334)
112. Karl Korsch, *Revolutionary Theory*, ed. Douglas Kellner (Austin: University of Texas Press, 1977), provides a good introduction and a representative selection of texts.
113. Antonio Gramsci, *The Modern Prince and Other Writings* (New York: International Publishers, 1957).
114. "The Southern Question" (1926), ibid., pp. 30-31.
115. Lukacs, *Geschichte und Klassenbewusstsein*, p. 300.
116. The most obvious is his disapproval of violent parties in "Opening Statement of the *Xiang River Review*" (*MZJ* 1:54) and in "The Great Union of the Popular Masses" (*MZJ* 1:59) and his characterization of such views as those of the small landlords and rich owner-peasants in "Peasant Classes" (*MZJ* 1:154-156). Another would be between the evaluation of the revolutionary role of the merchants in 1923 and the shift of focus toward the peasantry in 1926.

117. See "Opening Statement of the *Xiang River Review*" (*MZJ* 1:54). The same kind of thinking lies behind the set of exercises at the end of "A Study of Physical Education" (*MZJ* 1:44–47).

CHAPTER 3: RURAL REVOLUTION: 1927–1931

1. For a short description of the second most interesting base, that of Fang Zhimin in northeastern Jiangxi (Min Zhe Gan), see Ilpyong Kim, *The Politics of Chinese Communism* (Berkeley: University of California Press, 1973), pp. 40–46. See also Shi Feng, *Fang Zhimin*.
2. Quoted in "Zhonggong 'ba-qi' huiyi gao quan dang dangyuan shu" [A letter to members of the whole party from the 7 August CCP meeting], in *Zhongguo xin minzhu zhuyi geming shi cankao ciliao* [Reference materials for the history of China's new democratic revolution], ed. Hu Hua (Beijing: Zhongguo Tushu Faxing Gongsi, 1951), p. 217.
3. Text in Hu Hua, *New Democracy Materials*, pp. 191–223. Document in C. Brandt, B. Schwartz, and J. K. Fairbank, *Documentary History of Chinese Communism* (Cambridge: Harvard University Press, 1952), pp. 102–118.
4. Roy Hofheinz gives an account of this in "The Autumn Harvest Uprising," *China Quarterly* 32(October–December 1967):37–87; see also Liu Xing, "Qiushou qiyi qianhou di pianduan huiyi" [Memories of episodes surrounding the Autumn Harvest Uprising], in *Zhongguo gongchandang zai Jiangxi diqu lingdao geming douzheng di lishi cailiao* [Historical materials of the revolutionary struggle led by the CCP in the Jiangxi area], vol. 1, pp. 57–61; see also *Hunan History*, pp. 536–540.
5. *Hunan History*, p. 540.
6. The "Ning-Han War" from October 1927 to March 1928. See *Hunan History*, pp. 542–544.
7. Quoted in *SW* 1:98.
8. "Zhongguo gongchandang di liu ci quanguo daibiao dahui wenjian" [Documents of the CCP Sixth National Congress], in Hu Hua, *New Democracy Materials*, p. 234. In Brandt, Schwartz, and Fairbank, *Documentary History*, pp. 127–155.
9. See Chen, *Mao*, p. 153.
10. This resurgence of communism was noted throughout China. See "Zhongguo gongchandang di mingyun" [The fate of the CCP], in the *Tianjian Da Gong Bao*, 31 May 1930. Included in the *Gendai Shina no kiroku* [Record of contemporary China], June 1930. Keio reel 21.
11. "Xiang-Gan bianjie ge xian dang di erci daibiao dahui jueyian" [Draft resolution of the second congress of county party representatives of the Xiang-Gan border area], *MZJ* 2:15–23; *SW* 1:63–72.
12. "Jinggangshan qianwei dui zhongyang di baogao" [Report of the Jinggangshan front committee to the center], *MZJ* 2:25–66; *SW* 1:73–104.
13. *MZJ* 2:16; John Rue, *Mao Tse-tung in Opposition* (Stanford: Stanford University Press, 1966), p. 149.
14. My interpretation, which emphasizes the divisions among warlords rather than those among the imperialists, differs considerably from the more imperialism-oriented view advanced by John Gittings in *The World and China, 1922–1972* (London: Eyre Methuen, 1974), pp. 35–51. Our inter-

pretations are not completely different—for myself, Mao, and Gittings, the phenomena of warlordism and imperialism in China are closely related. But in my opinion Gittings makes a mistake by considering Mao's 1928 viewpoint to be identical with his more nationally oriented statements of 1936. Mao's basic problem in 1928 was surviving warlord politics, the vagaries of which were indirectly related to—but not derivable from—splits among the imperialists. The territoriality of warlord politics led to Mao's interstitial strategy of survival.

15. Given the ups and downs of factional politics, the persistence of many leaders is more remarkable than their circulation. Some examples would be: Duan Qirui, Wu Peifu, Feng Yuxiang.
16. *MZJ* 2:54.
17. See Edward Shils, "Center and Periphery," in his *The Logic of Personal Knowledge* (London: Routledge and Kegan Paul, 1961). However, Shils emphasizes the center almost exclusively. Behind my analysis of their interdependence are the Hegelian notions of *Ansichsein* and *Fürsichsein*.
18. Philip Kuhn, "Local Self-Government under the Republic," in *Conflict and Control in Late Imperial China*, ed. F. Wakeman and C. Grant (Berkeley: University of California Press, 1975), pp. 257–298.
19. *MZJ* 2:65.
20. Ibid.
21. *MZJ* 2:81–82.
22. Kuo, *Analytical History*, vol. 2, pp. 41, 43.
23. *SW* 1:124.
24. "Mao Zedong gei Yuan Guoping di xin" [A letter from Mao Zedong to Yuan Guoping] (1932), *MZJ* 3:96–98.
25. "Gei Lin Biao tongzhi di xin" [A letter to Lin Biao], *MZJ* 2:127–141; *SW* 1:117–128.
26. See the April 1930 letters supplied by Kuo, *Analytical History*, vol. 2, pp. 38–43. Zhang Guotao reports that the base areas were supporting Li Lisan financially at this time; see *Autobiography*, vol. 2, p. 166.
27. *MZJ* 2:129.
28. "Now, if your Majesty will institute a government whose action shall be benevolent, this will cause all the officers in the kingdom to wish to stand in your Majesty's court, and all the farmers to wish to plough in your Majesty's fields, and all the merchants, both traveling and stationary, to wish to store their goods in your Majesty's marketplace, and all traveling strangers to wish to make their tours on your Majesty's roads, and all throughout the kingdom those who feel aggrieved by their rulers to wish to come and complain to your Majesty. And when they are so bent, who will be able to keep them back?" See *Mencius*, bk. 1, pt. 1, chap. 7:18; trans. James Legge (New York: Dover, 1970), pp. 146–147. Maoist examples: the best propaganda to enemy soldiers is the treatment that captured and wounded soldiers receive from the Red Army (*MZJ* 2:44); the Red Army's behavior and regulations are real *(shiji)* propaganda to the masses (*MZJ* 2:105).
29. *MZJ* 2:130.
30. *MZJ* 2:132.

31. *MZJ* 2:16.
32. The first and typical usage is in "Analysis of the Various Peasant Classes" (1926), *MZJ* 1:155, where he describes the attitude of China's middle class as contradictory because it opposes both imperialism and communism. Other instances occur in *MZJ* 1:164 and *MZJ* 2:13.
33. *The Communist Manifesto*, sec. 4.
34. The spokesman of the revisionists was Eduard Bernstein; the most memorable reflection of the radical position is Lenin's *What Is to Be Done?*
35. Robert Michels, *Political Parties* (New York: Free Press, 1962), originally published in 1915.
36. The ambiguous usage of the terms "bourgeois" and "revisionist" in contemporary disputes can be considered the descendants of the initial acceptance of the Bolshevik universe of discourse concerning deviations.
37. *MZJ* 2:41.
38. Ibid.
39. *MZJ* 2:246.
40. Mao records that 40 percent of the village and district officials in Yongfeng district, Xingguo county, were middle peasants; *MZJ* 2:218.
41. William Skinner and Edwin Winckler, "Compliance Succession in Rural China," in Amatai Etzioni, ed., *A Sociological Reader in Complex Organizations*, 2nd ed. (New York: Holt, Rinehart, and Winston, 1969), pp. 410-438. This view was attacked by Andrew Nathan, "Policy Oscillations in the PRC: A Critique," and defended by Winckler in "A Reply," both in *China Quarterly* 68(December 1976):pp. 720-733, 734-750. Compliance is the leitmotif of Amatai Etzioni, *A Comparative Analysis of Complex Organizations* (New York: Free Press, 1961).
42. Skinner and Winckler, "Compliance Succession," p. 428.
43. This was also the basic organization of the NLF in Viet Nam. See William Andrews, *The Village War* (Columbia: University of Missouri Press, 1973), p. 105.
44. "Zhongguo gongchandang hongjun di si jun di jiu ci daibiao dahui jueyian" [Resolution of the Ninth Congress of the Fourth Army of the CCP Red Army], *MZJ* 2:77-126. Part 1 is in *SW* 1:105-116 as "On Correcting Mistaken Ideas in the Party." The congress was held in Gutian, in western Fujian province.
45. *MZJ* 2:51.
46. *MZJ* 2:52.
47. *MZJ* 2:51.
48. *MZJ* 2:79.
49. *MZJ* 2:81.
50. *MZJ* 2:90.
51. In fact, this part is deleted in *SW*.
52. *MZJ* 2:113.
53. Rue, *Mao Tse-tung in Opposition*, p. 193.
54. Philip Huang, "Intellectuals, Lumpen-proletarians, Workers, and Peasants in the Communist Movement: The Case of Xingguo County, 1927-1934," unpublished manuscript, July 1976.
55. Hsiao Tso-liang, *Power Relations*, vol. 1, pp. 110-111.

56. *MZJ* 2:145.
57. I would not have been struck by the significance of Lijiafang had Mao not pointed it out in the introduction.
58. *MZJ* 2:155–160.
59. "Xingguo diaocha" [Xingguo investigation], *MZJ* 2:185–252. This lengthy investigation is probably the most important of Mao's untranslated works from the pre-1935 period. A summary is available in Brantly Womack, "The Foundations of Mao Tse-tung's Political Thought" (Ph.D. dissertation in Political Science, University of Chicago, 1977), chap. 3.
60. *MZJ* 2:185.
61. *MZJ* 2:185. The pattern I am referring to can best be illustrated from Confucius: "The ancients who wished to illustrate illustrious virtue throughout the kingdom first ordered well their own states. Wishing to order well their own states, they first regulated their families. Wishing to regulate their families, they first cultivated their persons. Wishing to cultivate their persons . . ." (*The Great Learning* 1:4; Legge, *Analects, Great Learning, and Doctrine of the Mean* [New York: Dover, 1971], pp. 357–358). Mao's argumentation concerns similarity rather than moral causality, but the insignificance of the problem of scale for the model function (empirical or moral) is analogous.
62. "Fandui benben zhuyi." This interesting piece first appeared in *Selected Readings from the Works of Mao Tse-tung (SR)* (pp. 40–50 of the English edition) in the mid-sixties. It may well be more reliable than many of the post-1949 versions, which means that it is quite reliable for our purposes. My optimistic view of its authenticity is based on several factors. First is the generally high principles of editing evident in post-1949 editions. Second is the nature of the localizing references in the work. And third, the nonobjective attitude which leads to putschism and opportunism is called "idealism" in line with the original text of the Gutian Resolution (*MZJ* 2:86–87), rather than "subjectivism," the (more accurate) amendment of the 1951 *SW* text (*SW* 1:111–112). The frustrating problem with "Oppose Book Worship" is the absence of any indication of its intended audience.
63. "Nongcun diaocha yuyan" (*MZJ* 7:289–292; *SW* 3:11–13) and "Nongcun diaocha ba" (*MZJ* 7:297–300; *SW* 3:14–16). *Rural Surveys* was a 1941 collection of Mao's Jiangxi surveys, including all the ones considered here, published for the cadre study campaign of the Zhengfeng (Rectification) Movement. It was reprinted for general distribution in 1947, presumably to aid rural work in the civil war period by emphasizing investigation and giving models for it. Since these short pieces are Mao's generalizations and comments on the material just considered, they seem appropriate here.
64. "Bu zuo diaocha meiyou fayan quan, bu zuo zhengque di diaocha tongyang meiyou fayan quan," *MZJ* 2:255–257.
65. *SR*, p. 40.
66. *SR*, p. 49. The dialectical concept of leadership adumbrated here can be traced from Mao's articles on self-government for Hunan written in 1919 to the recognition of a problematic relationship between leader and led in "On the Correct Handling of Contradictions among the People" (1957), *SR*, p. 434, and on to the Cultural Revolution as an attempt to revitalize this relationship.

67. SR, pp. 47, 43.
68. SR, p. 42.
69. Ibid.
70. SR, p. 47.
71. SW 3:12; SR, p. 195; MZJ 7:290.
72. SR, p. 44.
73. SR, p. 45.
74. SR, p. 46.
75. MZJ 2:255.
76. MZJ 2:256.
77. In "How to Analyze Classes" (June 1933), MZJ 3:265–268, and "On Resolving Certain Problems in the Land Struggle" (10 October 1933), MZJ 4:43–65.
78. "Zhejiang sheng zhi nongmin zhengzhi jingji zhuangkuang" [The political-economic circumstances of the peasantry of Zhejiang province], by the party department of Zhejiang, in Chinese Peasant 8(September 1926):60.
79. See Arthur Stinchcombe, "Agricultural Enterprise and Rural Class Structure," American Journal of Sociology 67(2)(September 1961):165–176.
80. William Hinton, Fanshen (New York: Vintage, 1966).
81. Karl Marx, The Eighteenth Brumaire (1852), sec. 7.
82. Huang, "Xingguo County."
83. MZJ 2:204.
84. Hamza Alavi, "Peasants and Revolution," Socialist Register (1965):241–277, defines a rich peasant as a capitalist farmer (p. 244)—that is, someone who hires labor for production. A broader definition was used by Mao at this time; see Tso-liang Hsiao, The Land Revolution in China, 1930–1934 (Seattle: University of Washington Press, 1969), pp. 152–153. I think that Alavi is correct in identifying the rich peasants as the protocapitalist elements in the village, but rural entrepreneurial opportunities were manifold, and taking advantage of opportunities is more capitalistic than even production itself.
85. MZJ 2:205–210.
86. MZJ 2:52, 161–163, 217.
87. MZJ 2:217–218. These latter expenses could amount to one-third of a family's income. See Chao Kuo-chun, Agrarian Policy of the Chinese Communist Party 1921–1949 (Bombay: Asia Publishing House, 1960), p. 5.
88. MZJ 2:46–50.
89. MZJ 2:220–222.
90. MZJ 2:222–225.
91. MZJ 2:172; Hsiao, Land Revolution, p. 152.
92. It seems inappropriate to me to call these people lumpenproletarians because they have no relation to the urban proletariat and are no closer to the village wage workers than they are to other classes. "Lumpenproletariat" is merely the closest orthodox Marxist category. Marx's best-known use of the term is in The Eighteenth Brumaire, where it is used to designate the riffraff who composed Louis Napoleon's Parisian goon squads.
93. MZJ 2:246. See also Huang, "The Case of Xingguo."
94. Praetorianism, derived from the example of the Praetorian Guards of im-

perial Rome, refers to military domination of political leaders because of the military's physical superiority. In Rome the emperor surrounded himself with armed men, and then discovered that he was surrounded by armed men.

95. Document in Kuo, *Analytical History*, vol. 1, p. 455. This does not imply that Qu relied entirely on spontaneity. The next item of the circular is this: "The peasant's insurrection in Hubei and Hunan must begin on 10 September." But the circular is dated 14 September.
96. Kuo, *Analytical History*, vol. 2, p. 53.
97. *MZJ* 2:58, 244–246.
98. *MZJ* 2:53–55, 246.
99. Stinchcombe, "Agricultural Enterprise and Rural Class Structure."
100. Alavi, "Peasants and Revolution," and Eric Wolf, *Peasant Wars of the Twentieth Century* (New York: Harper & Row, 1969).
101. *MZJ* 2:46–48.
102. *MZJ* 2:162.
103. Alavi, "Peasants and Revolution," p. 259.
104. *MZJ* 2:48.
105. Trygve Lötveit, *Chinese Communism, 1931–1934* (Lund: Studentenlitteratur, 1973), p. 168.
106. Huang, "The Case of Xingguo."
107. Document in Kuo, *Analytical History*, vol. 1, p. 475.
108. Document in Kuo, *Analytical History*, vol. 1, p. 457.
109. See "Resolution on the Peasant Movement," in Brandt, Schwartz, and Fairbank, *A Documentary History*, pp. 156–165.
110. Document in Hsiao, *Land Revolution*, pp. 127–130.
111. See Hsiao, *Land Revolution*, pp. 5–11; also Hsiao, *Power Relations*, vol. 1, p. 21.
112. See Hsiao, *Land Revolution*, pp. 11, 39–40.
113. Document in Hsiao, *Land Revolution*, pp. 152–170; see also his commentary, pp. 34–37.
114. *MZJ* 2:179–184; in Hsiao, *Land Revolution*, pp. 130–135.
115. This tendency is clearest in "Gan-xi tudi fenpei qingxing" [The situation of land distribution in western Jiangxi], a survey of twelve localities; *MZJ* 2:155–160.
116. It is evident from the earlier discussion of the stages of land redistribution that this "concession" was quite tangled and hard-fought. But the propertied families who stayed in the village must have expected redistribution.
117. Mao estimates (*MZJ* 2:170) that only 25 percent of the rural population were capable of full labor, 37 percent were capable of half-labor, and 37 percent could not contribute to production. If a family had a high percentage of laborers it could, all else being equal, accumulate a surplus. But a per capita land redistribution would make it overstaffed for its own land.
118. *MZJ* 4:250, 256; *MZJ* 2:158–160.
119. For a particularly bad example of this type of interpretation, see Jen Chuo-hsuan, "An Analysis of the Thought of Mao Tse-Tung," in *Collected Documents of the First Sino-American Conference on Mainland China* (Taiwan: Institute of International Relations, 1971), pp. 307–324.

120. *MZJ* 2:51. For a critical view of the effectiveness of parliamentary democracy in protecting the interests of the rural poor in England, see J. L. and Barbara Hammond, *The Village Labourer, 1760–1832* (New York: Harper & Row, 1970), especially chaps. 2–3.
121. E. J. Hobsbawm, *Primitive Rebels* (New York: Norton, 1959), p. 80.

CHAPTER 4: GOVERNING THE CHINESE SOVIET REPUBLIC: 1931–1934

1. The early difficulties of coordinated leadership of the base areas are indicated by Zhang Guotao's claim that he was "not able to get any reliable news about the Party Central Committee until the Spring of 1932" (*Autobiography*, vol. 2, p. 262). This was five months after Zhang had been elected vice-chairman of the CSR. Establishing effective central coordination among soviets was a major goal of the Second National Soviet Congress in 1934.
2. See the map and explanation provided by Trygve Lötveit in *Chinese Communism, 1931–1934*, pp. 8–9.
3. Mao made the observation in 1958 that although several hundred Chinese had studied in Russia, there were only 28½ Bolsheviks. He gave the following explanation for this grouping: "It was because they [the 28½] were so terribly 'left' that they became self-restricting and isolated, thus reducing the Party's contacts." From "March 10 Talk at the Chengtu Conference," in Schram, *Chairman Mao Talks to the People*, p. 97.
4. William Dorrill attacks the "power struggle" thesis in "Rewriting History to Further Maoism: The Ningtu Conference of 1932," in Hsiung, *Logic of Maoism*, pp. 62–85. However, his assumption that any divergence of opinion was insignificant is even more misleading. Ilpyong Kim's view in *Chinese Communism* is much more balanced. He maintains that differences of opinion between Mao and the Twenty-eight Bolsheviks were not fundamental enough to prevent a working division of responsibility.
5. Since this group was in opposition to the Twenty-eight Bolsheviks, the suspicion was voiced immediately that they had been betrayed. This was countered with the claim that other rightist oppositionists had betrayed their brethren in order to create confusion. Warren Kuo, who is closer to the sources than most, says that the group attracted police attention by meeting in a Shanghai hotel for two days in a row and thus "had only their own stupidity to blame" (*Analytical History*, vol. 2, p. 257).
6. Zhang Guotao, *Autobiography*, vol. 2, p. 170.
7. Hsiao, *Power Relations*, pp. 155–156.
8. Quoted in Kuo, *Analytical History*, vol. 2, p. 389.
9. *Suweiai zhengquan* [Soviet power] edited by the General Political Department of the Chinese Worker's and Peasant's Red Army, p. 13 of the first edition (January 1932), which is the third copy of the pamphlet on reel 10 of the Chen Cheng microfilm collection.
10. Kim, *Chinese Communism*, pp. 38–39.
11. In the Stalinist purges, to have compromised was a far greater offense than to have been unrealistic.
12. See Carl Dorris, "Peasant Mobilization in North China and the Origins of Yenan Communism," *China Quarterly* 68(December 1976):697–719.

13. Derek Waller, *The Kiangsi Soviet Republic*, China Research Monograph (Berkeley: Center for Chinese Studies, 1973); Hsiao, *Power Relations*, pp. 170-184.
14. See Jürgen Domes, *Die Vertagte Revolution* (Berlin: Walther de Gruyter, 1969).
15. In 1958, Mao recalled the following difference of policy: "Because the number of rich peasants was very small we decided in principle to leave them alone, and to make concessions to them. But the 'leftists' did not agree. They advocated 'giving the rich peasants bad land, and giving the landlords no land.' As a result the landlords had nothing to eat, and some of them fled to the mountains and formed guerrilla bands." From Schram, *Chairman Mao Speaks*, p. 97.
16. *Douzheng* [Struggle] 72:16. Quoted in Lötveit, *Chinese Communism 1931-1934*, p. 168.
17. "On Tactics against Japanese Imperialism" (Mao's report to the Wayaobao Conference in December 1935), *SW* 1:164.
18. *MZJ* 4:379-397.
19. *MZJ* 3:44.
20. *MZJ* 3:118.
21. William Dorrill maintains that Mao's cooperative attitude toward the Fujian rebels was an invention of later Maoist "official history." The weight of evidence, however, clearly favors the official view. When Mao criticized the handling of the Fujian affair at the Zunyi Conference, one year after the event, he was not strong enough politically to fabricate an "official history" for an audience of recent participants. See William Dorrill, "The Fukien Rebellion and the CCP: A Case of Maoist Revisionism," *China Quarterly* 37(January 1969):31-53.
22. *MZJ* 4:389. In "Problems of Strategy in China's Revolutionary War" (*SW* 1:247; *MZJ* 5:164-165), Mao provides an instant replay of a military alternative available during the Fujian Incident.
23. *MZJ* 3:93-94.
24. *MZJ* 3:99-105, 107-112.
25. *MZJ* 3:96.
26. *MZJ* 3:101.
27. *MZJ* 3:107-112, 123-125.
28. *MZJ* 3:109-110.
29. "Guanyu jixu gaizao difang suweiai zhengfu wenti" [On the problem of continuously reforming local soviet government], *Hougse Zhonghua* [Red China] 35(27 September 1932); *MZJ* 3:131-133.
30. *MZJ* 3:132. This is the first occurrence in Mao's works of the important rectification trope *"xishua . . . xiyin"* (wash out . . . breathe in).
31. "Guanyu zhanzheng jinji dongyuan" [On urgent mobilization for war], *Red China* 38(16 October 1932); *MZJ* 3:143-148.
32. "Guanyu ge ji xuanju yundong di jiancha" [On the inspection of the election movement at all levels], *Red China* 43(5 December 1932); *MZJ* 3:169-172.
33. "Meiyou zong zhenzhi shang renshi gaizao," *MZJ* 3:169.

34. "Guanyu zhanzheng dongyuan yu gongzuo fangshi" [On mobilization for war and work styles], *Red China* 43(5 December 1932); *MZJ* 3:163–168.
35. *MZJ* 3:166.
36. *MZJ* 3:166–167.
37. *MZJ* 3:168. *"Gongzuo tuan"* and *"ziwo piping"* are used in this article for the first time in Mao's works.
38. See *Hongjun wenti jueyian* [Resolution on Red Army problems] passed by the First Congress of the Soviet Area Party and made available by the Soviet Area Central Bureau in October 1931; Chen Cheng reel 16. The same approach is evident in Zhang Wentian's essay on district soviets from April 1934 (Chen Cheng reel 10).
39. It should not be assumed that the party leadership in Jiangxi was in favor of bureaucratism. In fact, most of the principles of Mao's redirection of the election and mobilization movements can be found in a campaign for a "new leadership style" in the Jiangxi Party in June 1932. Bureaucratism, commandism, formalism, and so forth are all criticized in detail. See *Dang di Jianshe* [Party reconstruction], published by the Organizational Department of the Central Bureau, especially the articles in the first issue by Deng Yingchao (Teng Ying-ch'ao) and Chang Sheng. In Chen Cheng reel 17.
40. Judging from a February 1933 *Red China* investigation of district-level soviets in Ruijin, the reelection movement had no great success in revitalizing local government. See Yue Lin, "Ruijin ge qu jiancha gongzuo di chadian" [Weakness of inspection work in the districts of Ruijin County], *Red China* 52:4; Chen Cheng reel 17.
41. This campaign, "Jiesheng jingji bangju zhanzheng" (Save in Economics to Help the War), can be viewed as a direct ancestor of the Yanan "Better Troops and Simpler Administration" drive. See *Red China* 55(22 February 1933):3; 60(12 March 1933):6; both in Chen Cheng reel 17.
42. "Wei tiqian chungeng jizhong liliang fencui diren da ju jiangong shi" [Plant early in order to gather strength to defeat the enemy's big offensive], *Red China* 46(7 January 1933); Chen Cheng reel 17; *MZJ* 3:179–180.
43. See *MZJ* 3:213–214, 241–242. However, the combined harvests of 1933 were considerably better than those of 1932.
44. See Bo Gu (Qin Bangxian), "Weizhe Buersaiweike di chungeng er douzheng" [Fight for a Bolshevik spring planting], *Red China* 51(10 February 1933):1; Chen Cheng reel 17. Some of these policies were already in use in the CSR. "Revolutionary competition" is mentioned in *Ruijin Hongqi* [Red flag of Ruijin] 7(7 November 1931): 2, and some weeks later there was a call for inspection of land division. See *Ruijin Hongqi* 10(28 November 1931):1; Chen Cheng reel 1.
45. There had been cases reported in which the landlords retained their advantages; the poor peasants did not benefit and therefore did not actively participate in soviet work. See "Zhongyang zhengfu dui Huichang gongzuo di zhishi" [Central government directive on work in Huichang], *Red China* 30(4 August 1932):4; Chen Cheng reel 16.
46. "Qunzhong laodong reqing zuzhi qilai!" [Organize the work enthusiasm of the masses!], *Red Flag* 67(8 April 1933):2.

47. This is based on the account of the well-informed editors of *Chifei fandong wenjian lubian* [A collection of Red Bandit reactionary documents], 6 vols. (1935), vol. 3, p. 952. It is claimed by the former communist general Gong Chu that the initial stimulus came from the Comintern. See Lötveit, *Chinese Communism 1931–1934*, p. 155.
48. "Zhongyang ju guanyu chatian yundong di jueyi" [Resolution of the Central Bureau on the Land Investigation Movement], 2 June 1933; in *Reactionary Documents*, vol. 3, pp. 952–957.
49. This does not mean that the party leadership originated these ideas. The resolution starts: "Having heard the report of Mao Zedong and Hu Hai...."
50. "Shixing guangfan shenru di chatian yundong" [Execute a broad and deep Land Investigation Movement], *Red China* 87(20 June 1933); *MZJ* 3:223–226.
51. Actually the phrase used is "extremely important" *(ji zhongyao di)*, but no other mass organizations are mentioned. Mao probably used "extremely" instead of "most" out of deference to the labor-oriented party leadership, since "most" is far more characteristic of his style.
52. See, for example, "Chatian yundong zhong Xiaxiao quwei yu Ruijin xianwei di guanliao zhuyi" [The bureaucratism of the Xiaxiao District Committee (in Ruijin county) and the Ruijin County Committee in the Land Investigation Movement], *Red China* 95(23 July 1933):5; Chen Cheng reel 17.
53. "Report," *Red China* 86(17 June 1933); *MZJ* 3:243–244. Note the similarities of this framework of analysis to the one within which William Hinton's work team operated in *Fanshen*.
54. "Zenyang fenxi jieji" [How to differentiate classes], *Red China* 89(29 June 1933); *MZJ* 3:265–268.
55. "Chatian yundong di chubu zongjie" [Preliminary summary of the Land Investigation Movement], *Struggle* 24(29 August 1933); *MZJ* 3:341–356.
56. This course of events is well described in Lötveit, *Chinese Communism 1931–1934*, pp. 172–184.
57. "Preliminary Summary," *MZJ* 3:341.
58. *MZJ* 3:342–343.
59. *MZJ* 3:348. Such errors were not necessarily the sign of excessive enthusiasm, nor was the problem unique to the Land Investigation Movement. In an article from 1932 which reads like one of Mao's, "Central Government Directive on Work in Huichang," Huichang is criticized both for the lack of a deeply penetrating land struggle (landlords were still charging rent) and also for treating rich peasants like landlords and middle peasants like rich peasants.
60. "Guanyu tudi douzheng zhong yi xie wenti di jueding" [Resolution on some questions in the land struggle], *MZJ* 4:43–65.
61. Moreover, those who had uncovered large numbers of class enemies were well rewarded with favorable publicity, and the participating masses shared the confiscated goods.
62. *MZJ* 4:49.

63. "Guanyu jixu kaizhan chatian yundong di wenti" [On the problem of continuing to develop the Land Investigation Movement], *Red China* 164(20 March 1934):1; Chen Cheng reel 17.
64. See Lötveit, *Chinese Communism 1931–1934*, pp. 179–183.
65. "Guanyu 1933 liang ge wenjian di jueding" [Decision on two 1933 articles], *MZJ* 10:151–182. See also Hinton, *Fanshen*.
66. *MZJ* 4:23–27, 37.
67. *MZJ* 3:335.
68. "Changgang diaocha" [Investigation of Changgang], *MZJ* 4:125–171.
69. *MZJ* 4:125–126.
70. *MZJ* 4:154.
71. "Caixi Xiang diaocha" [Investigation of Caixi township], *MZJ* 4:175–196.
72. Mao was probably thinking of places like Caixi when he later referred to "sprouts of socialism" in Jiangxi. See Schram, *Chairman Mao Speaks*, p. 117.
73. *Red China* 92(8 July 1933):6.
74. Kuo, *Analytical History*, vol. 2, pp. 493–497; *Reactionary Documents*, vol. 3, p. 953.
75. See Waller, *Kiangsi Soviet Republic*, pp. 53–110.
76. See "Pinmin tuan zuzhi yu gongzuo dagang" [Organizational and work outline for the poor peasant associations], in *Chatian yundong zhinan* [Compass for the Land Investigation Movement]; *MZJ* 3:283–289.
77. "Chatian yundong di qunzhong gongzuo" [Mass work in the Land Investigation Movement], *Hongqi Zhoubao* [Red Flag Weekly] 63(December 1933); *MZJ* 4:199–205; *MZJ* 3:285–286.
78. *Qu xiang suweiai zenyang gongzuo* [How district and township soviets should work], April 1934; Chen Cheng reel 10. The first part of this pamphlet, on the township soviet (pp. 1–39), was written by Mao and appears in *MZJ* 4:337–352. The second part, on the district soviet (pp. 41–63), is by Zhang Wentian.
79. "Difang suweiai zhengfu zhenxing zuzhi tiaolie" [Preliminary articles on local soviet government], passed by the Central Executive Committee in November 1931; *Reactionary Documents*, vol. 3, pp. 703–725. Of seventy-two articles, numbers 5 through 17 deal with township soviets.
80. "Zhonghua Suweiai Gonghe guo difang suweiai zhangxing zuzhi fa caoan" [Draft provisional organic law for local soviets of the CSR], undated but evidently related to the Second National Congress; *Reactionary Documents*, vol. 3, pp. 725–793. Articles 33 through 55 of this 208-article behemoth deal with townships.
81. This is the first mention of this technique in Mao's writings, but it was suggested for party meetings in June 1932 by Deng Yingchao in the first issue of *Party Reconstruction*.
82. *MZJ* 3:344.
83. "How District Soviets Should Be Governed." An example of Zhang's approach: "The basic principle is, in making the district chair committee become the leader and organizer of all work in the district, make the resolution of every important problem pass through the chair committee,

and at the same time have the chair committee maintain appropriate relations with every department, and let the centralized leadership of the chair committee help rather than hinder the establishment of the various departments" (p. 42).

84. This summary is derived from Mao's announcement of the Second National Congress, *Red China* 101(13 August 1933); *MZJ* 3:303-305.
85. "Zhonghua Suweiai Gonghe guo zhongyang zhixing weiyuanhui yu renmin weiyuanhui dui di er ci quan guo suweiai daibiao dahui di baogao" [Report of the CSR Central Executive Committee and People's Commissariat to the Second National Congress]; *MZJ* 4:219-282. "Guanyu zhongyang zhixing weiyuanhui baogao di jielun" [Concluding remarks on the Central Executive Committee's report]; *MZJ* 4:283-294.
86. Waller provides a detailed description of the report in *Kiangsi Soviet Republic*, pp. 87-90.
87. *MZJ* 4:236.
88. *MZJ* 4:238-239.
89. *MZJ* 4:250-251.
90. "Guanyu changban liangshi hezuoshi wenti" [On the problems of initiating food cooperatives], *Red China* 94(14 July 1933); *MZJ* 3:269-270.
91. *MZJ* 4:253.
92. Included in *SW* (and in *SR*) as "Be Concerned with the Well-Being of the Masses, Pay Attention to Methods of Work," *SW* 1:147-148.
93. "Concluding Remarks," *MZJ* 4:286-287; and (somewhat differently) *SW* 1:147-148.
94. "Concluding Remarks," *MZJ* 4:288-289; *SW* 1:149.
95. "Zhong gong zhongyang guanyu fandui diren wu ci 'weijiao' di zongjie jueyi" [Comprehensive resolution of the CCP Center on opposing the enemy's fifth "encirclement and suppression"] *MZJ* 4:379-397.
96. The reason for this delay is given in *SW* 1:155n.: "However, as that meeting [the Zunyi Conference] took place during the Red Army's Long March, it had to confine itself to decisions on the most urgent military problems and on the organization of the Secretariat and the Revolutionary Military Commission of the Central Committee. Only when the Red Army had reached Northern Shenxi after the Long March was it possible for the Central Committee of the party to deal systematically with the various problems of tactics in the political sphere."
97. "Guanyu muqian zhengzhi xingshi yu dang renwu jueyi" [Resolution concerning the present political situation and responsibilities of the party], *MZJ* 5:19; "On Tactics against Japanese Imperialism," *SW* 1:153-178, *MZJ* 5:19-40; "Zhongguo geming zhanzheng di zhanlue wenti" [Problems of strategy in China's revolutionary war], *MZJ* 5:83-168, *SW* 1:179-254.
98. The first two points are made in *MZJ* 5:35-36; the last occurs throughout the "Resolution" and the "Report."
99. "Problems of Strategy," *MZJ* 5:126; *SW* 1:214.
100. *MZJ* 5:156-157; *SW* 1:241.
101. "Report," *SW* 1:156.
102. Compare for instance Waller's *Kiangsi Soviet Republic* and Dorrill's "Re-

writing History." Kim's thesis of a division of responsibilities is more accurate, but it tends to minimize the seriousness and chronological pattern of the disagreements.

103. Lowell Dittmer, " 'Line Struggle' in Theory and Practice," *China Quarterly* 72(December 1977):675–712.

CHAPTER 5: THE FOUNDATIONS OF MAO ZEDONG'S POLITICAL THOUGHT

1. See Chalmers Johnson, *Peasant Nationalism and Communist Power* (Stanford: Stanford University Press, 1962), and most recently "Peasant Nationalism Revisited," *China Quarterly* 72(December 1977):766–785.
2. See "Zhonghua Suweiai Gongheguo di zhongyang zhixing weiyuanhui mingling di er hao" [Order no. 2 of the Central Executive Committee of the CSR], 15 December 1935; *MZJ* 5:13–14. See also "Guanyu tudi zhengce di zhishi" [Directive on land policy], 22 July 1936; *MZJ* 5:63–65. It should be remembered that Mao's pre-CSR land policy tended somewhat in this direction and that he attributed the anti-rich peasant line to the Twenty-eight Bolsheviks. See Schram, *Chairman Mao Speaks*, p. 97.
3. "Decision on Two 1933 Articles," *MZJ* 10:151–182.
4. See Dorris, "Peasant Mobilization in North China."
5. See Thomas Kuhn, "Postscript," *Structure of Scientific Revolutions* (Chicago: University of Chicago Press, 1970), pp. 186–187.
6. *MZJ* 1:173. See also Chapter 2.
7. Bauer, *China und die Hoffnung auf Glück*, pp. 537–572. Since Bauer's theme is transcultural, his treatment of Mao is sensitive to Marxist influences. In my opinion, however, the analysis does not sufficiently take into account the changed practical context of Mao's thought.
8. See, for example, F. W. Mote, "China's Past in the Study of China Today," *Journal of Asian Studies* 32(1)(November 1972):107–120.
9. Thomas Metzger, *Escape from Predicament: Neo-Confucianism and China's Evolving Political Culture* (New York: Columbia University Press, 1977).
10. Ibid., p. 17. See also Metzger, "The Quest for Traditional Values in Modern Chinese Thought," *China Quarterly* 73(March 1978):166–171.
11. Metzger, *Escape*, pp. 49–51.
12. See An-che Li, "Notes on the Necessity of Field Research in Social Science in China," *Yenching Journal of Social Studies* 1(1)(June 1938):121–129, and Tung-sun Chang, "A Chinese Philosopher's Theory of Knowledge," ibid., 2(January 1939):161–189.
13. Stuart Schram, "The Marxist," in *Mao Tse-tung in the Scales of History*, ed. Dick Wilson (New York: Cambridge University Press, 1977), pp. 35–69.
14. See the series of articles by Karl Wittfogel and Benjamin Schwartz in *China Quarterly* 1–2(1960).
15. The series begins with an article by Ric Pfeffer in *Modern China* 2(4)(October 1976).
16. The best description of the complexity of Mao's background is Frederic Wakeman's *History and Will*.
17. Snow, *Red Star over China*, pp. 125–126.

18. *MZJ* 3:335.
19. These problems are also discussed in Womack, "Theory and Practice," pp. 21–28.
20. See "Comrade Mao Tse-tung's Talk at an Enlarged Working Conference Convened by the Central Committee of the Communist Party of China (30 January 1962)," *Peking Review* 27(7 July 1978):6–22.
21. See *Mao Zedong Sixiang Wansui* [Long live the thought of Mao Zedong], a Red Guard publication in three volumes reprinted in Taiwan and Hong Kong.
22. Mao, "Talk at a Conference of Party Committee Secretaries (27 January 1957)," *SW* 5:364.
23. "Comrade Mao Tse-tung's Talk" (1962), pp. 7–8.

Index

Alavi, Hamsa, 132
Anti-Bolshevik League, 115
Anti-Fengdian war, 48, 58, 82
Anti-Japanese War, xii, 142, 152, 153, 190; bases, 149, 190; Mao's policies, 134; national revolution, 182, 184
Anyuan Coal Mine strike, 27
August Emergency Conference, 86
Autumn Harvest Uprising (1927), 65, 76, 86, 87, 142

Bao An, 181
Bauer, Wolfgang, 196
Beijing University, 14, 36
Bo Gu, 162
Bolshevism, 78, 169, 199

Cai Hesen, 7, 35; Marxist viewpoint, 36
Cai Tingkai, 151, 153, 183
Cai Yuanpei, 8, 14
Caixi (township), 171; investigation, 172, 173, 175, 180
Canton, 40, 50, 52, 53; 1927 Commune, 142
Cao Kun, 42, 65
Capitalist roaders, xv
Central Bureau *(Zhongyang Ju)*, 145, 162
Central Committee, xiii, 34, 40, 56, 65, 67, 69, 76, 78, 80, 83, 86, 88, 93, 94, 99, 103, 110, 111, 112, 129, 140, 141, 144, 145, 146, 153, 168, 186; conference (1926), 63; land policy, 127, 135; Shanghai, 93; strained relationship with Mao, 96, 185
Central Government *(Zhongyang Zhengfu)*, 162, 166
Central Peasant Movement Institute (Wuhan), 66

Central Soviet Republic, 88, 110, 144, 176
Chaling, 87
Changgang (investigation), 170-176, 180
Changsha, 5, 13, 14, 18, 21, 22, 24, 26, 32, 36, 38, 58, 66, 69, 88, 98, 100
Chen Duxiu, 38, 44, 45, 46, 51, 56, 64, 66, 68, 69, 78; "The Chinese National Revolution and the Various Classes of Society," 45; "The Chinese Peasant Question," 51; criticism by 7 August (1927) Conference, 87; criticism by Sixth Party Congress (1928), 87; "Four Nots," 135; patriarchal style, 145; politics of restraint, 86
Chen Jiongming (rival government), 59, 63
Chen Qunpu, 52
Chen Yi, 87
Chiang Kai-shek, 88, 151, 157, 183; Nineteenth Route Army revolt in Fujian, 153, 184; system of encirclement, 182
China's Peasant Problem, 53
Chinese Communist Party, xi, xviii, 1, 7, 25, 27, 30-36, 38, 40, 43-46, 49-52, 56, 63-67, 69, 74-78, 81, 83-88, 101, 117, 120, 135, 140, 141, 145, 147, 153, 185, 186, 189, 197; CCP-KMT cooperation, 34, 40, 44-46, 50, 65, 69, 124; CCP-KMT United Front split, 84; control of peasant movement, 64, 65, 71; cosmopolitan, proletarian orientation, 129, 130, 203; distaste for the military, 130; First Congress (1921), 7, 24; Hunan Provincial Committee, 67; implications of CSR defeat, 189; Mao's writings, 193; rural leadership, 117; severance of ties with KMT, 50;

Shangyou branch, 132; "Sinify" thinking, 99; Third National Congress, 40, 51
The Chinese Peasant (Zhongguo Nongmin), 53, 55
Chinese Soviet Republic, 140, 144–163, 169–173, 176, 177, 179, 181, 183, 185–187, 189, 190, 192, 195; Central Executive Committee, 148, 153, 176; defeat (implications), 189; Mao's chairmanship, 148, 173, 195; National Soviet Provincial Central Government, 147; paradigms (clash), 187; People's Commisariat, 176; proclamation (7 November 1931), 144; Provincial Supreme Court, 153; self-image, 183
The Chronicle of the Three Kingdoms, 172
The Communist (Gongchandang), 51
Comintern, xii, 40, 64, 65, 88, 95, 140, 145, 149, 186; continuity in Jiangxi leadership, 145; forbids alliances (1928), 91; opposition to Li Lisan's land policy, 136
Communist Party: analysis by Gramsci, 79–81; analysis by Mao, 122; analysis by Stalin, 151
Confucius, 14; Mao's use, 199; Neo-Confucianism, 196, 197
Cultural Book Society, 9, 24, 25, 28, 30, 36, 38
Cultural Revolution, xiii, xv, xvi, xvii, 202, 203, 204; two-line struggle, 185

Da Gong Bao (Changsha), 22
Daoists, 129
Darwinism, 9
Deng Xiaoping (Teng Hsiao-ping), xiv, xv, 172
Dittmer, Lowell, 185
Duan Qirui, 49, 65

Eight County Land Investigation Conference (1933), 163–166, 169, 174
Encirclement and Suppression Campaign: first, 87; second, 134, 145; third, 145; fourth, 154, 157, 172, 177; fifth, 153, 154, 170, 173, 176, 177, 179, 181, 182, 201
Engels, Friedrich (inherence of opposition), 101
Etzioni, Amatai (theory of complex organizations), 107
Eyuwan Soviet, 157

Fang Zhimin, 66, 85
February Seventh Massacre (1923), 30, 31, 38, 39

Feng Yuxiang (National Revolutionary Army), 48
Fengdian Clique, 47, 48
Fifth Plenum of the CCP Central Committee (January 1934), 168, 173
First National Soviet Congress (November 1931), 146, 147, 148, 149, 151
First United Front, 50
Four modernizations, xiv
France, 36
Fujian, 110, 153, 154; Cai Tingkai, 153; Jiangxi-Fujian border, 88, 144; People's Government, 184; rebellion, 151, 153, 183
Futian Incident (8 December 1930), 88, 136, 145

Gang of Four, xiii–xv
Ganxian (county), 118
German Social Democratic Party, 78
Gramsci, Antonio, 78–81, 102; *The Modern Prince*, 80
Great Britain: treaty with China, 40; anti-Feng war, 47
Great Leap Forward, xiii, 203, 204
"Great Union of the Popular Masses, The." *See* Mao's works
Gu Shunzhang, 145
Gu Yanwu, 12
Guangdong, 52, 56, 63–66, 144; KMT-CCP alliance, 50; peasant movement, 63, 66; political situation, 46, 49, 51; salt, 126
Guangzhou National Government, 48
The Guide Weekly (Xiangdao), 36, 40, 56
"Gutian Resolution" (1929). *See* Mao's works

Hailufeng, 51, 59, 60, 90; peasant movement, 63
Han Suyin, 25
Hangzhou, 69
He Long, 85
Hengshan, 69
Hinton, William *(Fanshen)*, 125
Hobsbawn, Eric, 143
Hong Chao, 112
Hong Kong, xv
Hong Xiuquan, 112
Hu Hai, 162
Hua Guofeng, xiii
Huang, Phillip, 115, 126, 134, 201
Huangsong (district), 165
Hubei, 65
Hunan, 5–9, 14–16, 19, 21–27, 29–32, 35–41, 44, 46, 49, 50, 52, 63–77, 182–186; Jianxi border area, 89, 96; Mao's politics, 89; southern Hunan uprising, 94

INDEX 235

Hunan Communist Party, 26, 31, 38, 66
Hunan Constitution, 40
Hunan First Normal School, 3, 4, 6, 8, 10, 13, 24
"Hunan Report." *See* Mao's works, "Report of an Investigation of the Hunan Peasant Movement"
Hunan Self-Education College, 9, 12, 25-28, 30, 33, 38, 53, 81
Hunan Self-Government Movement, 9, 19, 21-23, 28, 29, 36
Hundred Flowers Movement (1957), 203

Italy, 80

James, William, 123
Japan, 16, 91, 152, 153, 182; anti-Feng war, 47; incursions, 177, 184, 189; Second United Front period, 183
Jiangxi, xiii, xviii, 65, 66, 84, 86-88, 99, 100, 110, 114-118, 125, 134, 140, 142-146, 152, 153, 158, 161, 173, 176, 181, 185; alliance policy, 153; base area on Fujian border, 88, 92, 99, 110, 114, 131, 144; Hunan-Jiangxi border area, 89, 96; Mao's beginnings, 189, 190, 201; Mao's investigations, 122, 148; Mao's land policy, 136, 143; peasant associations, 66; rural policy fluctuations, 107; pro-Li Lisan faction, 136; transfer of Central Committee, 144, 146, 184, 192, 202
Jiangxi Action Committee, 116; pro-Li Lisan/pro-Mao factions, 136
Jiangxi Provincial Soviet Government, 114, 115, 140, 144
Jinggangshan, 77, 85-88, 90, 93, 94, 96, 99, 103, 108-110, 115, 125, 127, 129-133, 135-137, 142, 147, 158, 160, 186; Front Committee, 89, 93; insurrections, 132; land distribution, 126, 133, 136, 137, 150, 167; Mao's beginnings, 142, 189, 190; Mao's first guerrilla base, 85-88, 90, 93, 94, 96, 99, 131; rural policy fluctuations, 107
Johnson, Chalmers, 189

Kang Youwei (*Datong Shu* [The book of great harmony]), 19
Korsch, Karl, 78, 79, 81, 102
Kropotkin, Peter, 20
Kuomintang, xii, 31, 35, 37, 40, 43-53, 56, 58, 59, 63-66, 69, 71, 75, 76, 84, 86, 88, 90, 91, 94, 95, 98, 130, 144, 145, 149, 157, 172, 181, 182, 184, 194; agrarian policy (1926), 64; anticommunist "new warlordism," 66, 90, 91; arrests of cadres, 145; blockade, 172; CCP-KMT cooperation, 34, 40, 44-46, 50, 65, 69, 124; Central Executive Committee, 46, 47, 48, 63; conquest of Hunan, 75; consolidates power, 98; control of Republic of China, 144, 152; First National Congress, 40, 46, 56; Guangdong KMT, 50, 56, 65; Joint Declaration (1927), 45; KMT Propaganda Bureau, 52; Nineteenth Army revolt, 184; Second National Conference (1926), 53, 63; severance of ties with CCP, 44, 50, 84, 86; Shanghai KMT, 46; threatens Jinggangshan base, 88; Western Hills clique, 49, 56, 65

Land Investigation Movement of 1933, 123, 147, 150, 161-169, 173-175, 178, 187, 190
Lenin, Nikolai, 22, 102; agitation (concept of), 44, 45, 61; in Europe, 78; Leninist-Stalinist theories of a socialist state, 187, 203; paradigm, party, 32, 34; paradigm, revolutionary, 92, 198; proletarian hegemony, 130; revolution, view of Bolshevik, 92; "revolutionary real politik," 78; struggle against imperialism, 38, 136; vanguard of the proletariat, 103
Li Dazhao, 38, 40
Li Lisan, 39, 88, 90, 96, 99, 100, 135, 136, 145; "Land Law," 135, 136; personal hegemony, 145; roving guerrilla strategy, 130; rural policy, 99; "take the cities" campaign, 100, 115
Li Rui, 2, 9, 10, 25; *Comrade Mao Zedong's Early Revolutionary Activities*, 2; "The Ideological Trend of Mao Zedong in His Youth," 2
Li Weihan, 35
Li Zhuang, 112
Liang Qichao (Liang Ch'i-Ch'ao), 6
Lijiafang, 116
Liling, 69
Lin Biao, xvii, 85, 88, 92, 98-100; general pessimism, 100; roving guerrilla strategy, 130; theory of genius, xvii
Liu Shaoqi, 39, 202
Liu Zhitan, 85
Lo Ming (line), 172
Long March, 85, 107, 148, 188, 189; importance of interstitial tactics, 98; Zunyi Conference, 173, 181
Lötveit, Trygve, 161
Lukacs, Georg, 78-81, 102; "Methodisches zur Organisationsfrage," 78

McDonald, Angus, 22
Mao Zedong: anarchism, 20, 21, 37, 193;

chairman, Chinese Soviet Republic, 89, 146–148; Chinese political culture, 195–198; collective wisdom, xvii, xviii; first example of Maoist ideological rectification, 110; Great Helmsman, xv; guerrilla tactics, 96–98; involvement in peasant movement (1926–1927), 34, 50–52, 80; land policy, 136–138; law and mobilization, 155; May Fourth politics and articles, 29, 30, 37, 40, 53–59, 62, 77, 80; May Fourth views, 14–17, 33, 40, 43–44, 77, 81, 189–194; pacifism, 21; paradigm, initial revolutionary, 92; paradigm, Marxist political, 188; paradigm, political, 84, 85; Marxist period, 1, 7, 17, 20, 21, 29, 30, 36–38, 81, 90, 129–131, 141, 185; pre-Marxist period, 1, 2, 7, 31, 62, 81; political thought (CSR period), 185–187

Mao's works: "The Strength of Will" (1915), 9; "A Study of Physical Education" (1917), 10–13, 26, 28, 31; "Great Union of the Popular Masses" (1919), 17–21, 25, 26, 28, 29, 39, 40, 44, 46, 49, 52, 54, 141, 180; "Opening Statement of the Xiang River Review" (1919), 8, 14–16; "What Is Socialism? What Is Anarchism?" (1919), 8; "A Proposal to Convene a 'Hunan Peoples Constitution Convention' by the Hunan Revolutionary Government 'to Enact' a 'Hunan Constitution' for the Purpose of Constructing a 'New Hunan' " (1920), 22–23; "Hunan Self-Government" (1920), 21–23, 28–30; "Introductory Statement of the Hunan Self-Education College" (1921), 25–27; "Report of the Affairs of the Cultural Book Society" (1921), 28; *Collected Correspondence of New Citizens Study Society Members* (1922), 8; "An Introduction to *New Age*" (1923), 32, 35; "The Beijing Coup and the Merchants" (1923), 42, 82; "The Chinese KMT's Propaganda Outline for the Anti-Feng (Fengdian) War" (1925), 47–50, 82; "An Analysis of the Classes in Chinese Society" (1926), 55–58, 62–64, 78, 82; "An Analysis of the Various Classes among the Chinese Peasantry and Their Attitudes toward Revolution" (1926), 53–55, 57, 58, 62, 82, 126; "The National Revolution and the Peasant Movement" (1926), 58–61, 83; *The Peasant Problem* (1926), 60–61; "Report of an Investigation of the Hunan Peasant Movement" (1927), 68–76, 83, 89, 117, 118, 122, 172, 200; "Draft Resolution of the Second Congress of County Party Representatives of the Xiang-Gan (Hunan-Jiangxi) Border Area" (1928), 89–93, 99, 101; "Jinggangshan Land Law" (1928?), 137; "Report to the Central Committee" (1928), 141; "Gutian Resolution" (1929), 104, 108, 110, 113, 130, 141, 160, 199; "Oppose Book Worship" (1930), 119, 121, 201; "No Investigation, No Right to Speak, No Correct Investigation, Still No Right to Speak" (1931), 119, 123, 201; "The Situation of Land Distribution in Western Jiangxi" (1931), 116; "Xingguo Investigation" (1931), 117, 118, 121, 122, 126, 138, 170, 201; "On Mobilization for War and Work Styles" (1932), 158, 159; "On the Inspection of the Election Movement at All Levels" (1932), 158; "How to Differentiate Classes" (1933), 165, 167, 169; "Preliminary Summary of the Land Investigation Movement" (1933), 165, 166; "Resolution on Some Questions in the Land Struggle" (1933), 167, 169; "Report to the Second National Congress of the Chinese Soviet Republic" (1934), 176–180; "On Contradiction" (1937), xii, 101; "On Practice" (1937), xii, 77, 122, 200–201; "New Democracy" writings (1940), 46; "Preface to *Rural Surveys*" (1941), 119, 121; "The Foolish Old Man Who Removed the Mountains" (1945), 12; "On the Correct Handling of Contradictions among the People" (1956), 101

Mao Zetan (Mao's brother), 172

Marx, Karl, 17, 20, 23, 102, 120, 125; categories of class struggle, 77; Chinese political culture and Marxism, 194–196; class analysis, 82, 194; European Marxism, 78–81, 102, 104; ideological hegemony, 198; *Manifesto*, 102; orthodox Marxism, 104, 131; political traditions, xii, 79, 84, 101–103, 120, 121, 186, 194, 202; problems of consolidation and construction, 101; proletarian hegemony, 130; social democratic parties (Europe), 78; study group, 24; structural predictions, 103

May Fourth Movement of 1919, xi, 6, 8, 13–16, 18, 21, 23, 30, 32, 33, 35–38, 81

May Thirtieth Movement of 1925, 47–52

Mencius, 100

Mensheviks, 45

Metzger, Thomas, 196, 197; *Escape from Predicament*, 196

Michels, Robert, 104

Mif, Pavel, 144
Miller, S. M., 62
Modern China, 197
Modern Schools, 3, 4, 26
Moscow, 87; Sun Yat-sen University, 144
"Mukden Incident" (1931), 152

Nanchang, 88, 100; failure of attack (1930), 98, 114
Nationalism (Western), 19
National Revolutionary Army (Guominjun), 48
New Age, 33, 35, 81
New Citizens Study Society, 13, 14, 21, 23, 28, 29, 35, 36, 38
New Culture Movement, 14
Nineteenth Route Army (of Cai Tingkai), 153, 183
Northern Expedition, 34, 58, 61, 63-65, 68, 71, 76, 77, 81; conquest of Hunan, 72; failure of communist participation, 85; peasant movement contributions, 67, 75; politics, 56, 78, 83; troops of Autumn Harvest Uprising, 86
Northern warlords, 37, 47

Owen, Robert, 25

Paper tigers, 30
Party Center, 87, 88, 90, 103, 111, 138, 141, 186; land policy, 136-138
Paulsen, Friedrich, 8-10, 16; *System der Ethik*, 8, 9; "Metaphysics from below," 9
Peasant Movement Training Institute, 53, 58, 60
The Peasant Problem, 53, 60
Peking, 14, 21, 38, 49, 52, 82, 94
Peng Dehuai, 186
Peng Pai, 51, 60, 90
People's Republic of China, xiii, xv, 85, 107, 143, 197, 203
Politburo: Mao's election as chairman, 145, 148; Mao's retirement, 87
Political Weekly (Zhengzhi Zhoubao), 46, 49, 52

Qing (dynasty), 40, 94
Qu Qiubai, 86-88, 90, 129, 135, 136; peasant policy, 87, 124; land policy, 135, 136
Quan Shan (Wang Fuzhi) Society, 25

Red Army, 86-88, 90, 93, 98-100, 105-108, 110-114, 124, 125, 127, 130-132, 137, 141, 142, 145, 153, 157, 158, 163, 166, 170, 171, 181-184, 193; Chinese soviets, 145; democracy, 105; discussion with soldiers, 117; five conditions, 93; Fourth, 110, 121; land sharing, 137, 178; midwife of the rural revolution, 131; recruitment, 116, 161, 163, 171; rural, nonproletarian character, 99; vagrants, 129
Red China (Jiangxi newspaper), 158, 163-165, 181
Red Flag, 23
Red May recruitment drive of 1933, 161
Rentian (district), 166, 167
Republic of China, 144, 152
Revolution: 1911, 6, 18, 38, 72, 75, 82; Chinese, 84, 99, 199; Hunanese, 32; land, 131, 178, 181; Lenin's view (Bolshevik), 92; national, 50-63, 71, 75, 82-84, 90; October, 78, 92; rural, 71-74, 78, 84, 99, 131-132; social, 131; urban, 99; world, 92
Roosevelt, Theodore, 12
Rue, John, 115
Ruijin (county), 132, 165; capital of the CSR, 147; Fifth Plenum of the CCP Central Committee, 168
Russian Revolution, 15, 23, 45, 144; bourgeois-democratic, 45
Russian Study Club, 36

Schram, Stuart, 1, 2, 10, 18, 197; discontinuity thesis, 2
Schwartz, Benjamin, 197
Second National Congress, 171, 173, 175-181, 186
Second United Front, xii, 183
Selden, Mark, 149
Shandong, 40
Shanghai, 14, 17, 21, 27, 32, 35, 46, 90, 96, 117, 140, 144, 145, 153; Central Committee, 93, 144; mass movements, 47; Twenty-eight Bolsheviks, 145
Shanghang (county), 154, 155
Sixth Central Committee, Fourth Plenum (January 1931), 145
Sixth Party Congress (July 1928), 87, 130, 135, 136; peasant policy, 135, 136
Skinner, William (compliance model), 107
Snow, Edgar, 50, 55, 181
Socialist Youth Corps of Hunan, 24, 36
Solomon, Richard, 1, 2, 20; *Mao's Revolution and the Chinese Political Culture*, 196
Soviet Land Law (December 1931), 134
Soviet Union, 18, 24, 52, 99, 136, 146, 151, 201; model of urban revolution, 99; peasant experiences, 51, 60, 61, 103, 136, 151; relationship with Yanan, 190
Stalin: inherence of opposition, 101; Leninist theories of the socialist state, 203; liquidation of rich peasants, 136,

150; personal hegemony, 151; retentions of CSR, 186, 189; "socialism in one country," 146; strains with proletariat (Korsch), 79
Stinchcombe, Arthur, 131
Sun Quanfang (Zhili Clique), 47
Sun Yat-sen, 35, 44, 67; death, 49; "land to the tillers," 135
Sun Yat-sen University (Moscow), 144

Tan Pingshan, 86
Tan Yankai, 49
Tang Junyi, 197
Tang Shengzhi, 49, 58
Three Dot Secret Society, 115
Three Peoples Principles, 44, 49
Tongshan Upper Primary School, 6
Twenty-eight Bolsheviks (Russian Returned Students), xviii, 140, 144–151, 160, 181–184, 186, 187, 189, 191, 192, 199, 202; Stalinist faction, 136, 146, 181–184, 186, 187; Zunyi Conference, 181–184, 191

United Front, 31, 50, 68, 84, 85
United States of America (anti-Feng war), 47
"Urgent Mobilization for War," 157

Versailles Peace Conference, 6

Wakeman, Frederic, 1, 2; *History and Will*, 1
Wanan (county), 118
Wang Jingwei, 45, 46, 52; reorganization efforts, 91
Wayaobao Conference, 181–184
Weber, Max: authority, 155, 160, 173, 176; bureaucratic structure, 186
Weihaiwei, 40
West Jiangxi Action Committee, 116
White Forces, 90, 91, 94, 105, 109, 116, 125, 133, 154, 158, 174; overrun Jinggangshan base, 90
Wilson, Woodrow, 22
Winckler, Edwin (compliance model), 107
Wittfogel, Karl, 197
Workers Night School, 13, 14, 16, 43
World War I, 6, 17
Wu Peifu, 38, 65; Zhili Clique, 47
Wu, Yuzhang, 14
Wuhan, 65–67, 69, 76, 86, 88, 100; Central Peasant Movement Institute, 66; KMT, 65, 67, 76, 86
Wuping (county), 154, 155

Xian (Sian) Incident (1936), 98
Xiang River Middle School, 26
Xiang River Review, 14, 15, 17, 21
Xiang Ying (cochairman, CSR), 148
Xiangdao (The Guide Weekly), 36, 40, 42, 64, 68
Xiangtan, 69
Xiangxiang, 69
Xiao, San *(Comrade Mao Zedong's Boyhood and Youth)*, 2
Xiao, Zisheng, 36, 37
Xin Qingnian (New Youth), 4, 6, 8, 10
Xingguo (county), 117, 118, 126, 127, 134, 201; concentration of landownership, 126; reoccupation by the KMT (April 1931), 134; land law application, 137
Xingqiri (Sunday), 17

Yan Yuan, 12
Yanan, xiii, 143; campaigns of 1942–1945, 187, 189; Mao's writings, 148, 181; Yanan period, xii–xiii, 107, 189–190; "Yanan Way," 149
Yang Changji, 4, 5
Yenching Journal of Social Studies, 197
Yong Feng (border district), 117, 118, 126; artisans, 128; farm laborers, 128; landlord families, 126; middle peasants, 127; rich peasants, 126; vagrants, 129
Yuan Guoping, 154
Yuan Shikai, 13

Zeng Guofan, 12
Zhang Guotao, 13, 28, 64, 65, 68, 85; cochairman, CSR, 148; Eyuwan Soviet, 157
Zhang Jingyao, 15, 21, 23
Zhang Wentian, 166, 168, 176
Zhang Zuolin (Fengdian Clique), 47, 48, 75; suppression of Shanghai mass movements, 47
Zhao Hengti, 23, 30, 40, 49, 50
Zhejiang (province), 124
Zhengzhi Zhoubao (Political Weekly), 46
Zhengfeng (Rectification) Movement, 190
Zhili Clique, 47, 48
Zhongguo Nongmin (The Chinese Peasant), 53
Zhu De, 87, 88, 93, 110, 145
Zunyi Resolution, 91, 151, 153, 181; conference (January 1935), 145, 148, 151, 173, 181, 191